Praise for *Spinning Thread*
*Endorsements appear in full
(All from USA un*

CW00543986

Reading this book recharged my
practices that cultivate a meaningful, nonviolent and joyful existence.
— Betty Burkes, life-long educator and activist

Miki Kashtan presents an urgent challenge to connect personal
growth with social justice.
— Deborah van Deusen Hunsinger, Princeton Theological Seminary

Through this volume Miki Kashtan has yielded an inspirational
bequest: a moving account of a life's journey that is simultaneously
personal, spiritual, moral, and political. It is remarkable for its depth
of revelation, its intelligence, and its honesty. She moves freely from
her own intense life experiences to a creative synthesis of insights
and practices of Marx, Freud, Gandhi, and Martin Luther King. She
makes salient the human needs and emotional dimensions in life and
tempers the adoration of the rational throughout human history. She
offers principles of thought, feeling, and practice that are
simultaneously cosmic and down-to-earth. Readers with spiritual and
moral sensitivity will resonate with Kashtan's compelling life
accounts and the therapeutic and social lessons she has woven from
them. Everyone will gain in them in the reading. Thanks to her for
this brave endeavor.
— Neil J. Smelser, Emeritus Professor of Sociology, UC Berkeley

Miki Kashtan has written a wonderful book that invites us to change
the way we change ourselves, and thereby also the way we change the
world.... This is a work of profound social theory, with exactly the
visionary breadth that we need to help lead humanity from our
current path of collective self-defeat, into a future of breath-taking
possibility. It is also a most unusual kind of "self-help" book. It
demands a great deal more of the reader in terms of inviting new
ways of thinking about ourselves, our problems and our possibilities,
while at the same time being practical and accessible...
— Victor Lee Lewis, Founder/Director, the Radical Resilience
Institute

Reading Miki Kashtan's new book, I felt warmly and passionately invited into a totally new way of seeing myself and what life could be.
-- Tom Attlee, founder, The Co-Intelligence Institute, author, The Tao of Democracy.

Because of Miki's work — summed up in this book — I have transformed aspects of my life and work so that I no longer avoid difficult conversations but have begun to embrace them as growth trying to emerge.
— Cindy Mercer, Co-Founder, Planet Heritage Foundation

May it feed the fire of your heart as it has mine.
— Talli Jackson, dancer, Bill T. Jones/Arnie Zane Dance Company

This book demands courage and rewards it with passion, aliveness, and joy.
— Nichola Torbett, Director, Seminary of the Street

If you believe in and want to put into action Gandhi's understanding about being the example of the change you want to see in this world, this book is a wonderful guide to start.
— Ozgur Gelbal, psychologist, Turkey

In this provocative and visionary work, Miki Kashtan challenges the very foundations and assumptions we have inherited in our western society about the truth of human nature.
— Sarah Proechel, co-founder of Midwife International

Spinning Threads provokes and challenges me to deeply examine the stories I hold about the world.
— Kanya Likanasudh, compassionate communication trainer, Thailand

As a person committed to social change, yet who works mostly with individuals who have been traumatized, I will turn to Miki's words again and again to remind me of, and inspire me with, the vision for which my heart yearns, of a world where everyone's needs matter.
— Shulamit Berlevtov, CNVC-certified trainer, Canada

Spinning Threads of Radical Aliveness

Transcending the Legacy of Separation in Our Individual Lives

by
Miki Kashtan

the *fearless* HEART

Fearless Heart Publications

Published by
FEARLESS HEART PUBLICATIONS

55 Santa Clara Avenue, Suite 203,
Oakland, CA 94610
www.thefearlessheart.org

Copyright © 2014 by Miki Kashtan

This work is licensed under the Creative
Commons Attribution-NonCommercial-
NoDerivs License. To view the license terms,
visit http://creativecommons.org/licenses/by-
nc-nd/3.0/deed.en_US

In addition to the above license, the author grants
permission for short quotes inserted within other
works even for commercial purposes. Please
request permission for use of longer quotes from
the publisher.

ISBN-10: 0990007308   Paperback
ISBN-13: 978-0-9900073-0-2   Paperback

ISBN subject categories: Interpersonal Relations, Social Sciences

Library of Congress Control Number: 2013951209

Cover design: Mili Raj (miliraj.com)
Formatting: AAM Iqbal (ebook.aamiqbal.com)

For all the children

Table of Contents

Introduction

Reexamine all that you have been told in school, or in church or in any book. Dismiss whatever insults your soul.

– Walt Whitman

The purpose of this book is simple and radical: to support readers like you in doing three things:

- Increase your awareness of what has gotten all of us and you into the kind of unsustainable and mostly unsatisfying existence that we call human life;
- Discover a systematic process that you can learn to apply to undo the effects of socialization and trauma and reclaim your full humanity;
- Learn a way of living in integrity within a world that, in essence, is not changing with you.

If your experience of reading this book is what I hope it will be, you will regain your faith in humanity. You might experience immense compassion and a sense of tragedy about the internal and external alienation we have created and which we pass from generation to generation. You will be inspired and moved by your own and others' basic heroism of surviving childhood. And you will learn much that can help you know what you need to do in order to get the kind of support that can help you make the transformation that will bring you back to yourself, ready to live as you might remember yourself wishing early on in life.

If you want to embark on this journey, I want to stress that this is not exactly or primarily a self-help book. Although it does contain practices, you will likely do better with them if you can get support from others. The practices, as well as the ideas and stories that are in this book, are here in the hope that your desire to live fully will awaken and you will then take additional steps towards yourself, including the ones pointed to within the book.

The title of this book derives from two sources. One is the metaphor which gave rise to this project in the first place: the felt sense I've had for some time that the human fabric has a tear, and that if we let this tear continue, there may come a point of no return.

I felt it, keenly, one night in 1995 when two young men falsely accused me of having run over one of them in an attempt to get me to give them money. I called on every human faculty that I had to try to reach actual engagement between us, and I failed. I never became a person in their eyes as far as I could tell. Within minutes after the interaction was completed, I saw them walking with the ostensible limp mysteriously healed, and I was inconsolable that night. It wasn't blame or judgment; more a sense of helplessness, a tragic alarm at the conditions that pit people against each other in such ways. I wanted to reach them, and didn't know how.

At this time, this tear in the human fabric has reached a state of global crisis characterized by a growing polarity between and within nations, manifesting in complex combinations and juxtapositions of material deprivation and spiritual depletion increasing social disintegration in many parts of the world; a more and more imminent threat to the carrying capacity of the planet; all leading to a persistent possibility of global civilization and population collapse. These phenomena are portrayed daily in the media, and their existence is not hugely controversial.

What's even more frightening to me is that solutions to these crises are often sought within the same set of core beliefs and practices that have contributed to the crises in the first place: more technology is believed to address the problems that technology created, and more capitalism-style development is believed to do away with poverty created by capitalism. Alternative explanations or solutions are regularly dismissed or rejected, often by arguing that the ideas or suggestions cannot be proven, are not cost effective, or are in opposition to human nature. We have effectively bought into a belief that no alternative exists.

I am not willing to settle into this framework, because I haven't lost touch with a vision I've been carrying with me since my childhood. Nor do I believe that I am alone. In fact, I believe that all of us carry somewhere in us a deep longing for and vision of a world that works for all. I frequently encounter traces of this buried vision in the most unexpected moments and places, as soon as someone's heart opens up to love, if nothing else. If this vision and possibility are, indeed, part of who we are, why is it that we have created a world based on separation, scarcity, and powerlessness that barely works for the few?

When this question is asked, more often than not the answer is that it's human nature that has brought us here.

I am here to tell you a different story about who we are, why we got here, and what we can do to move towards our longings for a different world.

I sometimes wonder who is truly naïve – those who think that we cannot trust ourselves to collaborate, and therefore must rely on control, coercion, and incentives, or those who think we can, and that collaborating with nature and with each other are entirely possible. Is it not our reliance on control, coercion, and incentives that has brought us to our current impasse of longing for change and not seeing options, personally and globally, for creating it?

Spinning Threads of Radical Aliveness puts forth the bold vision that there is one single key to getting us out of the stuck place we have created. It can open the door to profound changes at all levels, ranging from creating more satisfying personal lives all the way to a world that works for all, in Sharif Abdullah's resonant phrase.

This key is to embrace a major transformation in our relationship with our human needs.

This may be challenging at first. Later, it may come to support every turn in your road.

The first premise underlying this vision is that *all* human needs are fundamentally life-affirming and common to all. There is no need of yours or mine, or of anyone else, for that matter, of which we need feel ashamed. It is only the strategies we pursue to fulfill our needs that can be harmful to others and ourselves, not the needs themselves.

The second premise is that conflicts, suffering, and the many destructive aspects of human life are *all* the result of ignoring, mistrusting, denying, and suppressing rather than understanding, accepting, and embracing our needs.

Learning to use this new way of relating to our needs to guide our choices and actions is the path to a world that works for all.

The full scope of this project is quite ambitious. It rests on the deep faith that what we have created is at odds with – rather than an expression of – our human nature; and that therefore it is entirely possible for us to move towards a future that is more aligned with our core humanity and a social order that is attuned to the core needs of humans and that collaborates with the natural world, without having to control it.

In this book, I focus on our individual existence and what we can do to reclaim our full humanity and live lives of meaning and dignity in a chaotic and complex world.

In this sense, spinning threads is about the individual foundation of any other practice we might want to engage with: each of us is a thread that ultimately can be rewoven into the human fabric.

The other source for the spinning metaphor comes from Gandhi's core practice of spinning, which was intended to be both symbolically and materially a path to reclaiming the power to attend to needs without requiring large institutions. Spinning was also a path to taking action for each person right where they are, which is what I hope we can all do. Lastly, Gandhi's spinning invokes the commitment to nonviolence which informs everything I do and write about. In that sense, this book is an invitation to recover our individual ability to choose nonviolence in the face of difficult circumstances.

I. Transcending the Legacy of Separation

Part One: Transcending the Legacy of Separation, starts with tracing what led us to where we are: the path of negating our needs and emotions. Several thousand years of this path have created a world profoundly at odds with human thriving. The consequences of this path are known to all of us: disconnection from our deepest selves and separation from each other; immense challenges in handling differences and disagreements; and social structures which reinforce separation on all levels.

This is the setting that we want to change, both the internalized legacy and the persistent social structures that reinforce and maintain it, such that each generation anew finds itself gripped in the legacy of a difficult-to-change past.

Understanding the patterns of reproducing the past provides us with some clues, and sets the stage for the concrete invitation to each of us to recover from the powerful burden of socialization and to reclaim freedom and aliveness as well as the capacity to engage critically and lovingly with the world around us. We can liberate ourselves from the legacy of the past, find inner freedom, and cultivate a radical consciousness that calls into question what we have inherited and reclaims the capacity to envision and the courage to live out our vision. Once awakened to our human needs, we can embrace the practice of nonviolence through honoring our own and others' humanity in full by focusing on everyone's needs.

II. Pioneering a Future of Collaboration

Once we are on the path to liberating ourselves, Part Two: Pioneering a Future of Collaboration, outlines how each of us can become a one-person model of what life could be like. This is no small task, since any social reality has mechanisms that make it resistant to change and that will continue to put pressure on each individual to adapt back into it. This is why we need guidelines that we can lean on. Making needs central entirely reshapes how we relate to others. Resolving conflicts, supporting each other, knowing how to love, offering each other feedback when our needs are not met, and just about every aspect of relationship take on a new light when filtered through the lens of human needs. We shift from evaluating, judging, and the either/or way of living into an open-hearted commitment to make things work for everyone involved in any situation.

Key to this possibility is the core insight that conflicts only take place at the level of strategies, because, contrary to just about everything our culture tells us, human needs are not in conflict. With a modicum of skill and/or support from uninvolved parties, every conflict situation can turn into a shared exploration of which human needs are at the root of everyone's actions, opinions, and perceptions. When done in partnership, such explorations yield a shift into goodwill, which tends to result in mutually viable ways of attending to both parties' human needs and finding strategies that maximize meeting as many of them as possible. When done internally, such exploration tends to transform antagonism into empathy for another person, which can already create a profound shift in the relationship even without that person's collaboration.

This book, as you may recall, is only one part of the project I initially started. Our work doesn't end with changing ourselves. Especially given how much effort is required to maintain the changes we embrace, even for many of us to work on ourselves is not going to be sufficient to create the future we want. No amount of individual change alone will suffice to change the rules of the game –

the way our institutions are set up – that make it so difficult to live a life of integrity, meaning, and love. Even improving our relationships will not be enough. If we are going to change those social structures, we will need to grapple with them directly. At least some of us will need to work together with others to create systemic change. For this, I invite you to look at my second book, *Reweaving Our Human Fabric*, where I take on the task of showing us how we can work together for change, and paint a detailed picture of what the world to come could look like.

Why This Book

In addition to a revolutionary view of human nature, this book offers practical and concrete suggestions for:

- Overcoming the effects of the stultifying socialization so many of us endured;
- Restoring our capacity for meaningful relationships with self and others; and
- Putting nonviolence into practice in all areas of life.

This is a book for an era in which many feel profoundly afraid of the future and baffled by how to help our culture meet the challenges we are facing. Whether you are a political activist, an organizational consultant, or "simply" a human being trying to live your life with integrity and meaning, this book will offer you unexpected hope. By challenging some core assumptions about the nature of being human and what is possible for humanity, and by inviting you into a luminous vision of a livable future, this book invites you on a new journey, one that can profoundly alter how you live, relate, and work.

How to Read this Book

I hope that anyone reading this will feel free to follow their own curiosity and not be constrained by the order in which I have written the book. For example, I realize that some people are fascinated by how our civilization got to this point, while others may find the history or analysis of people like Freud and Marx not relevant for their own inquiries. You may want to skip that section (Section One), and perhaps read first about how our childhood upbringings made us who we are today (Section Two). If you then find yourself curious about how our civilization got here, you could then go back to Section One, or skip it altogether.

There are a number of different styles in the book: for memoir and my personal story, you can go to the sections headed "Early Hardships" and "Finding Me Finding Vision." If you want my teaching and experience about how to respond to the hard emotions of shame, despair, anger, and grief, you can go straight to the section "Strategic Discomfort." And so on. Happy traveling!

Part One:

Transcending the Legacy of Separation

An Invitation

The Past and the Future

Imagine that the time is somewhere in the twelfth or thirteenth century in feudal Europe. You are a traveler from the future, coming into that time. Your base is, perhaps, the late nineteenth century. You are meeting with people of different social locations, and your task is to introduce them to the absolutely revolutionary and radical idea that the world could be organized on the principle of competition and merit.

In case you are not familiar with medieval history, the people you would be talking with in this imaginary scenario knew a different sort of arrangement. In their world, whatever your station in life was when you were born determined to an extremely high degree what your life would look like. The idea that one could end up in different social locations – that a farmer's son could simply choose to be a tailor, for example – would have been unimaginable to them. They could likely imagine that for a few rare and exceptional situations, not as an organizing principle.

In response to your proposal they would pooh-pooh you, they would tell you that you were naïve or dangerous or both. They would tell you that no one would ever do anything if they weren't compelled to do it based on the strong coercive structures that existed at that time on all levels. They would say it was against human nature, and against God, who had specifically endorsed the existing order. Chaos would ensue, in which no one would do anything without the fear of God and expertise would get lost when not transferred carefully from father to son. They would dismiss you and ignore you.

And yet something like that transformation has happened. Our society is not perfectly meritocratic and the competition is largely fixed to benefit the haves, but meritocracy and competition are highly regarded by most and are in reality far more prevalent than in medieval times. The industrial revolution and the political revolutions that arose in tandem with it created an entirely different social order that would have been impossible for our ancestors to fathom.

I invite you to stretch and imagine what it would be like to live in that medieval world and have someone come and tell you that something else is possible.

This is exactly what happens these days when I attempt to invite people into my vivid picture of a fully collaborative world order based on need satisfaction and willingness, without external incentives, without money, without exchange, and without coercion. I am told, repeatedly, that my vision goes against human nature. That no one would do anything without external incentives in the form of money; that competition is what drives excellence and that generosity and kindness are not sufficient to run the world. A fully collaborative society is just as unthinkable in a world based on competition as competition was for an authority-based society.

If competition as the foundation of a social order emerged from medieval times, is it, perhaps, after all, possible to create a collaborative future from our own competitive present?

Indulge me, and yourself, and imagine that future with me for a moment, even if you think it's impossible.

Let's imagine that we can create social structures and institutions organized around caring for everyone's needs through willing collaboration. As this vision is at odds with our current reality of scarcity and conflict, to even imagine it requires some new understanding of and a positive relationship with what it means to be human. At the heart of this approach is an entirely revised theory of human nature which places human needs at the center, viewing them as the core of what makes us who we are, the core that motivates and animates all our actions as human beings.

Before embarking on describing this approach to human nature, I want to name a dilemma common to anyone who puts out a visionary perspective: they are, inherently, unprovable. Although I am making my best effort to put forth a cogent argument for this theory, I feel called to quote Peter Gabel, whose understanding of this dilemma leaves no need to add words beyond his. Although the specific theory he puts forth in that article is not the same as mine, there is enough alignment to warrant this full quote:

> It is in the nature of the intersubjective, spiritual-political theory that I am proposing that its truth-value to you depends upon whether you can recognize it as true rather

than any analytical proof or capacity to explain diverse facts that is the measure of the truth of more scientific ways of seeing and thinking.

All phenomenological or descriptive theory depends not upon a theory's ability to explain facts from premises or theoretical postulates, but rather upon its self-evidence, upon its capacity to produce an experience of recognition in the reader. Since the theory itself begins with a social-spiritual understanding of the very thing that the theory is addressing and talking about, the only claim to validity that it can make upon the reader is the extent to which the reader can recognize it as adequate to fully reveal what is being described.[1]

An Outline of a Needs-Friendly Theory of Human Nature

The suggestion of affirming and befriending our needs stands in stark contrast to millennia of assumptions that our needs, emotions, and desires form an unruly substratum, which interferes with the possibility of an orderly life of virtue and social order. Even in today's world, when we are often advised to "get in touch with our feelings," we are still socialized to be ashamed of having needs, to refrain from asking for what we want, and to continue to believe that we must tame and control ourselves in order to be acceptable members of human society.

This negative view of human nature runs through Eastern as well as Western worldviews, ancient and modern alike. The Buddha identified desire and ignorance as the roots of suffering. St. Paul puzzled that "that which I want to do I do not do, and that which I do not want to do is precisely what I do." The great effort of the Enlightenment was to apply reason, typically seen as being in opposition to emotion. Freud collapsed all our needs into two insatiable drives, at least one of which he saw as destructive, and both of which he construed as asocial, positing a fundamental and intrinsic conflict between individual and society, pleasure and reality.

The insight at the core of *Reweaving Our Human Fabric*, building on the work of Marshall Rosenberg, is that human needs, properly

---

[1] Gabel, Peter. A Spiritual Way of Seeing *Tikkun* 28(2): 17.

understood, are simply the building blocks of and motivation for all our actions, feelings, and reactions. Rather than a source of difficulty, they are what unite us, because we all have the same set of basic needs. In fact, nothing that we do has any purpose other than being an attempt to meet one or more of our human needs.

Needs, understood in this way, are finite in number, and distinct from the infinite variety of strategies we employ to meet them. In Marshall Rosenberg's words:

> Needs, as I use the term, can be thought of as resources that life requires in order to sustain itself. For example, our physical well-being depends on our needs for air, water, rest, and food being fulfilled. Our psychological and spiritual well-being is enhanced when our needs for understanding, support, honesty, and meaning are fulfilled.[2]

Needs as I discuss them here are abstract, common, and general enough that there is, by definition, a range of options for how to attend to them. The more removed from immediate physical survival, the larger the range. We need oxygen, or we incur potentially permanent brain damage after four minutes. There are no known substitutes for oxygen even though it's a strategy to attend to the need for survival. We have much more flexibility when it comes to love or meaning, even though our well-being depends on them being fulfilled just as much as our survival depends on oxygen.

If, then, needs are anything required for a human being to have a truly satisfying life – including physical needs, emotional and psychological needs, relational needs, social and communal needs, and spiritual needs – then it is the very attempt to suppress our needs, and by extension our desires and emotions, that has resulted in the level of suffering, trauma, and destruction of life that we have come to accept as normal.

Even when we are consumed with fury and take revenge, or when we set up structures that allow us to dominate other people, those actions, under this perspective, would be motivated by basic human needs that are common to all people, such as respect, autonomy, or love.[3] Every single one of the many familiar drives and behaviors that are usually seen as "proof" of our destructive

---

[2] Marshall Rosenberg, *We Can Work It Out*, by Marshall Rosenberg, page 2.
[3] James Gilligan, for example, in *Violence: Our Deadly Epidemic and Its Causes*, makes the case that all violence is an attempt to create justice. I found his approach both loving and compelling.

tendencies, including violence, domination, greed, or surviving at another's expense, can be seen as strategies to meet underlying, life-affirming needs: the need to survive, to be safe, to eat, to give and receive love, to be appreciated or respected, to contribute to the group, and many others, (see Appendix A for a basic list of human needs).[4] Rather than continuing the millennia-old tendency to believe that kindness, caring, and virtue are by necessity derived from fighting against "selfish" elements of our nature, which would logically lead to the attempt to get rid of our pesky "needs," this view then suggests that it is in and through accepting and befriending our needs that we can find our way to a livable future.

Instead of focusing on reason as the be-all and end-all of what it means to be human, and engaging in a losing battle to control an unruly layer of our being, a focus on human needs maintains a hopeful perspective. A rich multiplicity of human needs, and the realization that our experience of needs is not insatiable (a point elaborated below in the description of Section Two), means that suffering is not inevitable. In addition, the perennial conflict between individual and society, so poignantly captured by Sigmund Freud in *Civilization and Its Discontents*, can dissolve into a collaborative paradigm in which debate and war, with their inevitable winners and losers, become obsolete and fully constructive dialogue, with equally inevitable win-win solutions, becomes the new norm.

In a world structured at odds with human needs, we are socialized to expect that our needs will not be valued or attended to, and to fear that they will not be met. These expectations, in and of themselves, contribute directly to our conflicts, destructive behavior, violence, and suffering. Such behavior, in turn, reinforces the prevailing views about the negative aspects of human nature, thereby making it even more difficult to embrace human needs and maintain any hopeful views about who we are.

Part of the difficulty, as I see it, is that what is or isn't human *nature* is extremely hard, in my view, to prove. As a species, we exhibit many behaviors or urges – such as dominance or the drive for status – that I consider to be strategies and yet have habitually been seen as "negative" human needs. Viewing these as merely strategies,

---

[4] While this understanding of needs follows the trailblazing work of Marshall Rosenberg, who made the radical proposal of putting human needs, more than any other aspect of human life, at the center, a similar approach, from a different perspective, has been proposed by economist Manfred Max-Neef. See, for example, *Human Scale Development: Conception, Application and Further Reflections*.

or a means to an end – such as "survival," "order," or even "contribution," – rather than as needs or ends in themselves, is a choice. This way of viewing humanity is not something that is given by observation per se. This choice is reinforced by seeing the dramatic effect that happens when a person who is deeply motivated by these kinds of urges finds a way to contact the deeper and much more vulnerable needs underlying these behaviors, needs which are, indeed common to all people. This choice also finds support from the work of Abraham Maslow, a man who dedicated much of his life to the specific study of human needs. He was deeply aware of anthropological data, having been a student of Ruth Benedict, and nonetheless didn't include dominance in his list of needs. Nonetheless, this is a choice and not a scientifically provable hypothesis; it is a choice about how we define what is or isn't a need.

The power of this choice is that it opens up a path of transformation – internal as well as global – that is not dependent on recreating the cycle of control, suppression, or punishment of "evil" within or without. It is a choice that recognizes that we are capable of extreme harm and cruelty, while seeing an entirely plausible possibility that such harm is the outcome of conditions we have created rather than a given arising from the nature of who we are. I return to this question – the origin of violence – further below (page 108, "Whence Violence").

As I conclude this portion, I want to note that so much of who we are is formed in a context of human *societies* in which we are removed from a raw state of nature, that I don't see how we can really know what "human nature" is. It is also the case that we've always had individuals and societies that operate without violence. Because of these factors, because of my studies in social theory, because of my vision, and because of my persistent experience in my work with people and organizations, I am no longer able or willing to go along with the prevailing views of human nature. I believe we have choice, both individually and collectively, in which path we follow as we aim to attend to needs, since we are clearly capable of both cooperation and competition, love and fear, togetherness or separation.

Rather than attempting to settle this matter, I accept a certain kind of limitation – an inability to prove anything about humans –

and, instead, am choosing to adopt a worldview that is, perhaps, radical and unusual.

Beyond a theoretical lens on human nature, this view of all human needs as common, universal, and benign has ramifications for every facet of life:

- Internally, this view spells a path that allows us to create inner peace, self-acceptance, freedom, and integrity by finding the needs underlying inner conflict, depression, shame, self-judgments and other forms of internal strife.
- Interpersonally, it means that we can learn how to distinguish between our needs and our strategies, so that we can make connection with self and others around our *needs*, and in the environment of goodwill that emerges in the process strive towards solutions that address, in some fashion, everyone's needs.
- It also means changing how we relate to children, so that socialization itself becomes a process in which needs are affirmed, vulnerability is celebrated, and dialogic approaches to conflict are internalized from the start.
- When working within groups and organizations, this approach lends itself to processes that make collaboration dramatically more feasible.
- In working for change, the needs-based approach provides practical tools for living nonviolence fully, thereby reducing the chances of recreating the existing order while working to change it.
- Lastly, building institutions, allocating resources, and creating systems of governance that put human needs at the center remain an indispensable foundation for the possibility of creating a sustainable human life on this planet.

This centrality of human needs provides the core unifying principle of the multiple threads that the entire series provides. This principle suggests that the unity of all human beings, and indeed of all living beings, is far deeper and yet far more practically accessible than our current philosophies teach. That unity is based on sharing the same life-affirming needs that all of us, humans and all living beings, are continually trying to meet, every moment of every day, with the best means available to us.

With this understanding of human needs, imagine putting human needs at the center, and organizing life around them. If this is hard for you to do, there is a reason for it.

An Ancient Longing and a Current Reality

As far back as I look, I see evidence of a deep longing that our species has had: the dream of a world that works for all, where we live in harmony with each other, where peace prevails, and where nature provides in abundance.

Sometimes the longing shows up as a myth of an ancient place or time, such as the legendary land of Lumeria, the Golden Age in Crete, or the Garden of Eden. At other times the longing focuses on an afterlife. And at times the longing appears as visions of a future, such as the vision of turning swords into ploughshares or of having the wolf live in peace with the sheep (never mind what the wolf will eat). Wherever such images are located, they tend to be evocative and resonant. Even when we call them naïve and don't believe they are possible, we are still somehow drawn to those possibilities, and would likely prefer the reality they invoke to the one in which we live if we could only believe it possible.

If so, why is it that we live in this reality and not in one of those versions? This is one of those questions to which I don't believe anyone can provide a full response. The very short version of my own response is that we separated ourselves from nature at some point in our history, and eventually developed a view of ourselves as creatures that need to be controlled in order for society to exist at all. The result is the world in which we live, which is based on separation, scarcity, and powerlessness.

I don't believe this is the only reality possible. I see myself as part of that long tradition of dreaming a different world. I also have very clear ideas about how we can, individually and collectively, recover from the legacy of what was done to us over millennia, and create a society that does, indeed, work for all.

This is what I start to lay out here in Part One.

How We Got Here

The first section in this part condenses years of research I have done as part of my dissertation into an explanation of how the particular theory of human nature that we have inherited has affected our social reality and continues to be affected by it. I look, in particular, at the role that rationality has played in our view of human nature, and pose some serious questions about what I see as devastating consequences of assuming that our non-rational life needs to be tamed and controlled. This section is likely to be of interest primarily to people who love theory. If you are not one such person, you can probably take a look at the diagram on page 24 (in "the Power of Stories"), skip the rest, and come back only if something later becomes obscure.

How Separation Keeps Going

The second section (starting on page 41) builds on other aspects of my research, my work with people over the years, and my own childhood experiences, to describe the power of socialization to perpetuate and reproduce the social order from generation to generation. One of the ways that socialization prevents change is precisely by making us unable to believe that anything else is possible. This happens through a systematic process of being prepared to live in a world that doesn't work for all – we are trained either to accept having unmet needs, even repressing our needs, or to be willing to accept our own needs, at least some of them, being met while others' needs aren't. A significant portion of this section follows my own experiences as an example of the way that socialization affects our capacity to maintain our full human vibrancy, our access to our needs, and our ability to live as we want.

Rethinking Human Nature

The third section (from page 85) provides more details into the theory of human nature I have outlined above, which is dramatically different from what most of us have been brought up to believe. Placing human needs at the center of everything allows for an integration of reason and emotion, individual and society, and self and other. Given how accustomed we are to believing that we are either "sinful," in the older versions of prevalent theories of human nature, or have "drives" that are insatiable and destructive, as the modern versions have it, putting needs at the center calls on me to address some profound age-old questions such as the origins of violence and what it would really mean to meet human needs.

Going against the Grain

The last and longest section (page 121) is where things get practical and personal. If you are inspired by the vision of a world designed to meet human needs; if you recognize what has been done to all of us to bring us here, and, in particular, the cost to you of living in and complying with the dictates of this society; and if you want to liberate yourself, you will find here a possible path forward. The primary key to this liberation is reclaiming the fullness of your humanity by walking towards your emotions and learning about your needs. The courage that you develop in doing so allows you to find true choice and to develop what I call a radical consciousness, by which I mean being able to look at the world through the critical lens of a radical vision.

Section 1:

How We Got Here

The Power of Stories

As far back as I can remember I have been drawn inexorably towards questions of theory. I've always wanted to understand why anything is the way that it is. Continuing to question everything led me to challenge core assumptions that have been part and parcel of the Western way of being for millennia, and to develop an alternative frame based on a fierce faith that human beings have the option of transforming what seems unchangeable.

We live in extreme times. Unless we change the world, we may be left with nothing to change, or no one to change it. The neat distinctions between theory and practice are becoming meaningless and dangerous. What we think, what we say, and how we say it matter and have real and material consequences, and conversely, what we do and how we do it matter and have strong implications for how we think, individually and collectively.

Many people believe that war, greed, abuse, and all social ills are ultimately caused by human nature. Instead, I have come to believe that our *views* of human nature, rather than human nature itself, are at issue here. We have created social institutions based on negative views of human nature and of nature more generally, and on the perspective that both must be controlled to make social life possible. Our institutions then reproduce themselves and lead to humans acting in ways that confirm the very negative views we have inherited.

Here's a diagram that illustrates this process, based on the work of Marshall Rosenberg:

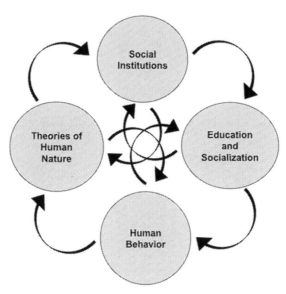

The story we have inherited is that we are fundamentally motivated by a narrow version of self-interest and that underneath our surface sociability we have base and unruly impulses that present a permanent danger to the functioning of society. Based on this picture, we collectively created institutions that constrain, control and manipulate people. It's no surprise that we base our process of education and socialization on punishment and reward and on fear of spontaneity. Being raised in such a manner almost guarantees that as adults we behave in ways that appear to lend evidence to the view of human nature as innately aggressive and with insatiable drives. Moreover, most of us emerge from our childhoods with emotional patterns and conditioning that leave us focused on adapting to what is rather than attempting to create change, thereby reducing the chances of coming together to create significant social change.

Stories are powerful. Therein lies a possible freedom: we can choose new stories. Choosing to enact a story based on more hopeful perspectives about what is humanly possible is likely to create different effects.[5] In the process, change happens, personally or collectively. When we form a social movement, in particular, we become a group of people who are enacting a different story of

---

[5] See Appendix B for a list of the assumptions and intentions that underlie the work I am presenting in this book.

what's possible, and so are sometimes able, collectively, to create a different social reality.

Before we can look at creating new understandings about what it means to be human and what kind of relationships and institutions we can have, I want to examine more deeply the path that has led us to where we are. How did the stories that we now have come to be? When did these views of human nature start? What have they led to?

Committed to Rationality

It is reason alone that should rule our actions and beliefs.
— Stephen Nathanson, *The Ideal of Rationality*

It is clear that the rule of the soul over the body, and of the rational element over the passionate, is natural and expedient; whereas the equality of the two or the rule of the inferior is always hurtful.
— Aristotle, *Politics*

Passion … no man wants for himself. Who wants to have himself put in chains when he can be free?
— Emmanuel Kant, *Anthropology from a Pragmatic Point of View*. Emphasis added.

In 2000 I completed a Ph.D. dissertation in which I examined deeply the origins and consequences of the views about human nature that have come to dominate the Western worldview. I identified a profound bias toward rationality that permeates this worldview, implicit in which is a dark view of human nature.

Because this is not my own view of human nature, understanding its origins became a deep personal and intellectual quest. Ultimately, such questions remain a mystery we cannot know, no matter how much anthropological and archeological data we collect, because the data must be interpreted and extrapolated. What follows is my own view, without any claim to final truth.

As I see it, the idea that our nature, our bodies, our needs and desires, and our feelings require the rule of reason and rationality had its original seed in the shift from foraging to food production. Previous to agriculture we relied on nature to provide, and trusted that it would. When the Mbuti people, hunter-gatherers in the Congo rainforest, experienced major problems they traditionally concluded that the forest, their mother and father, must be asleep or it would be taking care of them, so they would sing to it to wake it up. Singing to the forest as mother and father implies a relationship with nature that assumes humans are part of nature, and implies a level of trust that subsequently disappeared with the appearance of agriculture. I repeat my acknowledgment that how we lost our original trust in nature is ultimately a mystery we cannot know. The consequences, however, are still with us.

Agriculture rests on a fundamental mistrust of life that suggests that we need to control nature in order for us to have enough resources and protection. The introduction of reason and rationality as the key method for controlling our own nature arose many millennia later, likely as a logical extension of that initial loss of trust in what is natural. With that loss of trust, we have come to believe that we must transcend our relationship with nature, which has become suspect, so we can convince ourselves that we are not part of that which cannot be trusted.

The big jump in what got us here, especially in terms of current Western views of human nature, occurred more than two thousand years ago, during the period of Greek ascendance. It was Greek philosophy, starting at least with Parmenides, which introduced the faculty of reason as the hallmark of being human, the characteristic that separates us from animals and allows us to "rise above nature."

The Modern Worldview

The theme of reason as the antidote to what is "base" in us reappeared more strongly during the Enlightenment, when reason came to be the symbol and instrument of progress and rational thought was seen as a triumph over superstition and blind faith. This valuation of rationality comes together with a denigration of everything labeled "irrational," including needs, desires, emotions, imagination, and intuition. This perspective ultimately rests on a fundamental despair about human nature. We are seen as having a "base" and "dark" side that cannot easily be controlled and that is quite destructive if uncontrolled.

The Denigration of Emotions

Since the Enlightenment, our dominant culture holds that emotions cannot serve as a source of knowledge and are dangerous if applied as a guide to moral action.[6] Even within social circles that encourage "getting in touch with our feelings," e.g. the New Age movement, the word "irrational" remains a derogatory term, a way of discounting the feelings, needs, or thoughts that are being communicated. When

---

[6] Even in the partly diverging view of Rousseau, pity without reason is not a good foundation for moral action.

a supervisor tells an employee, "Your feelings are not part of my job," the message conveyed is that feelings are banned from relevance, unimportant in the world of work. When an instructor in a continuing education class for lawyers says, "When an opposing attorney displays anger, this can mean one of two things: either it is a ploy, or he [sic] is incompetent," the message is that anger must be masked and controlled in order to achieve competence.

Human Beings as Essentially Self-Seeking

As the theme of rationality developed, the idea of "rational" self-interest became more and more pronounced. In the words of Adam Smith: "It is not from the benevolence of the butcher, the brewer or the baker that we expect our dinner, but from their regard to their own interest. We address ourselves, not to their humanity, but to their self-love, and never talk to them of our own necessities but of their advantages."[7]

The assumption of unbounded egoism is currently so prominent that so-called altruistic behavior is considered a problem to be explained. This "problem" has haunted evolutionary theorists. Indeed, the very concept of altruism implies the abnormality of such action, assuming selfishness to be the natural motivation and acting on behalf of others to be an aberration.

The Need for External Authority

The combination of seeing us as self-seeking and hard to control leads to another negative conclusion about us: that if left to our own devices we would act selfishly and aggressively, and would not be able to erect a social order that is stable.

In this view, human association is formed not out of an interest in others, but solely as a result of self-interest. The quintessential form of human association is a contract, a form of exchange that results in common action taken by individuals, all of whom are looking after their own interests alone. On the societal level, the social contract, which is the willingness on the part of individuals to give up some freedom in exchange for security, is the only guarantee that social stability will prevail.

---

[7] Adam Smith, *The Wealth of Nations*, 18 (originally published in 1776).

Reason, Science, and Progress

The 18th and 19th centuries were characterized by real buoyancy about what science would make possible along with contempt for what was perceived as the ignorant and superstitious past. In this worldview no authority exists except that of reason, science, and empirical sense perceptions. This secular faith intensified towards the 20th century and became the new Western credo: the belief, itself not grounded in any empirical evidence, that science will in the end find the answers to and solve all human problems, and that these answers cannot exist anywhere else; the conviction that what science cannot explain or find answers for does not actually exist;[8] and the hope that eventually the same kind of scientific thinking and method could be applied to the human and social dimensions.

The belief in the power of reason to ensure progress exerts a powerful force on people's imagination. So much so, that the valuation of rationality, especially in its incarnation as science and technology, is common to approaches which are otherwise disparate and antagonistic to each other, such as market economics and traditional Marxism.

What is particularly ironic about the persistent power of the commitment to reason is that many who accept the primacy of reason repeatedly invoke images of faith and religion to describe it. Here are a few:

- "… unconfessed theology of reason."[9]
- "Reason, like the deity whom she replaced … is inherently a jealous and exclusive mistress."[10]

---

[8] A few examples will illustrate the point. 1) There have been cases of people diagnosed with cancer who proceeded to treat themselves successfully with alternative medicine alone. At times, when such individuals return to conventional medical doctors, the original diagnosis is reversed. The scientific outlook could not accept the possibility that a method of treatment not recognized by it can be efficacious. At other times such events are called "spontaneous remissions," as if no treatment was administered. 2) In the early part of the 20th century scientists argued that differences in the quality of sound produced by pianists could not have a physical cause, as they could see no mechanism that would cause it. Later, such a mechanism was discovered. (Michael Polanyi, *Personal Knowledge*, 50). 3) Western medicine claims that homeopathy cannot work, since the substances used are diluted to the point where no visible traces of them exist in the solutions produced. At the same time, regular scientific research conducted by physicians who are skeptical about homeopathy discovered empirically that in double-blind controlled experiments homeopathy does have an effect. This result creates a profound puzzle for the scientific method. Ironically, the shift in the understanding of piano tone quality and the insistence on the absurdity of homeopathy are on opposite pages of Polanyi's book (50 and 51).

[9] Radest, *Humanism with a Human Face*, 48.

[10] Ernest Gellner, *Reason and Culture*, 54.

- "... the mythological importance of reason obscures all else."[11]
- "It is a fact of profound irony that assured confidence in the efficacy of reason requires an act of faith."[12]

For many today, any perceived decline in the faith in reason provokes profound despair and fear. What declines is the faith in reason's ability to deliver its promise, while the belief that reason is the only available channel for progress remains intact and creates enormous tension.

The value of reason and rationality has become a new article of faith, re-asserted again and again regardless of any evidence. Indeed, I cannot imagine what *could* count as evidence, even as I recognize that the very requirement to produce evidence is itself rooted in the acceptance of the value of reason. No simple exits exist any more.

Why does this matter?

---

[11] John Ralston Saul, *Voltaire's Bastards*, 15.
[12] Rescher, *Rationality*, 230.

Controlling to Death

The significance of the theories we have created and the so-called "common sense" stories to which they give rise is in how they affect our individual actions and collective institutions. This holds true for the fundamental theories we have inherited about our human nature just as much as any other story or myth by which humans have lived.

Think about this for a moment. Here's the assumption we have inherited: that there is an inherent opposition between how we ought to be and how we actually are. In this story we ought to be ruled by reason and we actually are impulsive creatures interested only in maximizing pleasure and minimizing pain, without concern for anyone else's welfare. This way of looking at ourselves will inexorably lead us to an endless drive towards control.

The fear of being at the mercy of our drives, of acting without any ability to control ourselves, or of seeing others, whether individually or collectively, act without any control, leads us to attempt to suppress or repress feelings, passions, needs, and desires. We believe ourselves to be dangerous if left to our own devices. Reason is both the ideal we strive for and the tool for controlling our untamed nature. We look to an external authority to coerce us to cooperate with each other. We expect parents to control their children lest they be wild and willful, and employers to control their employees lest they slack off.

While the attempts to control our emotional life may be more or less successful in the short run, more often than not the suppressed aspects of our experience end up erupting down the line. Since we see unrestrained actions based on emotions, impulses, and desires as "irrational" and responsible for violence and destructiveness, the insistence on controlling emotions is likely to increase the more eruptions occur, resulting in a vicious cycle of eruption and control reinforcing each other.

The same difficulties extend beyond individuals. The profound bias toward rationality, and the implicit despair about human nature that supports it, together generate and contribute to what I see as a major tear in our human fabric.

1. We live in fear and isolation as a way to protect ourselves from others – both individually and as members of certain groups. The

accusation of "irrationality" and the attribution of uncontrollable emotions and passions have been leveled at many despised and oppressed groups such as women, African-Americans, lower-class people, or indigenous people the world over.

2. Under capitalism, which involves the application of "rationality" to the economic sphere, everything is reduced to money and exchange. "Rational" pursuit of self-interest leads to viewing others as instruments or obstacles rather than full human beings in their own right. Even personal relationships become a commodity (e.g. the infamous question: "What's in it for me?"). Generosity, community, and connection diminish in significance as monetary value and maximizing success gain in significance.

3. The fear of being perceived as less than rational leads to loss of authentic connection. Based on my experience of working with thousands of people, this phenomenon is very widespread: people are frequently ashamed of what they feel or what they want, and dismiss it by naming it irrational.

4. The organization of production, distribution, and consumption on "rational" principles masks the relationships between people, groups, and countries. It takes enormous effort of information gathering as well as emotional fortitude to recover feedback loops, and to trace, understand, and experience the effects of our actions on others, especially if they are far away from us.

5. The insistence on pure rationality deprives life of meaning. We owe this insight to Max Weber, a sociologist at the turn of the 20th century who dedicated decades to an exploration of rationality in social life. Weber saw an impasse that is still with us. We have painted ourselves into a corner in which we see dignity and freedom as emerging from sober rationality, while at the same time we know, and Weber named for us, the inadequacy of modern, instrumental rationality to the task of providing meaning. Older forms of existence, predating modern rationality, contained more possibility for meaning because human life was more whole and connected. We are progressively less able to find meaning in life the more we apply rationality to it.

6. Two aspects of the suppression of our emotional life have been the occasion for much harm in current times: the tendency of suppressed elements of the human spirit to erupt in destructive ways, and the numbing and denigration of natural caring to the

point of blind obedience to the voice of reason. These two
extremes are two sides of the same coin: the first being a
rebellion against, the second a submission to the insistence on
rationality and the suppression of emotional life. The Holocaust,
one of the most extreme events of the 20th century, is a
manifestation of both reactions to suppression. The eruption into
mass anger of the suppression of shame in Germany has been
seen as a potential contribution to the Holocaust. What is less
commonly explored, and is, to me, perhaps even more horrifying,
are the passionlessness, matter-of-factness and methodical nature
of the Holocaust. Zygmunt Bauman, in what I see as an
immensely brave analysis, argues that what is unique about the
Holocaust is precisely its modern character, not the fact itself of
mass murders:

> Once armed with the sophisticated technical and
> conceptual products of modern civilization, men can do
> things their nature would otherwise prevent them from
> doing. To put it differently, one can, following the Hobbesian
> tradition, conclude that the inhuman pre-social state has not
> yet been fully eradicated, all civilizing efforts notwithstanding.
> Or one can, on the contrary, insist that the civilizing process
> has succeeded in substituting artificial and flexible patterns of
> human conduct for natural drives, and hence made possible a
> scale of inhumanity and destruction which had remained
> inconceivable as long as natural dispositions guided human
> action.[13]

---

[13] Zygmunt Bauman, *Modernity and the Holocaust*, 95.

The Trap of Inherited Stories

The march of rationality, science, technology, and capitalism that has brought us here has not gone unchallenged. In each generation some of us have refused to accept the constrictions that have been placed on us. So far, however, I haven't seen evidence that our collective attempts over the last few centuries to block, question, or transform this progression have been successful. Even in those cases where there have been superficial successes in achieving goals, such as revolutions, regime changes, or some social movements, my reading of history doesn't compel me to believe that significant and fundamental changes have happened.

I want to learn from these failures. In all my actions, including in this writing, I aim to show the possibility of a world that truly works for all life, based on peaceful sharing of resources within a context of interdependent living. I also hope to contribute to this dream actually happening. This passion has made it imperative for me to gain understanding about what might be missing from the heroic efforts that have so far happened, and perhaps learn what we could do, individually and collectively, that could truly bring about a transformation of the systems and thoughts within which we live.

Because I am a theoretician and not a historian, I am drawn to focus on what I see as the tragic limitations of two intellectual giants – Karl Marx and Sigmund Freud – rather than to look at specific failed revolutions or social movements.

I am not picking them at random. I chose them because both of them have left a profound mark on the world and have legacies that continue to affect our own times directly and indirectly. I chose them because they came so close to breaking free of the dominant threads and yet didn't. I chose them because each of them bequeathed to us gifts I want to salvage and with which I want to engage to make sure we don't lose gains already made. I am using the word "salvage" mindfully: the radical potential of their gifts was ultimately lost because they didn't manage to release themselves fully enough from the legacy they had inherited. These losses have not been neutral. Marx's limitations have led to unspeakable social tragedies in the form of totalitarian regimes, and Freud's limitations have led to pervasive personal suffering through reinforcing the dark views of human nature and their attendant consequences.

Despite their limitations, I also chose them because, with some significant modifications, their insights provide a foundation on which I can stand to weave a radically hopeful view of human nature and of what's possible for us to create in this world.

What did they each challenge and where did they fall into the trap?

The Visionary Passion of Karl Marx

Marx challenged both the idea of an essential and unchangeable human nature as well as much of the specific version of the theory of human nature he inherited from 18th century Enlightenment thinkers. His core insights have become so integral to critical thought and to the vision of social movements that many people refer to them regularly without necessarily knowing that they originated with him.

1. **Humans are malleable creatures of practice.** Against a background of theories of human nature that speak of a fixed and unchangeable human nature, Marx suggested that how we think, feel, and act is invariably a product of the particular forms of human social life and organization that define the time and place into which we are born. A simple look at the radical diversity of human forms of living that has existed over the years and exists cross-culturally has convinced me beyond doubt that this is so.

2. **Human beings are interdependent.** Marx painted a clear picture of the extent to which every single person depends on others to satisfy the most primary basic needs, as well as the way in which we co-create the conditions of our living.

3. **Material conditions shape consciousness.** I see great wisdom in identifying and calling attention to the enormous influence that the material basis of human life, both individually and collectively, exerts on our consciousness and who we are.[14] I see the significance of this insight on an almost daily basis when I observe how challenging it is for people I work with to change their consciousness about money, for example, when the entire thrust of our current existence makes money and exchange the core strategy for fulfilling most needs. Marx painstakingly showed

---

[14] Despite seeing this influence, I question Marx's apparent insistence on the one-way causal relationship of the two.

how it is that capitalism truncates the richness of human needs and condenses them all into one desire, the desire to *have*, either to have more, or simply to have enough.

4. **Change is possible.** Through his analysis of historical change, Marx illustrated that no social order is permanent. He also identified what he saw as the engine of change: human beings, coming together to change the material conditions of their existence.

And yet, with all the depth of his understanding and the prophetic clarity of his critical analysis, Marx only challenged and questioned the social dimension of human life. He stopped short of questioning the personal and familial dimension of human living. He retained a primarily male-centered perspective on reality: a near-complete silence on the activities of women and children, impatience with subjective experience, and distaste for the language of emotions.

He never devoted serious attention to how families operate, how experiences within the family change over time in complex interaction with the changes in production, how individual experiences within families within social structures affect the internal life of individuals, and what effect such experiences have in terms of the possibilities for creating the kind of changes he so wished for.

To a large extent, Marx viewed gender relations and the sexual division of labor as naturally given, not as themselves subject to historical change. His future society is an association of free producers, and the examples of their activities are remarkably male: fishing, hunting, and philosophizing. They do not feed people, care for the young or the infirm, or sustain families. However sketchy his accounts of the future society are in terms of how production would be organized, there is even less detail about how, if at all, relationships between men and women, or between adults and children, would be different than in the society in which Marx lived.

As a result, Marx's perspective on human social life simultaneously underestimates the possibility of significant individual change within existing social structures, and overestimates the possibility of personal change within the context of revolutionary change.

I consider his failure to be particularly tragic, because his limitation resulted in a different kind of suffering for so many millions in Communist regimes that he has been thoroughly discredited, and the astonishing wisdom and depth of insight that he left to us have been mostly lost. He has been so discredited, in fact, that I feel an active tension and worry that *I* will be discredited automatically by even saying that I learned so much from him, even though untold numbers of people, including many who discredit him, follow in his footsteps, I believe, without even knowing it.

Freud: A Failed Radical

Freud was one of the few social thinkers who have left behind them a changed world. Psychoanalytic insights and concepts permeate twenty-first century consciousness and affect the lives of countless individuals. Freud devoted his entire life to the study of those elements of human experience that had been shunned or seen as inferior: our emotional and psychic life. His studies yielded some core insights which have transformed much of our thinking about what it means to be human.

1. **Much of our inner life is unconscious.** Freud crystallized, deepened, and solidified the fundamental insight that our vital energy, the drama of our life, is more often than not hidden. He also provided a clear explanation for why such unconsciousness is necessary and not accidental. He proposed that the tension of having awareness of our needs and wishes yet being unable to have them met is more than the human psyche can ordinarily contain, which forces us to repress our knowledge of our true inner processes.
2. **What happens early on in our lives affects the entire rest of our lives.** Freud opened a window into the lived experience of childhood, a world of intense needs and frustrations, dependency, and betrayal. The realization that childhood is fraught with painful experiences, and that those experiences affect adulthood in powerful ways has become a mainstay of contemporary thinking, a background assumption which is hardly questioned.
3. **Healing is possible and can greatly diminish our suffering.** Although the possibility of healing has been a core feature of human life, Freud's investigations put a central focus on the belief that it is possible to alleviate suffering and heal from painful experiences. This insight laid the foundation for an entire human vocation of psychotherapy.

Freud's insights offer a potentially radical perspective which would explain human suffering as the result of mutable features of human society. This explanation would encourage and leave room and hope for transformation. The critique hatching in Freud's writings could center on how existing social relations and their assumptions about human nature and nature more generally are destructive of life, human and otherwise. The tool implicit in Freud's approach to therapy is the possibility of reclaiming, personally and collectively, a more direct link to the life force built into our humanity and residing at the hidden layers of experience to which Freud so poignantly called attention. That link could then assist us in gaining clarity and knowledge as well as being able to detect injustices and the violation of life and to stand up to them.

Because Freud challenged the *centrality* of reason in what it means to be human, it would seem that his legacy could be helpful in restoring balance to our view of human nature. He didn't, however, for a moment challenge the *value* and *necessity* of rationality. Instead, he maintained unquestioned the beliefs that if left to our own devices we would be insatiable and destructive. He reduced our core human experiences such as struggles for autonomy and integrity, the longing for connection, and the care and empathy we offer to each other, to unconscious drives with very little transcendent value. He postulated a sexual and an aggressive drive and maintained that both focus on immediate individual gratification, with no true concern for anyone else's well being. He postulated three dimensions of fundamental enmity: between humans and nature, among human beings, and between individuals and civilization.

As a result, beyond the initial shock they generated, Freud's contributions do not pose any major threat to existing social orders. His powerful insights remained, in the end, a conservative force. Each of his core insights ended up serving to prove that rationality is essential rather than serving as a foundation for an even larger questioning of our inherited beliefs about human nature.

Understanding the Trap

As I was reading the works of Marx and Freud, as well as books and articles about them, I came to realize that the stories and systems we have created live in us more deeply than we may even realize. Neither

Marx nor Freud liberated themselves fully from the legacy they had inherited. Marx tried to both immerse himself enough in the commercial world of his day and to achieve enough critical distance from it to expose and unmask the operational logic of capitalism, a logic in which he knew he himself was entangled. He didn't apply the same rigor to any other dimension of life, including the implicit valuation of rationality. Freud came close to questioning the authority of parents, the foundation of all systems of authority, when he believed his patients about their horrific childhood experiences. He didn't manage to hold on to this perspective and reversed his position after three years of struggles with his peers.

Transformation requires us to actively seek to liberate ourselves from the thinking that surrounds us and from the habits of action we have internalized, both as individuals and in groups. Simply put, we are likely to persist in thinking and acting on unconscious assumptions of separation, scarcity, powerlessness, and the importance of controlling the natural even when we no longer consciously believe in doing so.

Intellectual understanding of the devastating consequences wreaked by the legacy of separation from nature and from each other and the mistrust of both is not sufficient to create transformation. We could still re-create the old ways in our own actions because the inherited stories continue to live inside us. This is no surprise, because every social order reproduces itself through instilling such stories and habits in us through the process of socialization, the fundamental way in which the social enters the personal and persists. It is the very nature of this process – so personal, so deep, and so pervasive – that is one of the core obstacles to social change.

Section 2:

How Separation Keeps Going

What Makes Change Difficult?

I remain forever grateful to Marx for describing, with remarkable precision and often uncanny foresight, the direct effects of capitalism on individuals. He captured with great vividness the reduction of all needs to material ones, and finally to money; the inversion of means and ends which results in other humans existing only as objects for the satisfaction of our needs; and the degradation of the spirit taking place at work. Many of us feel these effects on a daily, sometimes hourly basis.

Still, I am left with profound questions. I want to understand, essentially, what makes it so difficult for most of us to develop a consciousness that's at odds with the prevailing systems, no matter how much we suffer under their influence. I want to understand why it is that capitalism, and any social order, for that matter, remains so resilient.

As I have been pondering these kinds of questions, I have come to appreciate the depth of human emotional attachments and the overall resilience of systems and cultural institutions. I know, because I have seen it historically and personally, that any attempts to create change that don't address the internalized subjective dimension directly and proactively crash on the wall of emotional resistance. An example close to home for me is the collapse of the Kibbutz movement in Israel. The founders of the movement created rather sophisticated institutions for economic equality, even some for gender equality, and yet they didn't, to my knowledge, attend to individual consciousness and to personal transformation.

So I turn to childhood for at least part of the answer. For most of us, our early childhood experiences result in deep wounds which hold us hostage to our (individual) past, as well as more vulnerable to the psychological effects of the culture as a whole. Life points backwards in time towards a past often filled with anguish, as Freud suggested, not only forwards towards an emergent future, as Marx would have it. This is why I want to look closely at the process of socialization.

Early Childhood in a Social Context

By and large we have created social systems in which human needs are routinely unmet. So to prepare us to be willing to put up with such systems we must become accustomed to tolerating unmet needs from early on. This is a major aspect of the process of socialization. Based in part on our culture and social group, and in part on the idiosyncratic nature of the individuals raising us, we all experience a process of selective granting and denial of needs. For example, girls in most cultures are given more freedom of emotional expression – within limits – than boys. Boys are allowed more physical freedom. Children who attend schools designed for the middle to upper classes are provided with intellectual stimulation and are encouraged to think, write, and be creative. Children who attend schools for lower classes are often discouraged from creative thinking and directed towards obedience and rote learning.

The ways people react to our expressions of emotion when our needs are being met or unmet are an additional factor in the process of socialization and subsequently of any attempts to create change within ourselves. When we accumulate painful or frightening experiences without anyone offering us the comfort of empathic understanding, we learn to avoid actions and situations that result in those kinds of painful experiences. Our need for safety comes to supersede other needs.

Similarly, when we have joyful experiences and are not received with love, appreciation, and empathic understanding of our joy, we are less likely to persist in seeking such experiences. In this case our needs, say for meaning, for being seen, and for recognition as uniquely ourselves, if unfulfilled over an extended period of time, are superseded by other needs. For example, we might choose belonging and acceptance over the authentic expression of our own being. However, in the presence of empathy, these outcomes are less likely to happen. Research on adults who function adequately despite childhood abuse has shown that the power of empathy is so significant that it is enough for abused children to receive support and understanding from one adult outside the abusive context to counter the abuse sufficiently.

As infants, we come into the world as a "bundle of needs." If we are lucky enough to be born into a family where the adults who raise us are able to negotiate their own needs as well as ours, then initially we will encounter a wholehearted willingness to respond to our needs as newborns except when doing so would seriously endanger the well-being of our parents. This is the foundation of the experience of being welcomed and cared about that is so vitally needed for any of us to thrive then and later. Over time, we will experience a gradual shift in emphasis on the part of the adults surrounding us, so that they will become progressively more attentive to their own desires as distinct and at times contrary to our expressed wishes. As more and more of what we desire as a growing child is further and further removed from the need itself, and is more in the realm of a specific strategy to meet that need, dialogue and empathy become more possible and often even more desirable than simply granting us our wish.

The complexity of the ensuing conflicts and their social context and significance are such that few societies have worked them out successfully, although the unique patterns of need thwarting vary widely between cultures. It is this almost universal experience of need thwarting which I see as the very basis of human suffering.

The basic flaw of child-rearing is that it masquerades as being for the child's good, while in reality the practices are largely geared towards the adults' perspective. Even when motivated by care for the child, which I believe to be almost universal on the part of parents, the child's expression of their well-being is a smaller part of the equation than the parents' assessment of what's good for the child, which almost invariably is partially colored by the parents' desire for peace of mind about the present and the future, and their own concern for social acceptability. In many situations it is even considered potentially harmful to children to provide for them an experience of full satisfaction with regard to their needs, or the experience of full connection about and respect for their needs even when it's not possible to satisfy them.

Especially early on, we are completely dependent on our parents and need their love to a degree hard to fathom. Even if our parents are not able to be supportive of us, we still remain dependent on and connected with them. Without their acknowledgment and support of our own sense of our needs, we gradually lose the ability to distinguish our individual needs and wishes from those of our parents, and learn to respond to their needs, do what they want, and internalize it as "right" only so that we can maintain a sense of reliable connection with them. This can become the basis of the lifelong sense of alienation from our authentic needs and feelings that so many of us experience.

Socialization and Human Variability

That conflicts around needs are likely to exist no matter what social arrangements we create may be part of why Freud and other psychological theorists created models that ignore historical changes. Essentially, he presented as innate human features that are actually outcomes of deep and widespread psychic wounds, which are the result of common childhood experiences – common, though far from inevitable.

As a result, the task of making Freud's deep insights useful again for the purpose of serving a visionary transformative outlook, invites us to integrate a revised view of human nature with an understanding of the social context of human life along the lines proposed by Marx, a task that remains, to my knowledge, undone.

Families don't exist in a social vacuum. Child-rearing practices change over time, between societies, and between social classes within the same society. Such differences can be quite significant. Nowadays we automatically assume that mothers would need to choose between being productive members of society and being mothers. This simply wasn't always the case for humans. When production was centered in the home, mothers, and therefore their children, were fully integrated into society. The consequences are far-reaching. The relationship between mother and child was significantly less intensive, and the child was more integrated into the social network as a whole instead of being in an isolated one-on-one setting or one of few other children of the exact same age with one adult. If a conflict arose, mother, or child, were less vulnerable to the interactions with one another.

Such differences may have dramatic influences on us, and are rarely looked at from this perspective of understanding their significance in terms of who we become as human beings. I treasure the few examples I have been able to find that illustrate how far-reaching they can be.

Ruth Benedict was an anthropologist in the early part of the 20th century who studied differences between cultures through a lens similar to mine. She discovered that even basic features of what it means to be a child that are taken for granted in modern Western families are not universal. We tend to think of submission and uselessness as inherent features of childhood, and yet they are wholly absent in some other cultures. She describes cultural contexts in which children are encouraged to be useful and active from quite early on by being given tasks that ask them to stretch their limits, while at the same time being treated with great patience and loving understanding of their limitations. Clearly, those societies she is describing have found integrated ways of responding to a child's need to contribute. It seems to me important to note, in addition, that these kinds of arrangements are much more likely to be found in the normal course of events in societies that have home-based, family-oriented production than they are in our current practices. Indeed, as we have progressed more and more in the transition to capitalism, with the shift of production away from home, more and more of us are unable to contribute in any meaningful way for many years, often enough well into adulthood.

Our acculturation into the particular social context into which we are born starts from the moment we are born. Our social context determines the process of birth itself, including who greets us (whether it is doctors and nurses, family and friends, or midwife), where the birth takes place, and what happens immediately afterwards. Subsequent to those first moments of life, our social context also determines how much physical contact we are allowed to have with our mother and larger family and community, as well as what and how often we are fed. Later, it determines the norms of child-rearing, as well as the possibilities for need satisfaction and empathy in the type of family into which we are born.

Jean Liedloff, another anthropologist who worked some decades after Ruth Benedict, compared the ways infants and children are treated in our modern world with the way they are treated in an indigenous culture in South America. In her book *The Continuum Concept*, in a particularly harrowing description of the first few days of life in contemporary Western society from the imagined point of view of a newborn infant, she depicts the isolation and helplessness resulting from average practices in hospitals. Newborns are thrust into a cold and brightly lit room, are handled brusquely, have stinging drops put into their eyes, and are separated from their mothers and placed in a room full of other infants without much individual attention. Liedloff suggests that "by the time [the infant] is taken to his [sic] mother's home (surely it cannot be called his) he is well versed in the character of life. On the preconscious level plane that will qualify all his further impressions, as it is qualified by them, he knows life to be unspeakably lonely, unresponsive to his signals, and full of pain."[15]

The overwhelming majority of Western infants sleep alone, without bodily contact, and are held in arms for only small portions of the day. They are raised in isolation from a larger community by overworked parents, at least one of whom, and more often than not both (if there are two), are away for many hours every day. They are disciplined, directed, instructed, rewarded and punished, and in many instances abused, on a regular basis. They receive little empathy or respect from their elders, and rarely grow up able to experience the tension of true mutuality and dialogue.

By the time we come into direct contact with larger social institutions, starting with schools, our new encounters overlay what are already embedded, often repressed, realities of need thwarting. As adults, when we are already shaped by prior childhood experiences that are reinforced by the societal context and cultural images, we interact with our children in ways that prepare them (consciously and unconsciously) for their roles in society, including that of socializing yet another generation. The circle is complete.

Historical Changes and Their Effect

An ironic consequence of the very phenomenon I am trying to describe – the ways that who we are, how we think, and even what we need are affected by the social context into which we are born – is that, at least in the U.S., the modern way of thinking tends to individualize and personalize explanations about who we are. We know we are affected by our upbringing, and yet we don't see its social and historical context, only the personal, familial, and psychological. Since I see the social context as essential for understanding how we came to be who we are, as well as for being able to transform the conditions of our living, I want to offer a few

---

[15] Jean Liedloff, *The Continuum Concept*, 62.

more sketchy notes about the significance of social conditions for human personal development.

The Contempt for Emotions

While it may seem remote, the change in values that prioritizes rationality and self-sufficiency has definite ramifications for the experiences of children. The growing significance of rationality and efficiency affects all institutions of our society. Overall we live in a world with little tolerance for emotions and emotional display. We are pushed to live in a state of autonomy and self-sufficiency from the moment we are born. In addition, the increased impersonality of relationships outside the family puts more pressure on our families to satisfy all of our emotional needs at the very same time that such needs are devalued. This setup makes it harder for parents to meet their children's emotional needs and is incompatible with the kind of experiences I wish for all children to have.

Child Abuse

While it would be hard to imagine that less abuse took place in earlier times, I wonder about whether it was more likely for people to recover from such abuse in earlier times because they had more support, connection, and empathy within their larger network.

Even when people leave their families damaged, not all of them are going to pass this damage on, even if they never had an informed witness. Our individual propensity to violence, emotional mistreatment, or sexual abuse may very well be given by our psychological history. Still, no matter what that history is, it is certain experiences of stress which serve as trigger events. As economic despair or other social stressors increase, more and more of us, with less and less of such a propensity, will find ourselves crossing our threshold into actual harmful behavior.

At the same time, the very same historical changes are creating cross-cutting effects. While we have less access to extended families and community, we have more access to personal freedom and cultural resources at large. This change can help explain, in part, how it is that the truth about harm to children is becoming more known.

Changes in Women's Lives

Although women's lives are more compartmentalized, more women do have access to avenues of self-expression and more men are being encouraged and challenged to open themselves to the world of emotion and nurturance. This change may result in more children experiencing less gender polarity, and having more access to identification with both parents, a change which could result in more overall capacity for sustaining the tension of mutuality and experiencing wholeness.

Psychosocial Analysis

All in all, psychological approaches are able to explain personal change much better than Marx did. At the same time, they are far less able than Marx to explain social change. In a manner almost symmetrically opposed to Marx, psychological approaches overestimate the amount of personal change possible within given social structures, and leave largely unexamined personal change created by social change, evolutionary as well as revolutionary.

In order to begin to understand what makes change possible on all levels, I want to fully integrate the contributions of the psychological and the social. I want to find a way to engage in what I would call psychosocial analysis: the analysis of an individual life as reflective and illuminating of social life.[16] Psychoanalysis, at least the Freudian version of it, sets out to find in a person's memories, associations, dreams, and conversation traces of their early psychological dramas, assumed to be both timeless and entirely contained within the family unit, and usually based on unconscious fantasies. What I propose instead is to find in a person's memories, stories, ideas, transitions, and even dreams and associations if necessary, traces of the social environment into which they happen to have been born.

This type of analysis relies on one of the fundamental insights we received from Freud, which was essentially unheard of previously: that what happens early on is of utter importance in shaping the rest of a life. Unlike Freud I see the family primarily as mediating social dramas and less as purely the source of psychic dramas. Bringing into the foreground, as much as possible, the social context in which family dramas are played out counters the tendency to locate every problem in individual, atomized, and disconnected life stories.

I find the very act of bringing the social into our personal lives both informative and hopeful. In addition to having the option of a deeper understanding of commonalities between people in similar

---

[16] Unfortunately, this term is already used by a group of people who recognize the same difficulties that I point to for both psychoanalysis and sociology. They have not adopted the path I am advocating here, and an exploration of their approach is quite beyond the scope of my current interests. If you are interested in exploring further, an internet search for "psychosocial analysis" yields some interesting results.

social locations, this kind of understanding opens up new avenues for alleviating suffering. It was precisely this kind of shared awareness of social context that made women's consciousness raising groups so effective in relieving women.

I am not in any way suggesting that there is no individuality or no level of individual variety. I only want to challenge the common understanding that we are a combination of genes and personal history. I question this notion, because our personal history doesn't happen in a bubble separate from social life.

The difficulty, of course, is in discerning the social in the individual. How do social processes actually influence individuals? Although I know of no social theorist who does not accept some version of this influence, I have repeatedly found that every explanation I have seen left me with more questions than answers. What is the actual mechanism that explains how material existence determines consciousness, or exactly how internalization works? How do individuals come to be who they are in the context of an existing social order? What makes it possible for some people to overcome their upbringing and develop radical consciousness?

I would like to believe that focusing on individual stories could provide insight and information on the actual way that the social affects the individual, and provide some clues about how we can recover from such ordinary and detrimental influences.

Because there is so much individual variation, I see it as a hopeful sign, an indication that the effects of social forces are never "complete." There are always places where each of us resists inherited meanings, challenges accepted practices, and deviates from expected outcomes. This happens at one and the same time as we "internalize" cultural shared meanings and practices through our exposure to the family and larger culture. I draw much sustenance and hope from this form of incompleteness. I see it as a resource that can be tapped into for purposes of social change. Whether in the gradual, slow, and unplanned social change, or in the sudden, intentional thrust of a revolution, our ability to retain any aspect of ourselves supports us in generating or adapting to change.

Psychosocial analysis can be a tool for understanding the process by which the social influences the individual, and a tool for exploring the complex tension between reproducing the existing social order through "internalization" and the possibility of significant change.

Many factors influence the extent to which the process of socialization for any one of us will be complete. One factor that I want to highlight in particular is the significance of needs and empathy in the equation. As is to be expected, to the extent that the powerful figures in our early life are themselves immersed in the culture of their social group, and to the extent that they use their power towards the goal of getting us socialized into that culture, they are more likely to restrict the expression of any needs that stand in conflict with the dominant culture.

This process starts as soon as we are born. To the extent that a significant number of our needs as infants are denied, we become more vulnerable to accept restrictions in order to get a modicum of our need for love fulfilled. However, the unique feature of empathy is that receiving an adequate amount of it allows us to hold on to our needs, at least internally, despite the restrictions. A girl who is restricted at home from engaging in so-called "gender inappropriate behavior," yet has a teacher who is warm and supportive and understanding, is more likely, on account of this teacher, to grow up allowing herself the freedom to choose her behavior regardless of her gender even though she was restricted at home.

Empathy can be the force that reverses what would otherwise be determining factors in our lives. This can happen either by chance when we are growing up (and I unfortunately believe this is a rarity), in which case it can mitigate the process of socialization, or it can happen later in life, in which case it can reverse the process which already happened.

Conversely, families in which opposition to the dominant culture exists are more likely to set the goal of critical thinking and the capacity to establish distance from the dominant culture. These different goals would result in different parenting practices, and different needs, which are granted or thwarted.

In recent decades common practices of parenting such as feeding on schedule, letting infants cry, or having infants placed in cages (aka cribs) in separate rooms, or in strollers, usually facing outward and away from the adults, have been challenged. A new movement of "Attachment Parenting" has been developing that stresses child-rearing practices similar to those Jean Liedloff found in the indigenous culture she studied. People who join this movement focus their attention on holding babies in arms until they are ready by their own request to be elsewhere, sleeping with them, and feeding them whenever they want. Since violence is highly and inversely correlated with ongoing physical contact in infancy (see "Whence Violence" page 108), would children growing up in such families be less violent than those still raised in the more conventional ways?

As another example, families with many children often enlist the support of older siblings to take care of younger ones. This practice, and the mere existence of multiple siblings, changes the nature of the mother-child relationship. It becomes less intense because it is mitigated by other relationships, in a manner similar to older extended family and community arrangements. Similarly, many families have other adults who care for babies, again bringing into question the significance of the mother-infant relationship. How do such practices affect the outcome of socialization? What is different and what is similar?

This would be my hope for what a psychosocial analysis would do. I would want to be able to answer such questions and show the direct and indirect influence of society. I would want to be able to imagine what would be different if the class position of this family were different, if the father did different work, if the mother worked outside the home or didn't, if the child had two mothers or two fathers, or only one parent, if there was an extended family or there wasn't.

I don't have answers now, only questions. The examples I used are only meant to illustrate my point and clearly don't serve as "proof." As an individual without institutional affiliation I have no capacity to engage in such research. This unique position, along with my great hope of contributing to the possibility of change, planted in me the seed of doing the only psychosocial analysis I can do with complete immediacy: that of myself. I am offering myself here as a gift – to encourage all of us to break free to ask, and ask again, and challenge what we have been told so we can think in ways that support our freedom, individually and collectively.

Why Me?

Unlike the gazer, the toucher cannot be at a distance from what she knows in touch. While active, touch is simultaneously passive. The gazer can see without being seen ... But the toucher cannot touch the happenings she knows without also being touched by them. The act of touching is also necessarily an experience of being touched; touching cannot happen without a touching back, and thus there can be no clear opposition between subject and object, *because the two positions turn into each other.*[17]

– Iris Marion Young

I am well aware that doing an analysis of self is a thorny issue.

There are precedents, most famously Freud's own self-(psycho)analysis.

The obvious appeal in self-analysis is that I am completely available to myself. I am, in fact, the only one who knows, in some meaningful way, my inner states.

Yet the appeal is also the potential danger: the infinite closeness to the subject matter does not lend itself to looking at myself as an object in quite the same way I would be looking at anything that is outside of me.

And yet…

While some may consider such objectivity as desirable, I think of it as neither fully possible, nor fully desirable. This is where shifting metaphors can be liberating. Our Western, scientific, and now so familiar approach to knowledge equates it with seeing. If we adopt, instead, the metaphor of knowledge as touching, everything changes. If telling a story is more a touching than a seeing, then telling the story of myself is not that radically different from telling a story about someone else: in either case the touching and the being touched are one; the difference is one of degree.

My Hopes

I am telling my story in two parts, each with a particular goal. The goals are interrelated. The first part is a case study of two aspects of

---

[17] Emphasis mine, from "Breasted Experience" in Iris Marion Young's *On Female Body Experience: "Throwing Like a Girl" and Other Essays*, Oxford University Press, 2005.

socialization. One is the effect on an individual child of repeatedly experiencing that her core needs are not met, and that she receives no empathy for this lack. Towards that end I use both memories and a rare document that I have – a diary that my mother wrote about me in the first few years of my life. In order to make this more of a psycho*social* analysis, I hope to show the social context within which I was raised, both in terms of the overall treatment of children in my culture, and in terms of the social dimension of my parents' lives and how it may have influenced my upbringing.

I tell the second part of my story in a later section (page 211 "Finding Me Finding Vision"), though the reason is significant to mention here. If the social affects the personal to the degree that I believe it does, then individualized efforts to create change are not going to be sufficient to create a society that works for people. In order to achieve freedom, we all need sufficient support to counter the social forces that continue to exert their power on us. I provide more detail in that section about the core practice that has liberated me to develop vision and radical consciousness in addition to and beyond simple personal healing. I hope that sharing my own story can provide support to others in embracing this practice and freeing themselves from the effects of socialization.

Because stories have coherence as stories, and to bring sufficient care to the telling to preserve the human dignity of the person whose story I explore (even when it's me, so as to honor the vulnerable sharing of my life), I am also including, especially in the early parts, events, interactions, and some memories that don't fall neatly into either of these goals. I hope to paint a fuller picture of who I was as a child, to provide a context and background for understanding both the immense challenges I experienced as a child and the unfolding of my inner and outer transformation later in life. To emerge from my upbringing into who I am and what I do today seems to me like a minor miracle. It is my passionate hope that this story may inspire others to embark on reclaiming their full selves.

One of the qualities of human beings that most inspires me is our capacity to create, innovate, and challenge accepted wisdom, and even stand up to authority in order to manifest a dream or pursue a truth. I sometimes have had an image of a brilliant chain with many luminous links, connected across millennia and continents, in which each link represents someone who received from somewhere the faith that another world is possible, and passed that faith on to others. I know I have received this faith and carry it with me everywhere I go. I'd like to believe that I have passed it on to others, and will continue to do so for as long as I live. My biggest hope for this book, and within it for writing about myself, is to inspire others in precisely this way.

My Challenges in Writing about Me

Writing about myself and expecting to derive anything meaningful beyond my own life is fraught with epistemological mines. I need to read into, interpret, infer, guess, connect bits of information, and in other ways go beyond the obvious and immediate layer of information I have – especially in the early part which is the core of the "psychosocial analysis" I am attempting here. In doing that, given my own immersion in this story, many traps await me. The first challenge for me as a writer is, hence, one of applying rigor and integrity.

Another difficulty stems from the dominance of psychological and individualistic explanations of life stories. Psychology, being a main element in the current cultural story about human beings, shapes perceptions, interpretations, theories, and even action. I recognize its temptation. As I think about any element in my life, I am almost involuntarily drawn towards interpreting its significance in purely psychological terms. My structures of thought are not trained to look for the social context of the events of my life. Accordingly, I am facing the challenge of inviting myself to use a creative act of will in order to step beyond the bounds of the dominant form of thinking about life stories and to engage with the very difficult questions I am bringing up with regards to the social and the individual.

Even in my own life, I don't know how to answer them. For example, in terms of social power differentials, my father was on top in every dimension relative to my mother. Obviously, he was a man and my mother is a woman. He was Ashkenazi and she is Sephardi[18]. He was nine years older. They met in a context of significant power difference, when she was fourteen and he was her teacher in high school. He was of a higher class background than she was, and he was earning money while she wasn't. Lastly, my mother was also the

---

[18] These are ethnic categories of social hierarchy in Israel.

unpaid, unofficial, many-hours-a-day assistant to my father's various intellectual projects without getting any recognition. That's six dimensions of power differentials in one relationship.

How does this affect the shaping of the individual that I came to be? Here are some connecting dots. With all these differences, and with the social context about marriage and parenting that existed at that time in Israel, my mother internalized fully the belief that it was better for me, her daughter, to have a united position from my parents, and that it was absolutely her only choice to follow and obey my father's direction in parenting even when she vehemently disagreed with it. I know of several instances, both in my older sister's life and in my own life, when she completely opposed his approach and we didn't know it despite her efforts, behind the scenes, to create a different outcome for us. Had she herself been living in a context which allowed women to have their own separate perspectives on parenting, and had she lived in a society in which standing up to an authority figure was common, she might well have intervened in some of the events I relate in this section and the outcome of my entire life might have been different.

My Doubts and Acceptance

And here's a huge caveat.

As I move forward in the unfolding of my life, I am less and less sure of connecting such dots. At a certain point the social context is no longer mediated by two powerful adult figures, and is, instead, endemic in all my interactions. In addition, from a certain point on I am already a fully formed human being. Although I and other adults continue to be affected by the social context, we are not as malleable, and change becomes multi-directional. This, while being a hopeful insight for me, also makes it difficult to know, in certain moments, whether and how to exit the narrative of my story in order to bring in more social context.

I am in full acceptance that I will die not knowing what was constitutional, what was the effect of the individual circumstances of my life, with the specific parents I had and their specific individual psychological challenges, and what was primarily affected by the social context. I am at peace about this because of my understanding of life – my own, anyone's, and life as a whole – as being fundamentally a mystery.

Early Hardships

Eleven years take more than 4,000 days to complete. Each of those days takes 24 hours. Each of those hours takes 60 minutes. No amount of retelling anything that's ever happened to any of us can convey to others, or even to ourselves, the tellers of the story, the vividness of the initial experience of living our lives. Although my own memories of childhood are vivid, I find it inconceivable that I survived my childhood, or that anyone else survives theirs. Part of what feels so oppressive is that as painful as my childhood was, I don't think of it as extremely unusual. It's the familiarity of it that presses on my heart more than anything, knowing how common it is for children's needs to be overridden by the adults around them.

My Mother's Diary of Me

My mother's diary starts when I was born, and has a few entries in the first two years of my life. It then breaks off for about three years, and the bulk of the entries are from a two-year period at the ages of five and six years old. Below are translations from Hebrew into English of some of these entries and below them my current reflections on the significance of these entries.

The Personal Context

I was born in 1956 in a small apartment in Tel-Aviv, the second daughter (five years after the first) to a family of teachers, although my mother was not working as a teacher at the time. In addition to raising children, large chunks of her time were spent being my father's unacknowledged assistant in writing, publishing, and educational projects. When I was eight months old, I lived through my first war. When I was about fifteen months old, my family moved to Argentina for two years, where my father taught in Jewish institutions. When I was a little older than four, my family made another move to a new and larger apartment in Tel-Aviv, where we stayed until I was twelve. My third sister was born when I was nine.

The notes (indented), incomplete and imperfect as they are, are primarily reflections on the selections from my mother's diary that precede them. In addition, I have a couple of memories that are significant to this unfolding understanding, and a letter that was written and sent to me when I was seven.

Part 1: The First Two Years

> They brought you to me for a 10 am meal. .... You were fast asleep and I couldn't feed you. The nurse spanked you on the butt until you woke up crying and started learning the craft of suckling. (2/19/56)

The day after I was born the Western forms of child rearing were already apparent: separation from the mother, and very rigid ideas about when babies are supposed to eat. One day into the world, and three of my most basic needs are powerfully denied: the need for connection, the need for nourishment when my body needs it, and the need for choice and respect. I was being spanked because of not being ready to eat for a "10 am meal." No infant has a need for a "10 am meal." This is so clearly based on following the rhythm of adults and institutions rather than attending to the specific and unique being that I was. Nor is it my own mother's choice independently of that context.

> Hurry up and grow, the milk is bothering me. (2/20/56)

> What a night you made for us. On grandmother's advice (and I decided to follow her advice), I responded to your crying and fed you. So you ate almost every hour and a half. This has got to stop. (2/22/56)

> It's been a few days that you have been a very bad girl. After dinner you start crying a lot. Friday night we had guests, but you were not considerate at all, and stayed up until 3 am. (6/24/56)

Two days into the world the polarizing of mother's needs and infant's needs became ever more apparent. For me, this is very personal. My mother was constructing me as a thing that was burdening her rather than as a human being with needs. I read this entry to mean that she was the only one with needs. In fact, it's my very assertion of my needs that is construed as "bad girl" or "inconsiderate." I see this as a clear example of the social context I have described earlier, where children's needs are systematically denied and seen as bad and insatiable.

How did these reactions in my mother affect her actual handling of me and my needs? How did she communicate her reactions to me? What was their effect on me? The silences in the story abound.

> Last night you had a terrible cough, and also a pain in your anus that couldn't be soothed with any ointment. You were very miserable – and I with you. I was also scared – alone, alone with you and your sister. (8/31/58)

[Later, while traveling by bus:] You lay in my lap and slept most of the way. My legs, especially my thighs – were insane with heat, and were sweating under your weight and your heat – I bore it all with love. We are, after all, getting closer to father. (9/2/58)

The cough is so prolonged – and I am so afraid and worried. I am alone with this illness. (9/7/58)

There are many gaps in the diary, and this chunk is at the time when I had whooping cough, around two-and-a-half years old, while traveling with my mother and older sister, Arnina, in South America (from Buenos Aires, where we lived for two years, to Medellin and back). I am awed at the image of this young woman, twenty-nine years old, with a seven-year-old and a two-year-old with a potentially lethal disease, traveling in South America in 1958. And once again I am struck with the emphasis, in a diary written about me and to me, on her feelings at a time when I am suffering so much. I am coughing, and she is alone with the disease. My own experience is invisible in the story. The part that is hardest for me to swallow is the entry of my father into the picture. As I read "I bore it all with love," I imagine, I want to believe, that this love is for me, but no! It's for the father who is absent!

And once again I step back, and take in the social context of the nuclear family, intensified by being in a foreign country, and the consequences of the mother having no support in the labor of raising children – not from her husband and not from the social network around her. These conditions, mixed with the dependence of the woman on her husband, create untenable situations, and lock women and children into emotional intensities around ostensibly conflicting needs.

The way I heard this story growing up emphasized what happened to my mother. As a result of the heat and the sweat, at the end of the bus ride she had pus and sores on her legs. I recognize in myself one trait, which I date back to this terrible time of facing death in the context of having my needs experienced as both a burden and the cause of damage to my mother. I still am battling to overcome a persistent message that says that I cannot go all the way for anything I need, because if I do someone will be hurt, something bad will happen.

And I suspect that this experience is not unique to me. I sense that the setup of mother against (especially) daughter in the context of an insular nuclear family is often fertile ground for the development of the sense that our needs cannot be met except, in some way, at the expense of another human being.

> You are remarkably independent, and it's scary what a strong character you have. It's very hard to get you to change your mind. … Usually you are also a good girl – you eat well and play beautifully. (9/15/58).

This text clearly indicates that being a "good girl" and being "independent" or having "a strong character" are mutually exclusive categories: the implication of the text is that when I am displaying independence or a strong character, I am not being a good girl. Once again, this means some needs of mine are not going to be attended to.

> We traveled by a small, poor village. Little children were walking around half naked. We didn't stop, and you commented: "The boy does not have an undershirt. I have an undershirt." (9/15/58).

This entry is the earliest indication of a budding social consciousness. Concerns about poverty and justice and evil will surface again later. Where did this social consciousness come from? Is there a social context for it? Is it "constitutional"? Do other children have it and keep it to themselves because of not being encouraged to talk and engage with adults around them? I am trying to excavate myself, reconstruct how I came to be me, with the intensity of concern for others' well being that I have, personally and globally.

Interlude: Two Memories from When I Was Between Four and Five

Both of these memories are extreme acts done from a position of helplessness, the ultimate experience of a small being who is at the mercy of others larger than her.

A). We were engaging in a large family visit. Suddenly I realized I needed to shit. I had a real reluctance to use toilets in strange houses. I remember weighing the situation carefully. How much longer were we likely to stay there? How long could I hold the shit in? I concluded quickly that the effort to hold it in would be futile, that sooner or later I would have to shit in my pants anyway. And so I *decided*, out of total desperation, to shit in my pants. I was fully toilet trained by then. I had to choose to do something that was going against how my body had learned to function, so it took active will to make this choice. The discomfort was enormous. I can still feel the visceral experience of it.

At about four, I already had no hope that my parents would take my needs into account. I was in real fear that if I told them about my situation they would force me to use the strange toilet, which was beyond what I could bear. I didn't even consider the possibility that they might be willing to accommodate me and leave early enough that I could shit in the safety of my familiar home toilet. All alone, I made my own decisions. Self-reliant, already withdrawn.

I tell this story because it is, to me, a poignant memory illustrating the result of earlier training, for me and I suspect other children as well. Not having received care and empathy about my needs, I lost sense that they would matter to others. Once I am reduced to a small, lonely child, I am less and less likely to stand up, more and more likely to accept what others demand, to succumb to others' power to meet or deny my needs.

B). I was running away from my father between the living room, dining area and kitchen, which were all connected. I knew – because this happened before? Because I saw it happen with my older sister? Because of some intuition? – that when he caught me he would slap me. Suddenly I realized my size and his, and that there was no way I could escape the slap. I stopped running, turned around, faced him, raised my face in his direction, tightened my facial muscles and closed my eyes. "Hit me," I was thinking, "so it can be over with sooner."

What is it that enables a grown man to look at his four- or five-year-old daughter – frozen in fear, recognizing her enormous vulnerability before him, not even trying to escape anymore – and still hit her? The psychologist would say that probably he himself was hit as a child, and he was passing on the abuse. I, looking for the social context, recognize in this act a willingness, in the name of social mores and accepted practices of child rearing, to turn off what I believe is a natural empathic awareness of the other, in particular in relation to our own children, and believe that hitting a daughter is doing the right thing.

I know from my mother, through conversations we have had years later, that my father had an explicit project of breaking my spirit. I also know that she made some feeble attempts to stop him or at least mitigate it. She would say to him when I was not present: "Why break? You can mold, bend, shape, but why break?" and he would insist that I needed to be broken! In my presence she would sometimes say what I thought were magical words, because she said them in English, which I didn't know at the time: "Let her!" Then there would be a moment outside time, when I stood tense and expectant. Sometimes he would relent, and sometimes not. She never stood up for me explicitly. The social context is, once again, a patriarchal order in which she would not stand up to him, certainly not in front of the children, and in which the presence of an independent, vibrant, spontaneous, and curious little girl was a threat to the entire order of values and social understanding that my father occupied.

Part 2: Ages Five and Six

The bulk of what's written is my mother's interactions with me, and her observations about me, mostly stories about my interests and my intellectual and imaginative abilities, with a few miscellaneous other entries. The diary is almost entirely silent on most of the traumatic events I do remember, including the ones I mentioned above. What can I infer from the choice about what to tell? The celebration of my intellect is paramount. Indeed, I have grown up to have a solid confidence in my intellectual abilities, a level of confidence that is unusual for a woman.

The image of myself I get from reading these descriptions is incredibly spontaneous, energized, curious beyond limits, very verbal and bright, and also perceptive and thoughtful. I was creative with words (including inventing words for linguistic gaps I noticed, words that followed the Hebrew morphological rules), with ideas and with images. I had very clear ideas about many things.

As hard as I look, I cannot find my inner experience in these entries. I completely love the little girl I read about, and I wonder about her, my experience. What was I hiding already that my mother couldn't know and didn't write about? What is the gap between how I appear to others today and how I experience myself inside? I know that many people have no idea that so much of life is a struggle for me. It's clear to me that I learned to do then what I still do now: without conscious choice I maintain an external appearance of being self-assured, able to navigate life, and free while having an inner experience of being on my own when the going gets rough. The freedom is true. It's just not the whole picture. The legacy of my childhood leaves me not trusting that my needs can be heard, let alone acted on, by others, especially those in positions of authority.

[The selections continue:] It is not simple to tell you stories. We stop at every line, every word. You investigate and ask and want to understand the root of words and their ultimate meaning. And indeed the understanding is fantastic. After one telling you know and understand everything. (1/2/61)

[One day when I was witness to a conversation between my mother, my sister Arnina (five years older than me), and her friend, my mother asked me what history was, and relates:] The explosive response, which left all of us wide mouthed: "History is things that happened, and some people didn't see, and that's why they wrote it down." (2/19/61)

There is no question that there was no judgment of my inquisitiveness and incessant commenting on the world. My mother seems to have given me a certain freedom. She had the patience to let me pursue everything that interested me to the nth degree. I had total room to cultivate my mind, although from an earlier age I was given no room for many of my other needs. My mind itself was no threat. It was physical and emotional needs that presented a problem. I mentioned earlier a very persistent message about good behavior meaning certain things and not others. From this entry and others I gather that, in the social and familial context into which I was born, a lot of talking and excitement about ideas was not inconsistent with being a good girl.

The need for proof is so strong, that you must demonstrate it to yourself immediately. (2/19/61)

Yesterday I found you jumping on the bed, and when I entered the room you said: "You see how the earth is pulling me? I am jumping and falling. The earth is pulling..." *[And also, trying to understand the incessant motion of the moon:]* "You see," you said bending over and explaining with hand motions, "the earth is pulling, pulling, down, down", invoking gravity to explain the lunar motion. *My mother concludes*: In general, the need to figure out the root of things and understand phenomena all the way is a real characteristic. (2/26/61)

One aspect of myself that is particularly striking is the combination of experiential learning, scientific experimentation, factual knowledge, and imagination. On the whole, it seems that the scientific bent was the strongest, and it was always based on my checking things out for myself. These entries, written only a few days apart, are two incidents of trying to make sense of scientific information through my own experience, and there are more such entries in the same timeframe.

[One day I asked my mother to read to me from the big bible. I am fascinated by the Garden of Eden story, especially by the collective punishment of everyone.] "Why, I didn't do anything, why does God punish everyone?"
   [A conversation ensued later:] "Let's go look for the Tree of Life – We don't know where it is – So we will look all over Israel – But maybe it's not in Israel – So we will look in all the countries – But there are many countries – Not true, there are only 109 countries – How do you know? – I saw in Arnina's atlas *[my sister]*. I counted the flags, there are only 109 countries." (3/5/61)

"Mother, you are still learning, right? (you know that I am learning to play the piano), but father knows more than you, because he teaches..."
   I: "But father is also learning, because there are always things we don't know and can still learn."
   You (with anxiety): "So an old person can still learn?"

I: "Yes."

You: "So, so a person dies and doesn't know everything?"

You were clearly frightened, and I could feel that you were looking for a way out of the horror of this absence of knowledge.

"I have a bible as big as this whole room ... (in general, your private bible is a special concept. You say about everything: "I will look in my bible") and in my bible, at the end, there are blank pages, and each time it gets written, automatically, and when the pages are done, new pages are added, automatically, and everything is written there..."

We were stunned, and you – completely calm, because you solved for yourself the problem of knowing everything.

I provoked you: "If you have a bible that is so big, how can you even open it?"

You: "When I want to read it opens automatically." (October 1961)

Yet as these entries illustrate, my scientific experimentation was never separate from my imagination, and my sheer passion for wanting to know and understand things. Almost every entry is suffused with this combination.

As I think about this peculiar mixture of experimentation and vivid imagination, I can't help thinking about the denigration of indigenous knowledge, which always sounds like these people were simply stupid, unable to think straight and make logical inferences. More than anything, these entries show me that the assumed contradiction between imagination, passion, and rigorous logical thinking is not the only possible interpretation of reality. I lived that combination.

My acquisition of knowledge was as far away from dispassionate as is possible. I conducted my own little scientific experiments and deductions with great excitement and enthusiasm. The range of problems that occupied my mind was all over the map – morality, science, math, creation stories, technology, prehistoric anthropology, and more.

"Mother," you said, "isn't it true that each year they make better and better tools? So look, I will draw you" (and here you quickly brought paper and pencil and in lightning speed you started drawing). "Look, this is the hammer they make today, and these are the nails. So next year there will be a better hammer, which will hammer the nail in with one blow ... and the second year there will be an even better hammer, such that one would only need to touch the nail and it will go in ... In the third year there will be a very large nail ... and in that year they will make such a hammer that only holding it above the nail will be enough for the nail to go in." (December 1961).

It is in and through constructing this imaginary scenario that I worked out for myself an understanding of what progressive change means. This understanding exploded out of me in great passion.

"What, God worked in the dark? How did he see?" When he was done on the seventh day you were puzzled: "What, he created everything so fast, how did he manage? He is so fast, God. And what, the knives and forks too?" (in other words, all the little details) I answered: "No, forks and knives are made by people." "Oh, right, they are made in factories. Tell me, mother, is there a different god in each country?," "No," I said, "god is of all the countries." "So when it is day here it is night in Argentina, so how? I know, it's from country to country to country to country" – you resolved for yourself a very difficult question. (3/5/61)

Last Monday we went to the movie "The Ten Commandments." Your first response was: "What language are they speaking, how come it's not Hebrew?," followed by questions about customs in Egypt, dress, food habits, why Moses was called Moses (because he was taken out of the water) *[in Hebrew the name is derived from the root of the verb for taking something out of the water]*, but he was named before Pharaoh's daughter found him in the water, and why did Pharaoh love him, and why when it became known that he was Jewish Pharaoh didn't want him – "What, if he is Jewish then he could not be the king of Egypt? And why did god talk with him only, why doesn't god talk with others, and did all the Jews see him? And what a shame that I didn't live in those times" ... "And why was Dotan a bad Jew? Did he learn from the Egyptians?" I: "Every nation has good and bad people." You: "There are good people among the Germans too?" – I: "Yes, but they have many bad people." And then your summary: "We have many good and few bad, and others have many bad and few good, and some are

medium, good and bad. ... And why are there bad people at all?"
(3/14/61)

Just as I added passion and imagination to scientific endeavors, I also refused to let go of my sense of logic in any context. I subjected everything to a precise scrutiny, including stories and myths. My passion was never an occasion for losing my sense of logic. Everything had to make sense, and so it is no surprise that when I first asked my mother to read to me from the bible, I immediately started quizzing her.

I completely recognize myself in this story: the need to make sense of everything, the critical questioning mind, the swift way of making connections, and the sheer intensity. And so the questions of continuity and change surface: how much of who I am now is simply a continuation of that?

When I read to you from the bible you exclaimed suddenly: "I feel the things, I feel how the Greeks fought with us, I feel how we fought the Arabs" [undated, sometime in 1961].

[At five and a half I discovered the negative numbers, all on my own, and proceeded to name numbers:] "all the numbers below zero – the sad numbers. And the numbers above zero – the funny ones. And zero – the sad and the funny one, because it is between one above and one below." (October 1961)

At the time it didn't even occur to me that to think meant to not feel. My discoveries and my insights were always suffused with feeling. Is it even possible that this very ability to blend faculties and have an integrated experience of my world is what enabled me to have this striking intellectual discovery?

[Having learned in kindergarten about a national hero famed in particular for having had only one arm, I declared:] "From now on I will do everything with one hand," and proceeded to recount all that this hero was able to do with one hand. (3/5/61). [And years later, at 11, I spent a whole winter without any sweaters or jackets after learning about certain Aborigines in Australia who slept naked in freezing temperatures, and concluded that it was humanly possible, and therefore I was going to do it too.]

Not only was my knowledge completely intertwined with my passion and imagination, I also had no separation between theory and practice. What I learned had an immediate impact on my actions.

This morning, when I read the paper, you approached me and asked: "Mother, why are you reading the paper?" – I said that the paper gives us much important and interesting news. "Such as?" you persisted. And I answered: "Here there is news about Africa, and here about the theater, and music, and here they tell about new elections to the government and on and on."

And you: "I will be a prime minister." "And what will you do when you are a prime minister?" "I will call the prime ministers of all the nations, and I will tell them to tell their people not to be bad." "How will you do this?" – "I am still thinking about that." Later I asked you if you had already thought about it. "A little, only a few words. I will tell them not to fight against us or raid us. But this is not enough, right? I will need to tell them many more things. I will keep thinking." (3/14/61)

While I clearly had a very national point of view on this as on other concerns, this entry vividly illustrates my preoccupation with bigger issues of the world. At five years old I had not yet succumbed to the messages of powerlessness that later on locked me in paralyzed despair. I still had a clear sense that I, personally, could make such a big difference in the world. I understood that the problem was complex, and that much thought had to be given to it, but it never occurred to me that I couldn't do it. My mother's challenge to me, here as elsewhere, is ambiguous: perhaps simply inspired by her curiosity, and perhaps trying to convey the message that it's not so simple.

At five I said: "I will keep thinking." At fifty-eight, I am still thinking.

[My mother's description of my learning style:] an independent form of learning, consisting of penetrating looking, comparison, inference, the deciphering of pictures, and of course, to summarize, my own reading [of a text]. (December 1961)

You went to sleep: "Mother, do the insane know what they are saying?" And you responded: "When they are healthy they do, and when they are ill they don't. But afterwards do they remember what they said when they were ill?" (1/24/62)

There never seemed to be a moment when I wasn't trying to figure out something. There was no topic – personal, political, or otherwise – that was outside the bounds of what I would think about. And the diary makes it amply clear that my mother gave me every opportunity and encouragement for that process.

Two weeks ago you said to me with a lot of joy: "Today Leah spoke with me." (Leah is a one-of-a-kind quiet girl. It is hard to describe a silence as total as hers. I have already noticed your great interest in her. Occasionally you told me that she would say hello to you. That day you were glad to tell me that she actually spoke). I said: "You see that she is a good and smart girl," and you: "I didn't know if she was smart, because she didn't talk!" – "So why did you play with her?" – I asked, puzzled and curious to know what pushed you to her. You answered with passion and affirmatively: "I wanted her to talk to me." You see, you must solve and get to the core of phenomena which don't make sense to you. You couldn't digest the fact that she doesn't speak even though she has no physical disability (muteness as such you would easily understand), and so you "worked" on her for a month and a half – and succeeded. "How did you succeed in getting her to talk to you?" I asked. "I played with her, and played with her, and played with her," was the clear answer.

The following day I asked you if you played with her again. "No, she already talked to me!" In other words, having achieved your purpose, you were no longer interested in this problem, and you turned to other things." (2/19/61)

My mother's carte blanche extended, as far as I can see, into what I consider to be some of the darker sides of knowledge acquisition – the construction of others as objects. Nowhere in this story is there any real care for Leah. In fact, she remains mute despite talking to me. What she said, how she felt after the sudden drop of interest following a slow period of acquiring trust in me, will remain forever unknown. And that this was acceptable practice is evidenced by my mother's blindness to it as well. Leah silently joins the ranks of those who are made into the objects of knowledge without a voice of their own in the story.

> This afternoon you behaved ... shall we say poorly? Every time you don't get your way you threaten – "I will call the police" ... "I will hit you" – and other such expressions. There was no choice left but to throw you out of home. You cried and wailed and banged the door with your legs. Father opened the door and came out to you and suggested that you apologize. You came in, but by the time you got to me, you changed your mind. "In that case," said father, "I will let you out again, and I won't let you come in again." "Then I will get lost," you cried out in tears. "Go ahead and get lost," father was not frightened. "If I get lost, a police officer will find me and bring me back here." You were endlessly sweet, and we swallowed a smile. The end of it was that you came to me sheepishly and apologized. (1/22/60 or 61)

Leah's voice is not the only one silenced. This entry shows that, despite the freedoms, beyond a certain point a little girl cannot go. Once a boundary is crossed, my feelings no longer matter. The bit about the smile shows clearly that they had to put on a role in order to act like this to a small child. That role excludes caring for my feelings. In the role it doesn't matter that I am suffering. In the role, their power to meet or deny my needs is exercised, because they don't like what I am doing, the way I am manifesting my displeasure at not getting my needs met. In the end I cave in and apologize. My will got broken, perhaps, but it is hard to imagine I actually believed I had something to apologize for.

And I remember another incident of being kicked out of home, and sitting outside for many hours on the stairs leading up to the roof from our third floor apartment, and thinking to myself: "There is no way I am going to knock on that door and ask for forgiveness. I will sit here until they let me in." Was the memory of the previous defeat still burning in my consciousness? Will any parent, ever, know what is really going on inside their otherwise quiet child?

Pause: A Letter to a Seven-Year-Old Girl

It is amazing to me that so much of the diary is full of admiration for me, whereas actual contact with me was different. Sometime later, in August 1963, when I was seven and a half, I was visiting family friends in a Kibbutz while my parents were vacationing elsewhere. Here is a letter my mother sent me:

> Sweet M. – Hi!
>
> I am interested to know whether your memory is functioning well, in other words do you remember everything we told you in Tel-Aviv, in other words, are you behaving as you should be and can?
>
> What are you doing all day? Are you helping Ahuva *[the friend]* in the children's home? Are you sleeping in the afternoon without disturbing her? And in the sea – are you staying near her and do you get out of the water when she asks you? And how are you with Anat *[their daughter, my age]*, and the food, and discipline, and the clothes, and the order, and etc., etc., etc.?
>
> Write to me immediately as soon as you get this letter to this address...
>
> *[Description of their surroundings follows]*
>
> We miss you, M. When we take you and Anat home on Wednesday we will go places and have fun at home, all right? But bear in mind that your stay until Wednesday is dependent on your behavior. If you are not so good, we will come earlier and take you. Just bear it in mind.
>
> *[regards to friends and family]*
>
> Kisses,
>
> Your loving parents

Although the letter professes love, there is absolutely no interest in my experience, no question about whether or not I am enjoying myself, no wishing me a happy time. It seems like there was no faith that I could behave myself well. Was she assuming that love is there, taken for granted? Was she so preoccupied with her worry about how others, Ahuva in this case, would perceive me? Was she worried, perhaps, that her patience with my endless questioning and commenting would not be shared by others, and I would be a burden? Whatever the case may be on the personal level, as a trace into the social, this letter is an example of the neglect of the feelings of a child in the effort to control their behavior. An example of the gradual erosion of any sense of confidence in who we are as we are told to be different in order to fit in.

Blackmail

I started school in extremely unusual circumstances. I joined first grade in the third trimester, re-uniting with many children I knew from kindergarten, but still coming from the outside. I was the youngest in the class, having been born in February, almost a year later than some.

And so it was that I entered sixth grade at ten years old, when most other kids were already eleven. In very short order another girl started blackmailing me. She had found out I was taking money from my parents and threatened to tell them if I didn't give her money, which meant I was digging myself into a deeper and deeper hole, and I had no clue how I could ever climb out of it. I was in great distress, and this lasted for several months. A friend I had at the time came to my rescue one evening, ordered me to go home and not give the girl any more money, and the cycle exploded.

This could only have happened because I already experienced my parents as incapable of attending to my needs. I already had this conviction in place by the time I was four years old and didn't even consider turning to them for help, and it was repeatedly reinforced in the intervening years. For example, when I was seven two boys in the neighborhood tormented me regularly, sometimes even hitting me. One day, when the interactions were particularly extreme, I managed to run away from them and go hide at a greengrocer's store until my mother came and picked me up. The result was punishment, not comfort, because I had crossed a street in order to get there.

The reality of how the world is structured not to support children, not to believe them, not to offer them empathic presence, came clearest to me in the aftermath of the blackmail. My mother tells me that my father was adamant that I had a problem, because even if there was blackmail, it was my character defect to take money from them. In his eyes, I should have told them right away. Of course I couldn't have; I was simply too terrified. I wasn't terrified of the girl who blackmailed me. I was only terrified of being found out. And my terror was well founded. The night I was sent home by my friend I ran up three flights of stairs to our apartment screaming and crying, told my older sister Arnina, and swore her to secrecy which understandably she couldn't keep. All I remember next is being pinned down, emotionally, for days, interrogated about where I got the money to give her. I refused to answer, for days, and suffered so much. I have no memory of tenderness. Three days later I broke down and told them. I imagine they knew where the money came from, and the whole point of pressing on me was to get me to say it.

My mother, once again, took on the complex role of trying to work behind the scenes to support me, while maintaining unity with my father when she was with me. She asked Arnina to care for me, which was a futile effort, given the state of our relationship and the fact that, from my perspective, she broke my trust.

My mother also went to talk with the teacher in an effort to support me, again without my knowing at all. The teacher didn't believe me. When I came back to school a few days after the blackmail was exposed, I talked about what had happened. I cried, and the teacher named my tears "crocodile tears." In response, perhaps, I became the bad one, and was banned by my entire class for several weeks. Only two girls continued to talk with me, and only outside school. And still no warmth at home.

Writing about this now, as an adult, I am still and nonetheless shocked to re-discover, through my memory, the extent to which adults treat children as less than fully human. I have always felt both blessed and cursed by the fact of retaining my child-centered perspective. I often know exactly how a child would feel in a situation. It's part of what helps me work with parents, because I can give them an authentic expression of what their children are likely going through and won't tell them directly.

I was sent to a child psychologist. Not for support in recovering from trauma or in dealing with the situation in school. It could not have been further from that. I was sent to her in order to be evaluated. She ran dozens of personality tests on me, and completely and totally sided with my father on everything that he said and wanted. My own pain, my fear of him, were nowhere attended to. Children's needs are still seen through the interpretive lens of the adults who care for them, not through their own sense of what's important. The agony that I had just gone through, and my longing for the freedom to be, had no room in such a social order.

And so it came to be that I ran away from home. I was eleven years old, and I remember this event as if it happened yesterday. I wasn't trying to make a statement. It wasn't impulsive. I had planned it for some days, and I executed it with a lot of thought of where I was going and how I was going to get there. I lacked sufficient information, both about geography and about the legal structures of life, to know that my plans were impossible. I didn't even get to attempt them, however, because I got lost, and asked for directions in a way that totally aroused the suspicion of the person I asked. He took me with him to the boarding school where he was teaching, promised me that he would show me the way some hours later, and meanwhile called the police, unbeknownst to me. After lunch he invited me to go with him where he would show me the way where I wanted to go. We were walking towards the entrance of the school, on a shady trail with big trees. It was a lovely spring day. And then I saw the police car, and I started running away. Of course they caught me, and held me down, and brought me home against my will.

This was only one in many instances I remember in which adults, both in and out of my family, thought nothing of not telling me the truth. I still know this to be done routinely with children. What I wished he had done is to tell me the truth: that he was worried about me, that a girl my age didn't have the legal right to go where I wanted, and that he would have no choice but to let my parents know where I was.

I know in my body that in some way something in me completely gave up at that moment, for many years. The experience of doing all I knew to do to attend to my needs and being unable to do so was excruciating, and is still a theme. I couldn't even extricate myself from a situation that was so clearly toxic for me.

I don't remember the moment of coming home. I do remember that my father didn't speak to me for three months. I also remember the circumstances surrounding it. It was clear as day to all of us that I couldn't stay another year in the school where I was. I wanted to go live on a kibbutz. There was an established way for children to do this, where a kibbutz takes a child and provides a surrogate "adoptive" family. Being on a kibbutz, which I did over parts of each summer all through my childhood, was a heavenly respite from my home life, and I was aching for such freedom year round.

My father, on the other hand, had his own ideas about my future. He was very worried that his daughter, whose intellectual capabilities he admired while criticizing her for everything else, would be in a school that was academically inferior. As my father, he of course had the legal right to decide for me where I would be and what I would do. Instead, he told me that I was free to choose, and proceeded to not talk with me for as long as I insisted on carrying out my idea of going to a kibbutz for the following year. On top of that, the psychologist pressed on me to accept his plans. My mother maintained her silent support of my father. I withstood the pressure for three whole months, which I see as testament to the immense strength of my spirit, and which I imagine was incredibly worrisome for my father. In the end, I "voluntarily" gave up on my desire to move to a kibbutz. Had he simply enforced his view by making the decision, I would have been able to retain my inner resistance, my conviction in myself, despite my upset. I wouldn't have been crushed as I was by having to lose my inner sense of power in resisting him.

Like almost all other children, there was no way that I could have emerged from childhood without significant loss in the name of "socialization." The entire force of authority, including my father, the psychologist, and the police who brought me home, were united in an effort to make me adjust to the social order. I had no one to turn to in my anguish, no tenderness, and no empathy. I felt broken, and I lost hope. From then on, all I could do was wait.

Forced Exile

One of the biggest surprises of my early life, as I look back on it, is how my seventh grade turned out. Because at the end of my sixth grade I agreed, under duress, to accept a plan of action that was not of my choice, I would have expected to hate the following year. Instead, that year was the best experience I had for many years to come. These were days in which the Ministry of Education in Israel was exploring a shift from a model of eight years of primary education and four years of secondary to having six years of primary, three years of intermediate, and three years of secondary. I joined the first year of an experimental program with brand new curricula, hand-picked students, and the best of the teachers in the high school that sponsored the program. Finally, I was with many other children who, like me, were eager to learn, with teachers who could meet our eagerness, and with a lot of attention given to our well being. I simply loved it.

At the beginning of eighth grade the level of success was so dramatic that I was elected as a representative to the student government. For someone who was so severely ostracized as I was in sixth grade, this was simply heaven.

It was from this significant reprieve that I was plucked away, once again against my vociferous opposition, and taken, for two years, to another country, following my parents' decision to take on a position of Jewish education in Mexico City. My resistance to going was so intense that I was semi-seriously contemplating jumping off the ship and swimming back to Israel.

My parents had the legal right to take me against my will. That right is enshrined in millennia of social norms. Would I have wanted my parents not to go to Mexico because I didn't want to go? Not exactly. I would have wanted them to be open to considering not going as a possible outcome once all the needs were on the table. More than anything, I would have wanted them to hear and appreciate the horrible loss I was about to incur, to hear my plight and hold my needs alongside theirs. I would have wanted them to let me know, in full, their needs, their struggles, and their perspective that would lead them to want to go. I would have wanted to be invited into joint holding of all the needs and making the decision together. The experience of having no choice and no say in our lives

– which is endemic and pervasive in almost all children's lives, in many women's lives, still, around the world, and in other groups with little access to resources – is acutely painful and traumatic. I wish this kind of pain on no one, not even on people who have committed acts of horror against others, and certainly not on anyone on a daily basis .

The Israel I was raised in was established on the basis of what was known as "labor values." This meant, from my vantage point as a youth movement enthusiast, contempt for consumption and anything that came from "America," and a diffuse belief in equality, working the land, and some kind of pioneer mentality. When I left Israel, television was just beginning to be introduced. With this set of beliefs, values, and practices, I was thrown into an English school in Mexico (i.e. based on the British educational system with teachers imported from Britain) populated by children of diplomats and business people from the U.S. I was still the youngest in my class, and absolutely and completely clueless about the world at large. Juxtaposed against these sophisticated children, many of whom had already lived in several countries, I stood no chance.

And so it was that I was exposed to ever more social isolation and torment, on par with or even more extreme than what I had endured before. One night, while on a multi-night school trip, I was locked out of the cabin, on purpose, for the whole night. I stood leaning against a tree, freezing, having knocked and begged to at least come in and get a sweater. I regularly saw swastikas on the blackboard when I came in to school. Essentially no one played with me, though one girl sometimes took pity on me. At home I was subjected to intense pressure to learn both English and Spanish. I experienced complete and total alienation from my parents, as my own diary from that time testifies. My relationship with my older sister Arnina continued to be tense.

As part of the ongoing approach to raising me, and especially during this period, my father would routinely tell me how I would one day thank them for how they raised me (a day which, incidentally, is yet to come). In that context, he would often ask, in the middle of an intense stalemate between us, "Do you really believe we intend to harm you?" This was a question with a right answer, and I knew the right answer. Most of the time I also said it: "No." One day, sitting around the table, I had the strength, for a moment, to stand up to him. This was my great bitterly triumphant moment in these two dark years. I have no memory of what came before or after. I knew I would suffer consequences, and yet in response to the inevitable question I said: "Yes!" I don't even know whether or not I believed the answer. I just remember the immense and total relief, the sense of freedom, of truth-telling, even if my words didn't describe technical truth. What consequences I suffered I don't remember.

I survived this period like prisoners do: counting down the days. I knew that counting two years at once would be impossible to sustain, simply too depressing, and so I counted little milestones and when I reached them started counting again.

When we left for Mexico my parents promised me that if things were rough *enough* I would be allowed to travel back to Israel and live on a kibbutz, the dream I had had before seventh grade. I lived through the entire first year relying on this promise. When I came to them to make the arrangements they minimized what had happened to me, and prevented me from going back. The line I remember my mother saying is: "If things had been so bad, we would have known." I see this as one more installment of the prevalence of the adult perspective. The child's plight, my own, was disregarded, secondary at best. If they didn't know, it's because I didn't trust them to tell them what my experience of life was.

I dedicate this particular story to all the children who don't tell their stories because no one will listen, and to all the parents who want to learn to listen.

Turning towards Hope

In case it's not already abundantly clear, I am deeply troubled by the path that Western civilization has taken and to which it subsequently subjected the rest of the world. I don't share the belief that rationality is the essence of humanity nor do I see it as superior to emotions and needs. I don't believe that human beings are fundamentally selfish nor do I believe that we need to be controlled, either in childhood or as adults, in order for social life to function.

I have allowed myself to question these fundamental assumptions explicitly and directly, and to that extent I am no longer part of the inherited story about the superiority and necessity of rationality. Instead, as the previous book in this series illustrated, I have complete and practical faith in the possibility of creating human societies that work, where everyone's needs are cared for and routinely met, where resources are sufficient and are consciously shared, and where our various faculties are integrated into a whole that works to fulfill our own and others' needs with all resources, internal and external, that are available to us.

Towards that end, I see a great need for restoring balance, for renewing our appreciation of the orphaned aspects of our human experience. For the longest time many people's hope has rested on the assumption that reason is the only foundation for a working social order. That assumption leaves only two options: an optimism which downplays the significance of non-rational elements and considers them "conquerable" by reason, and a pessimism which is aware of these elements and cannot conceive of an integration.

With the pessimists, I maintain that human passions cannot be suppressed. Unlike the optimists, though, I argue that it is not necessary to suppress them in order to have hope. I want our needs, desires, emotions, imagination, intuition, and faith to be embraced as a route towards changing relationships with self, others, and nature.

At the same time, I am not advocating a romantic glorification of completely unrestrained expressions of emotions. Rather, I suggest that the faculty of reason is not comprehensive enough on its own to serve as a foundation for human social organization, and that the bias in its favor is at best problematic and at worst dangerous. The problem with reason is not its use, but its exclusivity. Rather than banishing reason altogether, I simply call for its de-throning. This call is grounded in a more hopeful view of human nature, one in which there is no intrinsic need for suppression of our natural inclinations in order to avert dangerous outcomes.

Reason, and by extension science and technology, can be instruments for the satisfaction of a variety of human needs, both material and spiritual. On the material level, reason can provide better means of feeding, clothing, sheltering, and protecting from harm ever larger numbers of human beings. On the spiritual level, reason can satisfy needs for making sense of the world, as well as help understand other aspects of human life. Moreover, rather than being used for suppressing our emotional life, reason can shed light on our emotional life and help us get clarity and insight by providing tools for articulating with precision the complexities of the psyche.

Since we are emerging from millennia of focus on and valuation of reason, restoring any kind of balance will require a conscious and deliberate effort to counter the dominance of reason. The so-called non-rational elements of our human experience, action, and motivation, which have previously been devalued, need to be re-valued as a precondition for dissolving the polarity. Such integration is the ground for my own hope in what's still possible

Section 3:

Rethinking Human Nature

Reintegrating Reason
with Emotion

Because so much hinges on how we relate to emotions – even more than on how we relate to reason – I want to change the terms of the conversation about emotions. I want to transform the root of the difficulty, which is the very polarity of rationality and irrationality. This dichotomy reinforces the denigration of our inner life, and renders invisible a variety of other possible ways of relating to our experience of the inner life.

What I see instead are other dimensions that define how we relate to our inner experience. One dimension is how close to or distant from our inner life we choose to be. Another is the degree to which we accept the content of our inner life. The third is the degree of control we exercise over our inner experiences and their expressions. A fourth is the degree of awareness with which we experience our emotional life. The fifth is our capacity to tolerate discomfort or psychic tension. And the sixth is the degree of importance we accord to our emotional life.

I have found enormous value in being able to look at different human experiences through this multi-dimensional lens, and I would like to use some examples to show why I find it so satisfying. Not all the dimensions are relevant in all the examples below, and I left some out which could go either way.

So, for example, the traditional stance of rationality would be characterized by a high degree of distance from our emotions, a low degree of acceptance of them, a high degree of (successful) control, and a low degree of importance that we accord to our inner life. Usually this stance also manifests in a low degree of both awareness of emotions and of tolerance for psychic tension, though neither of these appears to me to be inherent in this stance.

The stance characterized as "irrational" can often be characterized as a helpless resignation to the power of non-rational elements. It strikes me as a paradoxical stance, in that very often it includes a high degree of effort to control the emotions, albeit unsuccessful. Because this kind of state is so varied and so often viewed as failure, I am hesitant to formalize it into one characterization.

In rural China, research identified a frame of mind, or a state, of accepting emotions, being relatively close to them, exercising very little attempt to control them, being unaware of them, and attributing no importance to them whatsoever.[19] I was so astonished and delighted when I heard of this experience, because it's so vastly different from our habitually polarized way of viewing emotions that it supported me in having the freedom to see more options.

The state of mindfulness arrived at through Buddhist meditation is characterized by accepting our emotions, being distant from them, exercising very little attempt to control them, having a full awareness of the whole process, and tolerating psychic tension.

Learning from and healing through relating with emotions, what I often refer to as being in empathic space, is characterized by complete acceptance of our own and others' experience, needs, and emotions, staying very close to this realm, making no attempt to control it, being fully aware of it, having high tolerance for psychic tension, and considering the process to be of great importance.

Because I believe that liberating ourselves from the legacy of modern life requires a willingness to relate fully to our emotions, and in particular cultivating the capacity to tolerate psychic tension, I intend to come back to this aspect of the topic later. For the moment, my main hope in introducing this multi-dimensional perspective is simply to destabilize the dichotomy and the denigration of our emotional life.

Dissolving the Duality

While the valuation of reason has been a constant thread in Western thought, it is only since the Enlightenment that emotions are seen as mutually exclusive with reason, a view which leads to their blanket devaluation. This devaluation goes to extremes at times, as in this quote from Karl Popper, a prominent philosopher in the twentieth century, about what happens during a dispute: "There are only two solutions; one is the use of emotion, and ultimately of violence, and

---

[19] See Sulamith Heins Potter, "The Cultural Construction of Emotion in Rural Chinese Social Life." I had never considered this combination before reading this article, and am deeply indebted to Potter for opening my eyes to the possibility of assigning so little importance to our emotions while being so accepting of them.

the other is the use of reason, of impartiality, of reasonable compromise."[20] Popper gives voice to a mistrust of emotions so deep, that he cannot imagine a positive role for emotions in times of dispute. Similarly, emotions are seen as destructive of the ability to think, choose, and decide, and as interfering with knowledge and understanding. In all matters large and small, the assumption is that the use of unadulterated reason would yield the best outcome.

I question the idea that reason and emotion are mutually exclusive, and I do not accept the supremacy of reason. I consider the ideal of a disembodied, unadulterated reason to be not only undesirable, but actually impossible. This is why Antonio Damasio, who discovered that people without the capacity to feel (a rare brain condition) have no ability to make decisions, calls his book *Descartes' Error!*

Moment by moment, emotions and reason act as parallel and equally significant features of life, providing us with two different kinds of information. One provides comprehension, and the other meaning and vitality. Any attempt to use either of them for what the other faculty can provide results in impaired functioning.

My challenge of the dominant view goes to the core of what it means to be human, to act and exist within the world. Even if reason can exist without emotion, being human is not possible without them both. The ideal of humanity glorified by rationalists for centuries is in the final analysis not really an ideal of humanity, but rather one of a disembodied mind, existing outside time and space, which cannot have the full range of the experience of being human, its depth, meaning, and purpose.

However critical we become of our culture, we are immersed within it, and cannot transcend it beyond a certain point without fundamental change. As an individual from a Western culture, I have struggled both experientially and intellectually with just how far a deeper engagement with emotions can push and expand those limits and enable transcendence of the culture. Is it possible to consciously choose a different story from the one we have inherited? What would a story that integrates reason and emotion look like?

If the view of human nature is so core and central, is there any basis for thinking we have inherited a flawed one and can recover a different view on the basis of which we can treat ourselves and each

---

[20] Karl Popper, *The Open Society*, 441.

other differently, and, more to the point, build different institutions and pass on a different legacy to our children?

As I began to question the idea that we are where we are as a species simply because this is our nature, and to imagine the possibility that we are not, after all, isolated individuals who are self-seeking and dangerous creatures, I started asking new questions. Is there a way of understanding human life and human nature that is attentive to social and historical dimensions, inclusive of the possibilities and limitations of existing social arrangements, sensitive to their effects on human beings, open to the hope of creating a different social order based on need satisfaction, and cognizant of obstacles to its attainment? If suffering, scarcity, separation, and violence, for example, are not innately given, then why do we have them? What would make it possible to meet human needs on a global scale?

Putting Needs at the Center

I believe it's a useful philosophy to hold that people are neither good nor bad innately but are beings who try to meet their needs with the tools they have at hand. And those needs include wanting to take care of themselves, connect with and contribute to others. And if they see that they can get their needs met without harming others, they will only be happy to do so. In fact, my hope is that when they have this consciousness, they will see that their own needs won't get fully met until everyone's needs are met as well.[21]

– Jeyanthy Siva

Emerging from a millennia-old story based in fear, scarcity, and separation is no small task. Because I believe so strongly that the stories we collectively tell ourselves, each other, and the next generation are so powerful, I want to fully tell a different story, to offer a theory of human nature that truly integrates reason and emotion. For this task I follow the lead of others, primarily Marshall Rosenberg, and to a smaller extent Manfred Max-Neef, in proposing human needs as a core organizing principle for understanding human action at all levels.

Since understanding and connecting with our needs is a non-rational experience, while choosing actions to meet our needs relies on information and strategic thinking, placing human needs at the center is clearly an integrative move.

Additionally, the concept of needs has several peculiar properties which make it paradoxical, and thus well suited for the task of integration. Needs indicate limits on our freedom as well as possibilities for its expression; they contain what unites us with the non-human animals and life as a whole as well as what separates us and makes us "truly" human; they straddle the border between the biological and the psychological; they irreducibly contain universal as well as particular elements; they are neither purely essential/universal nor purely relative; they are both matters of fact and inextricably matters of value; and they contain both objective and subjective elements. Needs appear at the intersection between the individual, the interpersonal, and the social. As such they are uniquely suited for

---

[21] These words come from a letter I received from a friend and colleague, Jeyanthy Siva, who teaches Nonviolent Communication in Sri Lanka.

an exploration of human nature which seeks to rebalance dichotomies.

Understanding human needs can free us from the legacy of viewing our human nature as dangerous and in need of control, and restore a sense of dignity to who we are. That dignity comes from our ability to apply our mind and heart together to make choices based on clarity about our true human needs. Freud's image of only two deeply unconscious drives – an insatiable sexual drive combined with a destructive built-in aggressive drive – continues to permeate our common sense understanding, leaving us with a vague sense that we are hardwired in ways that make human sociability tenuous. It is these notions that we regularly invoke when we say anything that implies that nothing better could be expected because "this is just human nature." I want to challenge these notions by taking a deep look at what human needs are and how understanding them can restore faith in humanity and in the possibility of a livable future.

Basic Human Needs

As a starting point, I have accepted Rosenberg's profound insight that all life, including human life, is focused on the attempt to meet needs, and that every action taken by a living organism is motivated by needs. Although it may be intuitively appealing to create hierarchies of needs (just remember how hard it can be to think about anything but food when we are hungry), I believe such hierarchies ultimately fail to capture the human experience in its fullness. For one thing, studies indicate that failure to receive love and attachment in early infancy results in severe harm, including premature death, indicating that not meeting psychological needs can at times be as devastating as not meeting physical needs. Such harm can be long lasting, even if not fatal, or lead to harming others or nature.

Our relationship with needs is intricate. Unlike instincts, needs can be overridden, even if at a cost to us. As examples of martyrdom illustrate, we may even override the need for life preservation when some other value is more important. Perhaps one of the features unique to human beings is that the exercise of autonomy remains an option under almost any conditions. Sometimes we are even able to choose not to satisfy a need if the only option for satisfying it is at odds with some deeply held value such as dignity. And while it is true that persistent hunger may blunt the ability to become aware of other needs, it can also be the very occasion for becoming aware of the social causes for the persistent hunger, and subsequently for social action aimed at creating change.

For a sense of order, I have integrated Rosenberg's and Max-Neef's forms of cataloging needs and grouped them into four categories: subsistence and security, freedom, connection, and meaning. Viewed through this lens, the original claim made by Rosenberg can be restated: one of about 100 variations and sub-categories of the above four is responsible for every human action, choice, reaction, or even thought that happens on this planet.[22]

From Strategy to Need

By and large, we don't experience needs in these abstract forms. Instead, we usually encounter a multiplicity of large and small, urgent or calm, intense or mild wishes, wants, desires, and impulses which often mask the underlying need and keep it from becoming conscious. I see this challenge as the main reason why earlier attempts to categorize needs have floundered. They can only succeed when we account for the relationship between needs and their manifestations in the concrete and specific desires that we experience moment by moment.

Suppose I have 27 pairs of shoes in good condition, and I find myself believing that I need to buy a new fashionable pair. Clearly, a 28th pair of shoes would not find its place on any need list. Instead, most of us would consider it a luxury, the very opposite of a need. In fact, I would argue that at the abstract level in which I defined needs, needs are never for any specific object, person, or action. Specific objects, persons, or actions are always simply strategies for meeting needs.[23] Thus, my coveting of the shoes may result from a need for love, or it may express a need for celebration, for respect, for acceptance (by a peer-culture, for example), connection (to a peer-culture), self- expression and creativity, or a number of other possibilities. There is no clear, one-to-one relationship between a

---

[22] A proposed list of human needs is available for reference and reflection as Appendix A. This list is based on integrating Rosenberg's and Max-Neef's approaches.

[23] This construction of words tends to sound odd, even offensive at times, since we want to honor the independent existence of other people, for example, and uphold their dignity as individuals with their own life, center, and needs. The purpose of referring to it in this way is to drive home the point about the distinction, so that we can remember that we don't *need* any one individual.

specific strategy and our underlying needs, nor can it be inferred a priori. Additionally, the underlying needs may exist several layers deep: I want the shoes because I want to feel desirable; I want to feel desirable because I want others to notice me; I want others to notice me because I want love. These connections can only be discovered and examined in the moment, in the specific reality of the situation.

This image of an underlying need, often buried away from consciousness, and which requires effort of a particular kind to uncover, is my way of honoring the depth of wisdom that informed Freud's insight about the existence of an unconscious level of human experience. The similarity ends here, though. Because, based on my experience of working with hundreds of people, when we are equipped with the right tools, what we discover at that underlying level are core human needs, none of which are insatiable. There is nothing in our fundamental human design which would make it impossible to satisfy our needs.

This discovery has been key and central to me and many others transcending the legacy of suspicion toward our human nature. It is the foundation on which my more hopeful perspective about who we are rests. We are, like all of life, creatures that attempt to meet our needs, including those related to contributing to others and to life. We are designed to engage with others in free relationships of mutuality for the purpose of enhancing our collective ability to respond to human needs.

An unexpected corollary of this discovery is that the more we know and allow our needs and the less we try to deny or control our inner experience, the more we can be successful at living lives of fulfillment.

Mutual Recognition

Another pillar of the legacy of the Enlightenment that remains central to our common sense understanding of human nature and social life is the notion that we are isolated individuals. Here again, Freud emerges as a carrier forward of that legacy. He saw each of us as born in a symbiotic and unaware state from which we must gradually learn to separate. He held experiences of union and connection as regressive and dangerous to the boundaries of the self. While many of us have never heard of such theories, dominant parenting practices rely on them in insisting on early independence and separation.

And yet I know of growing evidence that from an early age we are able to recognize the existence of others and gradually become more attuned to their separate existence at the same time that we sense a basic togetherness. Rather than seeing what is commonly known as "separation anxiety" as an inevitable and necessary step grounded in our fundamental separateness, I see it as a reaction to having created social conditions in which our fundamental needs for connection are neither met nor honored. We grow up, in that way, without the visceral and learned experience of ongoing connection, of dialogue and relationship as the foundation of life.

Human life is inherently relational and mutual recognition is one of our essential and formative human needs. The capacity to recognize one another as human subjects, which is the essence of mutual recognition, is essential for any relationship between us to be possible. If I truly want to be recognized by you, I must also recognize you as a person whose recognition "counts." The only path to mutual recognition is treating each other like subjects instead of objects.

Mutual recognition is an ongoing balancing act, not a stable point of arrival. Even in our relatedness, others have an independent existence of their own. They are affected by our actions and choices, while at the same time affecting us by their actions and choices. This tension cannot be resolved, and must not be resolved. To maintain mutual recognition we can neither reduce others to the status of objects that exist to fulfill our needs, nor do we want to submit to their demands and give up on our own self.

Since mutual recognition is so crucial to our wholeness from so early on, we need our primary caregivers to show us that they can exist independently, precisely so that as children we don't feel abandoned. If our parents let us have everything we want, the message we receive, however implicitly, is that they are afraid of our disappointment. Instead, our well-being depends on our parents' ability to face the irreducible reality that they cannot make things perfect for us. No parent could ever have granted our every wish when we were children, nor could any parent have protected us fully from pain and disappointment.

Unless parents maintain a balance between their needs and the child's needs, a failure in recognition ensues. If, as children, our needs take too much precedence, the environment does not enable us to recognize the parents who have obliterated themselves. If the parents' needs take too much precedence, we don't get sufficiently recognized to form a sense of self.

The balance in all relationships is enormously precarious, and can easily break down into conflict between self and other. The only way to sustain the essential human need for mutual recognition without creating polarities is by maintaining the tension and the paradox between separateness and connection, difference and sameness. The earliest and perhaps most poignant expression of the paradox shows up in relation to toddlers' need for recognition of their autonomy and separate selfhood. Toddlers can only get this recognition of their independence from others around them, which means that at the core of the need for a separate self there is a fundamental attachment to others.

For mutual recognition to be a meaningful ideal, what must be accomplished and mastered is not so much sustaining the balance indefinitely, an image which still holds within it the fear of conflict, but rather being able to repair it when it inevitably breaks down. It is the confidence in being able to repair conflict which allows us to engage openly and take the risk of conflict. While as infants we may come into the world equipped with care and trust, and are able to exist in a preliminary state of attunement and recognition, as we grow up and discover that others may have different wants from ours, how our caregivers respond to us crucially affects our own ability, later on, to sustain relationships of mutuality with others.

Paradoxically, the ability to own our own needs would likely make us as parents more able to tolerate the tension of mutuality, and hence negotiate needs better with our children. Without this ownership and clarity, we are challenged to sustain the tension of recognition with our children whenever there is a conflict with our own needs. This challenge is likely one of the key causes of the polarity of permissive or coercive parenting, neither of which models or supports the development of mutual recognition and empathy in our children.

Empathy and Mutual Recognition

Mutual recognition presupposes empathy because the act of empathy is what enables us to overcome the tendency to view the other as object. Through empathy we can experience the other as both equal and different: neither a mere projection of ourselves that ignores differences, nor an incomprehensible other because of being different. No human connection could exist without some capacity to understand the experience of another. Empathy requires both the capacity to be fully present within ourselves, living our own lives, as well as the capacity to reach out and transcend our own self to enter into the other person's experience. I see this dual capacity and its paradoxical nature as fully resonant with the paradox at the core of mutual recognition.

Empathy is a central human experience in that it specifically calls for a joining together of emotion and reason. The gift of empathy is that it integrates mind and heart in the very same act as it brings together self and other. This may explain, in part, the satisfaction of being in empathy: in the act of giving, we also receive a gift. As Martin Buber said, "when we truly confront and encounter one another, we will meet more than we realize: we will also find the divine within our own lives." Empathy, in other words, is not only a means to some other end. It is also an end in itself, a process of discovery and connection with intrinsic value.

Despite its crucial significance, and the growing interest in the field in recent times, a single agreed-upon understanding of what empathy means remains lacking.

The literal translation of the word empathy, which was initially coined in Germany, can most closely be rendered by the phrase "feeling into another."

Empathy also requires a quality of open-heartedness, as well as a mental focusing on the other. The more we are able to focus on "simply" understanding and being with others in their experience, rather than with our reaction to it, the less of a burden it is to be with their experience, even when they suffer. From my own experience and that of others I have worked with, such presence, when achieved, amounts to "savoring" the other's experience, and can be quite blissful and expansive.

Obstacles to Empathy in Contemporary Society

Contemporary capitalist society stresses competition and individualism and pits our needs against each other in the context of manufactured scarcity. In Manhattan, for example, competition for the few "good" public schools is so intense that four-year-olds must undergo stressful entrance examinations which, if they fail, may bar their entry into school and permanently affect the whole of the rest of their lives. The scarcity is manufactured in the sense that it's based on the idea that only so many children can have access to educational experiences that are enriching and stimulating.

Empathy presupposes the ability to transcend the self and reach out to another. Since it calls for a temporary suspension of our own needs, it is not likely to emerge as a widely available ability in a society replete with rampant capitalism, immediate gratification through consumerism, and hyper-autonomy, mixed with violence and a general lack of generosity. In this kind of context most of us have an incentive to harden our hearts to be able to survive. It is a context which makes the gift of empathy both desperately needed and sorely lacking.

Despite these devastating conditions, I still maintain that connectedness and mutual recognition are our basic human reality, and extreme isolation a culturally manufactured illusion. To say, as I believe, that we are "hard-wired" for mutual recognition and empathy does not necessarily mean that we will always act in caring, compassionate ways. Rather, it means that to the extent that we ignore care and empathy and cultivate other emotional postures, we pay enormous prices: depression, apathy, nightmares, victimization, and anger on an individual level, and crime, neglect, and isolation on a societal level. Conversely, to the extent that we cultivate care and empathy and transform alienation, anger, and judgment, we improve our own well-being and contribute to that of others around us. Beyond the personal, as more and more of us embrace an empathic response to life, the culture that created obstacles to empathy in the first place might be transformed.

Meeting Human Needs

My vision is of a world in which needs are routinely met, in which the experience of need satisfaction is the norm rather than the exception. Considering how far this vision is from what we mostly know in our modern world, the question of the possibility of meeting human needs takes on a great deal of significance.

On a surface level, physical finitude makes it clearly impossible for all of us to have everything we want all the time. At the same time, it is clearly documented that, at least for now, we possess, globally, enough resources to feed, clothe, and shelter all of us. The question of whether or not needs can be satisfied depends on the connection between our needs and the myriad surface desires to which they give rise. Without making that distinction, we can easily get discouraged by the overwhelming amount of suffering due to unmet needs that exists in the world.

Freud confronted the fact that human needs were largely unmet from the premise that human needs are in principle not satisfiable. He effectively preempted any discussion of need satisfaction by postulating its impossibility. All he could focus on was the *consequences* of unmet needs, most especially during early childhood, and on attempts to mitigate the pain by renouncing needs. To the extent that Freud's legacy continues to permeate, unchallenged, our cultural framework of human nature, we will continue to accept a world of suffering as inevitable. If we want to create a different world, it's imperative that we identify and transform his legacy and arrive at a radically different understanding of human needs.

Juxtaposing the belief that human needs can in principle be met with the fact of the prevalence of unmet human needs leads me to focus on the *causes* of why needs have so far been unmet, and some of the *conditions* required to satisfy needs.

This is, again, one of the reasons why I chose to focus on Marx and to follow his lead in terms of the possibility of a satisfying human life. Like him, I believe that eternal renunciation of the kind assumed by Freud is not inevitable but rather socially necessitated and historically produced.

Unsurprisingly, Marx's view of human needs was positive, in stark contrast to prevailing notions of needs in his time and into ours. Instead of seeing them as weakness or a challenge to freedom, he saw them as the core of what it meant to be human, and predicted a future in which we will be "rich in needs."

Can Human Needs Be Satisfied?

At the level of strategies to meet needs, conflicts are ubiquitous, another reason it is difficult to imagine how needs can be met at the more abstract or deep level when more concrete or surface desires are not being met.

The key to disentangling this knot lies in a paradoxical property of needs: the more we are aware of the underlying need which is motivating us in a particular situation, the less strongly we hold on to the specific outcome in the moment. Although we are often unaware of our needs (a point I come back to momentarily), a process exists for becoming more aware. My experience of working with thousands of individuals in different cultures indicates that the more we become aware of deeper levels at which needs operate, the more options we can imagine for satisfying them. Thus, in the earlier example of getting a 28th pair of shoes, if my underlying need is for love, and I am able to embrace this need and experience it fully, the shoes are quite likely to lose their appeal.

One more difficulty with the claim that all needs can in principle be satisfied is that we often find ourselves wanting things that, even if motivated by some need, are in direct conflict with meeting some other need. Resolving this apparent conflict involves becoming aware of the two needs (or more) at the core of the inner conflict, which makes it possible for us to make a choice that takes all of them into consideration. If I long, for example, for connection with people, but act meanly towards others, I may discover that my meanness results from an attempt to protect myself from the pain I might incur by exposing myself vulnerably to love and not receiving it. I can then realize that this protection is not serving me, and over time release the fear which leads to meanness.

Ultimately, the question of need satisfaction can only be answered in practice. Unfortunately, as far as I know, no human society has been solely dedicated to meeting human needs, and the data for assessing this question on a large scale simply doesn't exist. However, on a smaller scale, my work over the years has shown me beyond any doubt for me that *more* satisfaction is possible even before changing social conditions.

This brings me to some deep questions that so far humanity as a whole has not found a way to answer. What would it take for optimal need satisfaction to become a societal goal? How can we produce and allocate resources in a way that's most conducive to meeting everyone's needs? What societal and individual changes are most likely to change patterns of consumption to make resources available more widely? In large part, these are the questions that led me to embark on the project of writing this book.

Sharing Resources

The claim that human needs are in principle satisfiable tells us nothing about whether or not they will be satisfied, or even can be satisfied in given conditions. Clearly, it is not possible to satisfy human needs if there is no limit to how many of us there are or to our consumption patterns and social habits. Human beings are now in a time and place where physical reality is imposing clarity on us. Because of physical constraints given by living on a finite planet, there is an upper limit to just how many of us can live on the planet and reproduce without destroying the planet. Determining this number is not simple, because part of what affects it is our consumption patterns as well as our collective ability to utilize and create resources for satisfying needs.

Two facts remain incontrovertible. One is that with each passing year there are more of us here and we have fewer natural resources. Sooner or later, unless we change our collective ways on the planet, we will exceed the earth's carrying capacity. The other is that many more people's biological needs could be met if consumption patterns were changed and/or resources were allocated differently.

Thus, although the underlying question of available resources is a true physical limit, we can only address it at the level of social organization. It is only at that level that the real moral and political issues become primary.

Every form of social organization includes in it implicit (or explicit) decisions about whose needs are prioritized, which needs are recognized and valued, and how resources are allocated towards meeting such needs. Our dominant liberal theories resolve the question by not addressing it, or by assuming, implicitly, that the function of the system is to use the mechanisms of the market to meet pre-existing needs. We regularly reduce the question of whether or not human needs can be met to an empirical matter of market supply and demand.

Under capitalism, a system of social organization pitting us against each other, the most valued needs are those relating to individual autonomy, narrowly defined. Our legal system, for example, is based on protecting us and our property from each other, not on fostering community and shared resources. Our economic system offers individual rewards for work that creates wealth for other individuals, while ignoring or under-rewarding work of equal or greater social importance that does not; so selling luxury goods nets a lot more money than providing childcare. Connection and community, primary in many other social arrangements, are increasingly left up to the individual to create in a world of shrinking time, increased mobility and dislocation, and growing mistrust.

Indeed, autonomy has become a fierce non-negotiable for many of us in advanced industrial societies, to the point of being used as an argument against social programs designed to provide universal services such as access to health care. Ironically, even autonomy often gets measured by or translated into consumption patterns and decisions.

In socialist and communist regimes, on the other hand, other needs have been prioritized. Autonomy, in the form of freedom of speech and in the form of life choices, has not usually been high on the priority list. Instead, access to education and healthcare has been prioritized. From the perspective of a Western, liberal democracy, conditions in such societies are entirely unacceptable. Indeed, the level of repression and horror in many such societies, including the killing of millions of people, has been a dark chapter in human history, equivalent only to other totalitarian regimes. From the perspective of many people in socialist regimes, however, including many who wish they had access to more consumer goods, the level of poverty and isolation within capitalist societies is unacceptable.

This level of poverty exists despite the fact that there is more than enough food to feed everyone in the world adequately. The reasons that a billion people or more are chronically malnourished lie more in the realm of distribution than availability.

The Problem of Inequality

How are we going to evaluate this disparity in access to resources? What makes it equitable or not? There is no simple answer to this fundamental question, because we have at least four different schemes for evaluating what counts as justice in resource allocation, and no method for deciding between them. Our current system for allocating resources is based on what is known as equity of output, namely how much we each produce in the market economy (traditionally ignoring, for example, women's output in the home or volunteer work for helping the community). The quantification itself is made monetarily, and it's our access to money that gives us access to resources.

Resources can also be allocated on the basis of equity of effort, which would imply some way of measuring how much effort we each put into attempting to contribute, regardless of how much contribution we are actually making. Paying employees on the basis of hours worked allocates resources based on effort. Paying employees on the basis of units of production is based on output.

Yet another method is allocating resources on the basis of equality, a numerical distribution where everyone gets the same amount. This system is the one we use when we set up a buffet of food that is being served by a caterer and where everyone gets an identical plate with the same amount of food.

The final method for allocating resources is based on needs. Regardless of what we produce, or how much effort we put into contributing, we get a share of resources that is related to our needs.

Allocating resources on the basis of output equity is the method least tied to empathy. It's a way of obscuring from view the fact that having fewer resources means we are less likely to be able to contribute, which means we receive less and continue to have our needs unmet. We have created a cycle which reinforces patterns of economic inequality while making them appear to be based on a just distribution. One result of such a system is insensitivity to others' needs, and an overall decrease in empathy.

Privilege works in part by masking the needs of others and habituating some segment of the population to having some of their needs met at the expense of others without even knowing this is so. In particular, many people with privilege protect themselves from recognizing the effects of their privilege on others by attributing others' suffering to their own actions. This is what I see as the common view that people are poor because of not working hard enough. Indeed, research indicates that people with lower income score better on measures of empathy than people of higher means. It is one thing to cultivate an abstract recognition that others have needs. It is a whole other matter for all of us who have access to privilege to give attention and consideration to how we might change our daily actions in order to be more responsive to others' needs.

Allocating resources on the basis of needs is most closely related to empathy. This method invites us to understand and care about each other's needs as we share resources. Whatever anyone produces, we all need to eat, for example. We cannot share resources based on needs without relating to each other and understanding our needs. In such a system empathy becomes invaluable, because cultivating empathy as a central value and a way of life increases the possibility of attentiveness to as many needs as possible, and to the unique and varied ways in which needs manifest themselves in people of different cultures, ages, and groups more generally. Conversely, when human needs are satisfied, empathy is nurtured and expanded.

Resolving Conflicts

The fact that needs manifest themselves in many forms and through a variety of images, objects, and specific desires precludes any simplistic notion of an unproblematic life. No matter what social arrangements we humans will eventually come up with, the fact of having many surface strategies to meet needs, and the fact of changing internal and external conditions pretty much guarantees that conflict is intrinsic and here to stay.

In the absence of clear mechanisms for addressing conflicting strategies between people, discussions of need satisfaction often fall apart because of the difficulty of finding adequate alternatives to centrally determined levels of satisfaction. One of the major attractions of markets is that compared to central planning they allow a degree of freedom and a more distributed method of allocating resources. Because for so many people centrally determined criteria are the only image they have other than market-based solutions, it's not surprising that the insistence on market solutions is so strong. What I envision, instead, is that an even more distributed and participatory system is possible. (I have written stories describing such a system in my book *Reweaving Our Human Fabric*.) I see dialogue as the true antidote to authoritarianism as well as to the harsh realities of capitalism. Dialogue, according to Martin Buber, is a conversation whose outcome is unknown. Such dialogue goes beyond the cognitive-rational level, beyond negotiating criteria external to the conflict itself.

Within a context of commitment to need satisfaction, and within relationships of mutual recognition, negotiation of conflict can transcend the requirement for external criteria, and result in an entirely different experience for the parties involved.

Conflicts between people more often than not result from having contradictory images of satisfaction rather than from having incompatible needs. What's needed for creating connection and transcending such differences is the capacity to sustain an empathic understanding of our own and others' needs even in times of conflict and disagreement. By focusing on reason alone we limit our ability to understand how we are constituted in relation to each other. The capacity for empathy, which is deeply embedded in our emotional life, rather than the capacity for rational discourse, may well emerge as a primary human feature, and thus as a different basis for hope.

Dialogue can then be based on the immediate, present conflict, with the goal of reaching understanding and transcendence. Such dialogue can lead to enhancing the satisfaction of all parties involved by becoming aware of all the relevant needs which are to be taken into consideration for an effective solution. Such a goal can be even more possible if tools and skills for effective dialogue become widespread within a given culture.

Within the context of such a dialogue, we can engage in empathy with self and other for the purpose of assisting each other to become aware of our own and hear each other's needs. One of the guiding principles of such dialogue is the irreducible value of the understanding itself. Restoring relationship and finding solutions to the conflict are inseparable from each other.

Another core principle is that the ultimate authority on needs rests with the affected party: no one else can decide what counts as a need. Any defensiveness, deception, and resistance to change can be contained and overcome with the presence of empathy. A rapidly growing body of anecdotal evidence suggests this possibility even though it may seem implausible within the context of the competitive, atomized, and self-centered culture prevalent in contemporary Western societies.

Once again, conclusive evidence for this claim would require extensive research. I nonetheless would like to illustrate the point with a concrete example. In the "Tzofe Sharon" school in Alfei Menashe in Israel, a training program was established in 1995. Everyone in the school was trained in Nonviolent Communication, a process which provides a foundation for this kind of dialogue, and learned specific tools for dialogue, need awareness, and empathy. In addition, a subset of the students were selected to serve as "peace seekers" and to help mediate and resolve conflicts when they arose. The program changed the atmosphere in the school completely, to the point where three years into the program the peace seekers came to the principal to complain that they were out of work because there were not enough conflicts that required their assistance.

At the very least, institutionalizing a culture of dialogue and empathy enables many more needs to be met than in its absence. I see several factors combining to make it so. First, given that becoming aware of a need reduces the attachment to any particular strategy for satisfying it, the universe of possible outcomes expands with growing awareness in the system. Second, one of the peculiarities of needs is that the importance attached to satisfying this or that need waxes and wanes continuously. Third, as all ancient and modern wisdom indicates, the experience of being heard and understood contributes to flexibility. Finally, in the context of empathic dialogue, truly hearing another's need expressed creates goodwill and a genuine willingness to respond to it.

Whence Violence

The realist perspective for a humane future is not the man who loves his enemies, but the man who has no enemies.

— Agnes Heller, *On Instincts*

People who know and feel *what happened to them in their childhood will never want to harm others.*

— Alice Miller, *Breaking Down the Wall of Silence*

Just as much as I am challenging Freud's notion that needs are insatiable and therefore dangerous, I also take issue with his way of explaining the presence of destructive human behavior. From his perspective, violence is simply an expression of human nature, a result of the fact that we each have an innate aggressive drive. Instead, although violence is prevalent in most human societies, I join Marx and others in having full faith that violence is nonetheless the result of specific conditions, and therefore changeable.

Simply put, I see violence as an expression of unmet needs, either in the present or in the past. It's hard to imagine why an individual whose needs are and have been fundamentally met would engage in violence *unless* we posit a fundamentally dark nature to humans.

The Freudian paradigm, steeped as it is in Enlightenment structures of thought, assumes self-seeking, innately aggressive individuals. The problem for that paradigm is to explain how such people come to care about each other and create any social order that sustains itself. Any attempt to question the view of inherent violence, any effort to present a needs-based perspective of human nature – including the assumption that empathic, caring, and pro-social behavior is an innate capacity – runs into the inevitable question that must be answered: how to explain violence, domination, and self-centered activity.

The Roots of Violence

To begin to answer this question, I want to describe, briefly, the work of two people who have undertaken to examine violence without assuming an innate aggressive drive. One is Alice Miller, who started out as a classical Freudian psychoanalyst and eventually parted ways completely with Freud's legacy. The other is James Gilligan, who worked extensively with violent criminals in the Massachusetts prison system for 25 years.

Alice Miller undertook a painstaking documentation of widespread mistreatment of children, and concluded that the only reason any of us would be aggressive or violent is because of first being the victim of violence.[24] Through careful case studies she reconstructed the process by which early childhood experiences translate into later actions. Miller took Freud's essential insight that early childhood experiences are a powerful force shaping adult life, and pushed it further by showing what actually happens in children's lives and what the consequences can be.

One of the most horrifying aspects of the cycle of violence she uncovered is that acts of brutality, even murders, often contain within them actual pointers to the original childhood experiences that preceded them. When people commit acts of violence, they often unconsciously re-enact on others (or sometimes on themselves) exactly what was done to them. "Those children who are beaten will in turn give beatings, those who are intimidated will be intimidating, those who are humiliated will impose humiliation, and those whose souls are murdered will murder."[25]

While I agree with Miller that only those who have suffered abuse will inflict abuse, I also know that not all those who suffered abuse pass it on. As much as I appreciate Miller's work, she didn't consider that the social context may well be what determines who among those who have been brutalized is likely to become a perpetrator, as well as which groups in society are more or less likely to endure and inflict violence, or even how many people will act out early experiences of abuse. For just one chilling example, during the Intifada (the 1987–1993 Palestinian uprising against the Israeli occupation of the Palestinian Territories) the incidence of domestic violence rose in Israel.

Focusing on the social context of violence is one of the ways that the work of James Gilligan complements Miller's analysis. Gilligan starts his exploration of violence[26] by looking at the meaning of individual acts of violence. Based on numerous conversations with

---

[24] Alice Miller, *For Your Own Good: Hidden Cruelty in Child-Rearing and the Roots of Violence.*
[25] Ibid.
[26] James Gilligan, *Violence: Our Deadly Epidemic and Its Causes.*

people who have engaged in violent behavior, including the most brutally incomprehensible acts, he concludes that all forms of violence are an attempt to right a wrong and create justice, however ill-conceived and fantastic the connection may be.

Clearly, not everyone who wants to seek justice chooses violence. What Gilligan so lovingly reminds us is that apparently an astonishing majority of incarcerated violent offenders are full of shame and untold rates of self-loathing. At the heart of their shame he uncovers the longing to be loved, so deeply unfulfilled as to create shame for even having the desire. In other words, the human vulnerability to violence is intimately linked to failures in mutual recognition. People who commit atrocities, as Gilligan repeatedly says, have hearts that are just as vulnerable as anyone else's. They defend their hearts to such a degree that the result is violence towards others. Because the search for dignity is also fundamental and core to human beings, experiencing profound levels of shame means that the intensity of the need for dignity can override other needs and lead to extreme actions.

This is where the social context comes in. Gilligan documents in painful detail how existing social structures in the U.S. lead to intense shame for some social groups, most notably poor people and people of color, especially African Americans. This loss of dignity combines with actual experiences of mistreatment to create the conditions for increased violence within those groups.

Gilligan is unequivocal in his statement that violence can be prevented by attending to such social conditions. His prescription is fully aligned with my earlier comment that having our needs satisfied is likely to create less violence overall. The wish to harm (self, others, or nature) will not arise except when needs are unmet to a degree which is alarming to the self. I love the words author Andy Schmookler used: "an urge to destroy is comprehensible for creatures whose fulfillment is blocked at every turn."[27]

Gilligan effectively advocates for a social order in which people's needs for well-being and dignity are routinely met. He believes that violence is more fruitfully seen as tragic than as immoral or even insane, and suggests that such a focus can actually contribute immensely to a drastic reduction in the incidence of violence. Although he doesn't say so explicitly, I believe that he would agree

---

[27] Andrew Scmookler, *The Parable of the Tribes*, 153.

with me that the tragedy, in part, is that our needs are unmet in large part on account of the attempt to control and subjugate our inner experience of being human.

Cross-Cultural Findings about Violence

Although few, some cultures do exist in which violence is either negligible or nonexistent. To me this settles the question of innate aggressiveness, and leaves open a host of other questions. Even if aggression is not universal, it is clearly endemic, and thus is a human possibility even if it's not an inevitable feature of human life. What factors contribute to individual variation in violence, and to there being more or less violence in a society? Approaching this question from a needs perspective, the question can be asked differently: Which needs, when met or unmet, are likely to result in increased or decreased violence?

Here is where cross-cultural studies can support our understanding. How do violent and nonviolent cultures differ from each other? What elements can support us in envisioning social orders or psychological environments which would result in less violence?

Two studies that include cross-cultural comparisons have identified three significant items that bear on these questions. The first is a study by Ruth Benedict. She concluded on the basis of cross-cultural comparative material that those societies in which aggression and violence are infrequent tend to be societies in which the presumed conflict between individual and society is also missing. In other words, such societies are ordered in such a way that individuals serve their own interests and those of the whole in one and the same act. She refers to such patterns as cultures with high synergy, and points out that synergy is an independent axis from many others; in fact, she even claims that high synergy can co-exist with great inequality in the society in question. It simply has to do with recognized mutual advantage. The conclusion from her work is that the antagonism between individual and society as institutionalized in most cultures of the world, and especially in modern capitalism, is the outcome rather than cause of aggression. A social order without such antagonism is possible, and indeed many societies have succeeded in implementing it.

More recently, James Prescott conducted another cross-cultural analysis of 49 societies[28], and found two factors which together were sufficient to predict violence or nonviolence in all of them. One was the degree of physical affection during early child-rearing (which correlated with degree of violence in thirty-nine of the societies), and the other was the degree to which adolescents were free to engage in sexual activity. Prescott's extensive review of a number of studies supports the hypothesis that harsh upbringing and sexual suppression are linked with increased violence. Prescott concludes, on the basis of this and other findings, that "the single most important child rearing practice to be adopted ... is to carry the newborn/infant on the body of the mother/caretaker all day long ... as a 'behavioral vaccine.'" Prescott's analysis provides a framework that sheds light on destructive tendencies we see in human beings. Rather than believing that childhood frustrations are incidental to destructive tendencies, or even that harshness is required in order to curb aggression, his framework suggests that the very frustrations designed to curb destructive tendencies are the ones which instill them.

Alfie Kohn conducted an exhaustive review of the literature on the related issue of competitiveness.[29] He concluded unequivocally that the majority of empirical studies as well as researchers indicate that competition is not innate. Kohn's claim, more generally, is that it is structural conditions rather than innate dispositions that determine behaviors. To substantiate this more general claim, Kohn cites the well-known study conducted in Stanford in the 1970s by psychologist Philip Zimbardo in which individuals were randomly assigned to being guards or inmates in a simulation that lasted six days. The study was intended to last two weeks, but was stopped because both guards and inmates assumed their roles so deeply that the researchers were concerned about their well-being. "Guards" were being mean and abusive to the "inmates," and the latter took on behaviors characteristic of real-life prisoners, such as passivity and deviousness.

[28] James Prescott, "The Origins of Human Love and Violence".
[29] Alfie Kohn, *No Contest*.

Beyond Impartiality and Impersonality

Despite centuries of efforts to establish morality on rational grounds, nothing in any moral theory of abstract principles answers the most painful question of all: What is it that enables so many people, in so many situations, to harm others? It is all too easy to imagine that people who participated in the Holocaust, for example, or who, on a smaller scale, take part in acts of torture, are monsters. It is much harder to try to grapple with what it is that makes it possible for otherwise ordinary and decent human beings to engage in such acts.

Blocks to Empathy and Extreme Destructiveness

"If I were there [meaning in Germany, during WWII], I would likely be one of those who would go along without asking questions until it was too late." So began an extraordinary conversation with a woman I met when I was in England. I had never imagined hearing anyone say this, so I had nothing but respect for her. "How can you know this about yourself?" I continued. Her answer amazed me even further. She told me she knew herself to not ask many questions, to go along with things. She could see how one little step could lead to another, and by the time she or anyone had an inkling of what was actually going on, they would be too entangled to back up. Their family and kids would depend on their income, or their standing in the community would be too precarious anyway. I am wondering if she is ultimately right about herself. After all, she is reflecting on these issues, and with such self-honesty. Wouldn't that kind of courage give her the requisite moral compass?

The movie "Saviors in the Night" bears directly on this question. It depicts a true story of a family of farmers in Westphalia that hid mother and daughter during the war under immensely difficult conditions and at high risk to themselves in a small community replete with Nazis. At first not even the entire family knew that their "guests" were Jews, in part because the teenage daughter was completely identified with the Nazis. One of the most extraordinary scenes in the movie shows the father taking the teenage daughter, after she discovered the truth, to hear some stories that would finally open her heart to the humanity of the Jews. I have rarely seen on screen someone's heart cracking open to truth, and I sense we can all learn from the choices the father made for how to reach people who are elsewhere.

What this film made abundantly clear to me is just how much courage would be needed in order to make a choice to stand up to the force field of Nazism, to the government, to the individuals around, and to the fear of death itself. It clarified for me why so few had done so. There are only a few hundred documented cases of people saving Jews in Germany. Between this movie and the conversation with the woman in England, I have ever more appreciation for the immense complexity and daunting challenges.

I saw the movie during a visit to Israel. Walking out of the movie I overheard someone comment to another about these numbers in a surprised tone in which I heard an edge of moral superiority. I was saddened. I so want all of us to grow in humility, to learn that we have no way of knowing, any of us, about ourselves. Later, as I poked around the web for more information about this movie, I came across a comment from someone that captures this intensity beautifully for me: "If your government was exterminating a despised minority, do you think you would refuse and resist? Or do you think you would go along?"

We know most people didn't resist. That would mean most of us wouldn't, either. What makes that possible? What force is powerful enough to be a block to empathy, to what I believe is the natural response to others' suffering? What conditions, internal or external, block access to empathy and make it possible to harm others?

Failure to empathize is a very common experience, and there are many everyday conditions in which empathy gets blocked. In situations of conflict, we often use a variety of strategies, frequently unconscious, to overcome empathy, since empathy, were it to be experienced, would likely create an incentive to change our own behavior.

Blocks to empathy can be strong enough that perpetrators or witnesses do not even see the harm done to victims as harm or suffering, especially when they hold a set of values, or "higher principles," which leave the harmed ones outside the moral domain. Such was the case in Germany, where Jews were not considered human. Similar clashes existed for white settlers in North America relative to native peoples where "manifest destiny" was the high principle. Similarly, for a significant minority in Israel, the value of national security renders Palestinians as less than fully human and makes them responsible for the measures imposed on them. The single most famous example of the phenomenon of blocked empathy is Eichmann, who likely suffered from a failing to *feel*. Not only did he dehumanize his victims, but also himself; he no longer saw himself as a human being ready to respond to others' suffering. Eichmann was not alone. Alice Miller also pointed out that people who participated in Hitler's actions often did it out of their inability to feel their own feelings.

Fear, Discipline, and Obedience

A particularly powerful block to empathy, and one directly relevant to the question of torture, is the power of discipline and obedience. The effects of obedience became chillingly clear in Milgram's famous experiments, in which the overwhelming majority of participants in the experiment willingly subjected others to electric shocks which, though in fact simulated by actors, appeared to them to inflict severe pain on the victims, and which they nonetheless continued to administer.

I had the enormous good fortune of actually watching Milgram's film, an experience that completely changed my perspective and understanding of what is significant about his experiments. What I found most striking was the degree of personal anguish so many of the participants experienced as they were administering the electric shocks, clearly indicating that their basic reaction was one of aversion to harming another. While people can be brought to ignore, overcome, suppress, or numb out their natural empathic responses, what Milgram's experiments show more than anything else is the enormous cost to us of overcoming natural empathy.

The kind of obedience exemplified in this experiment is directly a result of the rational ordering of life, and is directly related to events such as the Holocaust. Modern rationality, with its efficiency and impersonalism, created conditions that make it more possible for people to overcome empathy. In this case the block is not to the experience of empathy per se, but to the ability to *use* empathy as a guide to action. It appears that the ability to feel and then to act on our feelings is a key ingredient in the willingness to stand up to authority when what we are asked to do or refrain from doing results in suffering to others.

To my mind, Milgram's experiments serve as grounds to challenge the supremacy of reason. Although we clearly have been capable of severe cruelty, what modern rationality has done is make such cruelty possible on larger scales, and more effectively. Zygmunt Bauman, who studied the Holocaust with this specific question in mind, singles out as causes of this increased capacity for harm "those social mechanisms, also set in motion under contemporary conditions, that silence or neutralize moral inhibitions and, more generally, make people refrain from resistance against evil."[30]

Empathy is so ingrained, and such a powerful inhibition to harming others, that even during wars most people have historically refrained from killing. Up to and including World War II the firing-to-kill rate hovered at 20%-25% of soldiers in direct combat.[31] Dave Grossman, an army colonel, historian, and psychologist, who actually is supportive of the existence of armies and believes in the inevitability of war, nonetheless maintains that human beings have an innate resistance to killing, which must be actively overcome in order to make it possible for people to kill even in times of war.

Traditional military methods used up until the middle of the twentieth century were only partially effective in achieving this goal. Once studies started documenting the prevalence of non-shooting strategies, military training was changed drastically, with the specific intent of making more soldiers kill. Current military training actively desensitizes soldiers to the effects of killing and conditions them, through simulations containing immediate rewards for killing, to acquire behaviors that are almost reflexive, so that when in battle they will simply repeat the sequence before having a moment to reflect. The net result of such training was that the shooting rate during the Vietnam War rose sharply and was about 95%.[32]

Human malleability is such that it is clearly possible to do this; we can be, and often are, trained and molded to be and do almost anything. The crucial point is the cost we incur. Grossman's research indicates that only 2% of the population can kill without suffering serious psychological damage afterwards. He sees the forced increase in shooting rates as preventing soldiers from being able to integrate their actions into their sense of self. This is what he sees as the cause

---

[30] Bauman, *Modernity and the Holocaust*, 95.
[31] Dave Grossman, *On Killing*, 250.
[32] ibid.

of the staggering number of Vietnam veterans who suffer from serious Post Traumatic Stress Disorder (PTSD), with some estimates being as high as 1.5 million of the total number of 2.8 Vietnam veterans.

Even SS officers, who were highly motivated and trained to kill, were not always able to overcome their empathy fully. The act of killing and atrocities were always seen as demanding enormous costs, and in a distorted way were viewed as a sacrifice. Moreover, beyond a certain point, open-air shooting was discontinued, because no amount of training could create enough psychic numbing to continue with such brutalities over time. The severe psychological consequences were one of the factors named by Rudolf Höss as contributing towards the choice to replace open-air shooting with the gas killings, which were at a much greater distance, in addition to being technically more adequate to the horrendous task.

The tendency to ignore feelings and proceed with a destructive task at hand in the name of some higher value is most poignantly illustrated by the story of a man, a personal acquaintance of mine, who, at age seven, found a special insect, captured it, and delightedly told his science teacher about it. His teacher gave him alcohol to drown the insect in, and asked that he bring it to the school science laboratory. The child proceeded to do this with great enthusiasm, thinking of this as his contribution to science. The insect, meanwhile, had other designs. Struggling for its life, it repeatedly attempted to climb out of the alcohol, and succeeded in doing so several times before it was finally drowned. All this time the child was shaking, and used tremendous willpower to overcome his aversion to inflicting further damage on the insect. In the name of science, he set his feelings aside. As he later said: "I never questioned my actions, only my feelings."

The movie *Testimonies* provides one more dramatic illustration of the issues I am raising here. Made by Ido Sela in Israel in 1993, this documentary is a series of interviews with Israeli soldiers who humiliated, beat up, maimed, kicked, shot, and killed Palestinians in the course of the first Intifada, in some cases subjecting them to prolonged physical torture. Once again, the individuals interviewed in the movie appear to be ordinary, even caring, people, who nonetheless participated in acts of severe torture. Watching the movie, I was struck by the intensity of the feelings expressed during the interviews. The feelings were right there, very close to the surface, manifesting themselves in pauses, nervous fleeting smiles, a struggle against crying, and strong reactions to the interviewer's questions.

The willingness to ignore empathy in the name of some other value is painfully evident in the interviews. Some of the soldiers described quite intense responses they had to their experiences in the Intifada. Some of them even indicated that they had strong reactions while the atrocity was going on. "This disruption [of family life] killed me," said one of them, who also reported in excruciating detail the horrific nature of the typical scene of forcefully entering a residence in the middle of the night, breaking open the door and waking up a sleeping family. Yet, in all but one case, these reactions did not stop soldiers from carrying out their mission. Only one of the soldiers reported empathy strong enough that it prevented him from taking a particular action, when he compared a young girl to his daughter, and decided against shooting her. Of those who set their feelings of care aside, only one reported fear of consequences as his reason for proceeding. More commonly, interviewees responded with anger to suggestions on the part of the interviewer, who was not attempting to be "neutral," that their victims may be human beings just like them, deserving of care and compassion. Either explicitly or implicitly, they argued that "these people" were not of a category to merit such feelings.

One soldier attempted to resolve his evident anguish over the possible death of a two-year-old from tear gas by being angry at her father for not opening the door in the first place. This experience, especially not knowing if the girl was indeed going to die, was clearly traumatic for him. So much so that, to the suggestion of the interviewer that he might want to ask the forgiveness of the father, rather than of his friends, to whom he had been turning for support in facing this event, he eventually responded by arguing that the family, his victims, should ask his forgiveness, because "they led me into this kind of situation." Once the "cause" for the suffering is seen as the victim's actions, he is no longer called upon to empathize.

Who, Then, Stands Up?

Samuel and Pearl Oliner conducted a massive study of people who saved Jews during the Holocaust (*The Altruistic Personality*). Based on many hundreds of interviews, a couple of telling things stand out. One is that rescuers were asked to do so. This is also true in the movie I mentioned above. The farmer would not likely have offered to hide the Jewish family without being asked. When we are asked, we are confronted with the moral dilemma in a way that makes it harder to ignore and downplay. Let's not give in to the notion that others are too busy or wouldn't care enough. Let's give them the respect of asking, always, for what's truly needed.

The second distinguishing factor is that the people who rescued Jews tended to grow up in households where punishment was not the norm. They were raised on engaging with values rather than being punished for doing the wrong thing. As a result, they had less fear and more willingness to stand up. This has implications for parenting: we can raise our children without fear, without calling them to obedience. We can honor their endless questions, encourage them to make their own choices in matters of moral principle, and accept their mistakes as part of learning.

This brings me back to the woman who was so open to the possibility that she might have gone along. I like the idea that the more we are willing to stand up and ask questions, all the time, the more likely we are to maintain our moral courage. This is something we can do on a daily basis. We can ask questions, especially in relation to authority, about everything. We can reclaim this capacity we all had as children. We can cultivate it as an inoculation against complicity, against losing our humanity one not-asked question at a time.

Concluding Remarks on Emotions, Empathy, and Morality

One way of understanding hatred, the quintessential "dark" emotion that can lead to destructive acts (with anti-Semitism being a central example), is as a deficiency or failure in the faculty of empathy. Empathy, in a manner similar to language, is an innate capacity, but it must be learned in a human social context in order to develop fully. It can only be attained initially in relationships where it is expressed by others.

In our times, however, as we face unprecedented large-scale moral issues, hatred is no longer the prime force of immoral acts. As

Bauman reminds us, "mass destruction was accompanied not by the uproar of emotions, but the dead silence of unconcern."[33]

As difficult as it may be to take in, some of the conditions that enable people to engage in mass killings are remarkably similar to the very criteria of morality we still learn: impersonality, objectivity, and the impartial application of rules to the exclusion of empathy for the people involved. While I am clearly not implying a specific immorality on the part of people who espouse these views, this link gives frightening credence to Bauman's insistence that "the Holocaust did not just, mysteriously, avoid clash with the social norms and institutions of modernity. It was these norms and institutions that made the Holocaust feasible."[34]

Once again, I am coming to a similar conclusion: if we want to significantly reduce the level of atrocities and horror that take place in the world in the name of any number of principles and values, what is most desperately needed are changes in the social order that prioritize empathy and the satisfaction of needs.

If hostility and aggression result from social conditions, a social world in which people's needs for physical affection, pleasure, and tenderness are met is a social world with less violence than one based on discipline and restraint.

Creating a world based on meeting needs affects every aspect of life. It would mean a radically different approach to parenting and schooling, one in which punishment, reward, and coercion are transformed into dialogue, mutual recognition from early on, and natural limits based on adults' actual needs rather than on rules. It would also mean social institutions based on willingness, collaboration, and shared interests rather than control and enforcement. This would be a world designed for people to thrive and love.

---

[33] Bauman, *Modernity and the Holocaust*, 74.
[34] Ibid 87.

Section 4:

Going against the Grain

Getting from Here to There – Beginning the Journey

Even if you are attracted to the vision of a world that works for everyone, whether my own version or any other, and even if you resonate with the ideas I presented here about why we are in the mess we are in, you may still wonder why I imagine and believe that putting human needs at the center can support us in facing the dire circumstances we have created. Is that really necessary to enable us to end poverty, oppression, climate change, massive extinction of species, or any of dozens of other manifestations of the fundamental problems of separation, scarcity, and powerlessness?

Perhaps you will agree that our actions, however harmful, are all expressions of human needs, which are, in themselves, not harmful. If that is so, the next questions are not so much theoretical as practical: Can we ever reach a state in which we can have sufficient mindfulness to make different choices that are less harmful in moments of stress? If our emotions are simply information about the state of our needs, can we reach a state that will allow us to engage with them differently, so we can receive this information instead of being lost in the emotions or the actions that derive from unconscious needs we have suppressed? Even more significantly, how would any of this help any of us do something as personal as, say, stop smoking, let alone end cycles of violence in our families, learn to live interdependently with others, or participate in transforming our social structures into ones that truly address human needs?

My deep belief is that we absolutely can come closer and closer to such states of true choice, freedom, and connectedness. Given that I am overall seeking integration of reason and emotion, it is important for me to state clearly here that reaching mastery requires practice, and especially practicing how to engage with our emotions and needs. To get there, you will need specific practices, specific ways to learn about your emotions and your needs. You will need people to do these practices with, a community that learns together and creates the new reality in microcosm.

I have learned so much about how to do this myself, and I have helped so many other people walk on this path, that I now have fairly concrete guidelines that can make this "reboot" a reality. Everything I am writing about in this part of the book is practical and tested. The success of such practices is a big part of why I think a different reality can come true. I have seen too much not to believe it. What I write about here, my own personal practice of it, is also the very reason I had the gall to write this book.

There's no roadmap to the future, but there is a toolkit for how each of us can get started. This part of the book is my effort at describing the toolkit, with a warning. I didn't learn how to do this from a book and I don't know how much you can either. I am hoping only to provide you with a vision of possibility, an inspiration, the faith that you can reboot yourself over a period of time into the kind of emotionally skilled, integrated, radically conscious human being who can help make that future happen. If it inspires you in that way, then I hope you will go find the people who can support your journey in more direct ways.

Change Is Possible

If social systems are so seamless in their ability to reproduce themselves through socialization, how is change even possible?

Focusing on human needs makes it abundantly clear what specifically is oppressive in most existing human societies. We have created systems that regularly and frequently go against human needs, while cultivating in us entrenched complicity with existing structures despite their oppressiveness.

In this context empathy becomes the moment of hope. Through empathy we can begin to cultivate, individually and collectively, the hope and belief that our needs can be met, hope that may well be a key foundation for creating change.

Even though most of us grew up in modern families and had the particular constellation of unmet needs that such families generate, we can still engage in practices to cultivate and restore the radical consciousness necessary to ground social change. We are much more likely to cultivate radical consciousness and challenge existing stories and institutions when we have restored our hope that our needs can be satisfied.

To maintain the possibility of change is to assume that something in us remains capable of resisting the pressure of the social conditions in which we live. The possibility of personal and social transformation is never extinguished. The hope for change affirms our fundamental human wish for freedom as a given. So much of individual and social oppression relies on curbing our ability to know and act on what we want, and yet the dream of living a life of fulfillment never fully goes away. It only goes underground. Our human agency, the energy that fuels our life, resides in our deepest needs and emotions, rather than in a faculty of reason that is at odds with them.

The Process of Change

Working towards and creating change (as distinct from change happening, which is a constant in life) involves conscious choice and action. Whether personally or socially, three things need to be in place for conscious change to be possible:

- Clarity that what is happening is not to our liking, and a sense of what we want instead. Only knowing we don't like what is will not result in change. We need to have enough faith that something else is indeed possible to imagine mobilizing the resources necessary. This is where vision is so critical.

- Having or knowing how to materialize the resources needed to create the change, and trusting our capacity for accessing the resources. Resources here are both internal (in the form of skills, faith, consciousness, courage, presence and the like) as well as external (in the form of support from others, material resources where needed, access to people with influence and the like). The faith in our capacity to access and mobilize resources is an irreducible part of what's needed to move towards the change.

- Making the choice to take action. This is not a trivial step. Both personally and collectively we find ourselves in situations where we know we want something done, we know we can do it, and we still choose not to take action. The willingness to commit is the final element that moves us into action.

On the personal level, this means understanding and overcoming the conditioning of our socialization so we can live freely. Then we can become more the person we would like to be, create new options for ourselves, and choose how we want to engage with life, be in the world even when nothing has changed, and work to create the changes we long to see.

Reclaiming Ourselves

Intense and terrible, I think, must be the loneliness
Of infants...

— Edna St. Vincent Millay

One of the tools available to people who embark on studying Nonviolent Communication is a list of feelings divided into two categories: feelings that arise when our needs are met, and feelings that arise when our needs are not met[35]. When I first looked at these lists, I was struck by the imbalance between the two categories: there are about 150 feelings associated with unmet needs and only 100 associated with met needs.

I have often pondered why this is so. I hold a lot of respect for what language tells us about our experience, and this situation is no exception. Although this cannot be known, my own intuitive sense is that having more feelings associated with unmet needs means that having unmet needs is more common than having our needs met to our satisfaction. It could also mean, more simply, that the experiences of having unmet needs are more troubling, and so we give them more names in an effort to make sense of them and to gain some hope of being able to transform them.

Indeed, helplessness in the face of unmet needs accentuates and exacerbates the experience itself. This is true for us as adults. Given that as children we have reduced access to resources, and even more so as infants, I can only imagine how much more pronounced and acute the experience of unmet needs is for us in those early years, especially having such fundamental helplessness to change our circumstances right when we are most easily affected and formed.

For many years I was unconsciously waiting for things to change around me in order to feel better. I would even go so far as to say that I was somehow attached to this idea. I didn't want to take responsibility for making my life what I wanted it to be, because it would mean letting go of the desire to be taken care of.

---

[35] The list is available at baynvc.org/materials/Feelings_Emotions.pdf

As infants, being taken care of is a matter of survival. We all needed someone to give us their full attention, so they could sense, without any effort on our part, what it was that we needed, and prioritize giving it to us. As adults, unless we are specifically incapacitated, life is not set up for us ever to be able to receive this form of support from another in a sustained way over time. If unfulfilled in infancy, the desire to be taken care of may remain well into adulthood and can easily get confused with our fundamental dependence on other people to fulfill so many of our needs. We need other people to grow the food we eat, to provide essential services, to engage with, and for just about anything that we do.

The difference between the two primarily consists of where the responsibility for the needs lies. As infants, the responsibility was primarily with our caregivers. As adults, the responsibility is primarily with us. Learning what our needs are, attending to them, and making the requests necessary so others can support us, are essential building blocks of the socially-engaged interdependent living that I believe our evolution has prepared us for.

In many of our modern cultures, however, instead of a gradual and collaborative shift from being taken care of by others to assuming full responsibility for our lives, we experience neither. We are regularly thrust into premature independence (e.g. sleeping alone from the first few days of life). From early on our needs are questioned (e.g. we are often fed not when we express hunger). Our fundamental humanness is assumed to be in need of change and our actions are constantly monitored and even changed (e.g. the constant stream of instructions to small children about what to do, or, mostly, what not to do). Then, when we develop an interest in independence and exploration, we are not allowed basic freedoms that are available to children at surprisingly young ages in many indigenous cultures[36]. We usually emerge from such experiences without trust in others' goodwill towards us or in our own fundamental human acceptability. The result is a high degree of isolation, separation, belief in scarcity, and a prevailing sense of choicelessness. In addition, since our fundamental social institutions are designed to maximize profit and enforcement of power structures rather than to maximize need satisfaction, we continue to have an experience of overall unmet needs. In addition, the social milieu many of us live in requires us to

---

[36] See "Why parents should leave their kids alone" by Jay Griffiths, The Guardian, 3 May 2013.

hide our inner experience from others, oftentimes even from ourselves, and to act in ways that often feel inauthentic.

Aside from the sheer sadness that this is so, when we have such a frequency of having unmet needs, it is harder to tolerate even one more unmet need. We are then more likely to be reactive, which increases the chances of acting in ways that won't meet our own or others' needs. If others are then also affected, and they, too, react, the result can be a spiral of unmet needs that creates more and more suffering.

This is the common context we must engage with if we are to fully reclaim who we are. How can we choose authenticity, truth telling, courage, and love against the personal legacy and social constraints we face on a daily basis?

It is my absolute faith, based on my own and others' experience, that this personal journey is entirely possible and completely practical. I don't think of it as easy by any means. I've had to mobilize tremendous will, vision, and support in order to embark on it myself. There's nothing else I've done in my personal life that I feel happier about. I have so much more of a sense of power, freedom, and choice now than I did before I started. I am writing this piece in the spring of 2011, and in the last year the journey is even taking me to experiencing tremendous gratitude many times a day, more joy, and a breakthrough in my deep habitual beliefs about how much room there is, in this world, for my own full authentic self.

This is part of why I find it impossible to speak about my views without being grounded in my personal experience. In parallel with my own personal numbness that preceded my healing journey, I was also deeply steeped in the dominant view of emotions and needs. Through my journey I have come to appreciate the expansiveness and sense of meaning and possibility that come from attending to and cultivating my emotional life. I have also come to be impatient with and suspicious of any discussion of human life that isn't grounded in personal passion of one sort or another. I have learned quite viscerally both how my thoughts and beliefs, and changes within them, affect my emotions, and how those thoughts and beliefs change as my inner explorations shift my feelings. I cannot imagine one without the other, nor a satisfying life without either.

In addition, being on this journey has increased a million-fold my empowerment in relation to the world at large and with it my ability to imagine myself as a change agent with a significant contribution to make. I would never have been able to envision this book project even a few years ago.

There is much I have learned from my journey about what we can do to recover our fullness of life and develop a radical consciousness that allows us to step outside of how we were raised and to look critically at our society's norms and structures. To me, fullness of life means ease and flow in relating to a wide range of human needs and emotions both within us and around us. Then we can live an emotionally authentic life in which autonomy and interconnection are in a complex balance with each other. Such authenticity, and with it the capacity to be with whatever emotions exist in us, is one clear path to sufficient courage and inner strength to see and understand with great clarity the depth of challenge we collectively face, to live a life dedicated to love, compassion, and authenticity within the world as it exists, and to engage with others in actions to transform the world into what we see it can become.

Strategic Discomfort

It's a good thing that we feel pain, because then it wakes us up to the situation we're in, and to the fact that we care about it.

– Joanna Macy

Many years ago, before I even knew I had a journey of healing to do, a friend exhorted me to open up to experiencing pain and discomfort. At the time, I was miles and miles away from seeing any benefit to it. I was profoundly unsettled and even upset at the idea that I would need to feel, again, pain that I thought I had already left behind. What my friend didn't say clearly, and what I understood later, is that it's not the pain itself that would bring healing or other benefit. Rather, I learned that the knee-jerk reaction of backing away from discomfort is a form of un-freedom, and that the willingness to engage and be present with discomfort, rather than the discomfort itself, is what supports us in expanding and healing.

Our willingness to adapt to a world that isn't set up to support us came about as we gave up on certain needs because they were so consistently not attended to. That giving up was, undoubtedly, quite painful and uncomfortable. It makes sense to me that liberation will require of us the willingness to return to the discomfort and have a different outcome. Instead of giving up on the need, we can open to it, and embrace the humanity that the need expresses. As we begin to want what we want, again, we can reclaim our freedom.

I still, to this day, have some misgivings about the idea that engaging and being present with discomfort, refusing to run away from it, is the only way to move forward. I still hope I can find and share with others another way. So far, it's the only one that has reliably and consistently worked to give me a sense of mastery and freedom that I absolutely cherish.

The Gift of Emotions

Under the best of circumstances, which I wish were more common, our babyhood experiences of the most intense vulnerability and helplessness happen in parallel with the most complete satisfaction of needs. Instead, in modern societies, more often than not, our acute helplessness as infants is coupled with being denied experiences that would satisfy basic human needs for love, such as ongoing uninterrupted access to touch. It is, perhaps, because of this early experience that both individually and culturally we associate emotions and the experience of need with vulnerability and weakness, not with satisfaction and strength. Freud, who was perhaps the first to delve into exploring early helplessness, expressed what may be familiar disdain for needs and dependency in his description of this experience: "This biological factor of helplessness thus brings into being the first situations of danger and creates the need to be loved which the human being is destined never to renounce."[37] Rather than compassion and appreciation for our need for love, his description evokes distance and repudiation: it is as if the need for love is an undesirable, if unavoidable, consequence of helplessness rather than a basic condition of life. Because we internalize so early on, and within a context of such profound closeness, our aversion to vulnerability and our shame about needing love, it becomes extraordinarily difficult to overcome what we internalize, almost as if we have to tear out a piece of our own heart.

Overcoming Our Aversion to Emotions

In order to reclaim our full humanity, we are called to overcome the legacy of Western civilization's idealization of rationality as the quintessential human faculty and devaluation of and suspicion toward emotions. We also need to overcome our own personal histories of being steeped in such a cultural view, as well as the primal experience of helplessness without emotional support. The result is what one unusual psychologist, Kenneth Isaacs, refers to as "affect phobia."[38]

---

[37] Freud, *The Problem of Anxiety*, 100.
[38] Isaacs, *Uses of Emotions*. Isaacs describes a staggering amount of resistance within academic circles to his proposal to take emotions seriously.

Embarking on such an emotional journey requires significant courage and effort, and particularly a willingness to overcome our deeply ingrained aversion to emotions. On the practical plane, it requires us to be willing to feel discomfort. Why would we want to do that? What is the benefit that we can derive from engaging differently with our emotions?

Emotions, Needs, and Values

If we are able to overcome our aversion to emotions, we may discover and restore the central role that emotions have in human life. Simply put, emotions help reveal our values and needs. We respond emotionally to situations on the basis of our evaluation of the situation. Emotions provide us with an ongoing, incessant, and constantly changing stream of information about what is of meaning and value to us, both internally and around us.

When we experience joy, contentment, bliss, gratitude, delight, relief, or a host of other emotions, this means we evaluate a situation as meeting our needs. When we experience hope, excitement, and the like, this means we anticipate that a given situation will meet our needs, or continue to meet them. When we experience, among others, frustration, sadness, grief, disgust, agitation, helplessness, melancholy, loneliness, apathy, anguish, or resentment, it means that we evaluate a situation as not meeting our needs. Finally, when we experience anxiety, despair, impatience, fear, and similar emotions, this means we anticipate conditions which will not meet our needs.[39]

Needless to say, this evaluation doesn't happen in some deliberate, conscious, and spacious way. Rather, moment by moment our organism responds to our emotions as a signal, usually unconsciously. They impel us to action to prolong a situation that meets our needs or rectify one that does not. Without this steady input, our lives can be profoundly impoverished. Because our aversion to emotions prevents us from noticing and responding to these signals, it becomes a crucial obstacle on the way towards satisfying lives.

If this aversion is linked to very early helplessness, and specifically to the terror of noticing that our needs are not being met while being

---

[39] If you have noticed that I haven't included emotions such as anger, guilt, or shame, there is a specific reason for that to which I come back in a later section.

unable to do anything about it, then the ability to recognize the difference between an unmet need and the anticipation of an unmet need can be the requisite step towards overcoming "affect phobia" and cultivating a willingness to explore emotions. I am focusing specifically on unmet needs, since, for the most part, we are not particularly phobic about pleasurable emotions. (Only up to a point, though, since beyond a certain level even pleasurable emotions are also avoided, as witnessed by the admonition to children to curb their exuberance.)

When we are able to reach that openness, the experience of our emotions takes on a different flavor, and we can begin to recognize their gift. Emotions tell us something of vital importance, and point our attention to our needs, which is their deepest gift.

In that sense, emotions are responses to present conditions, and contain an irreducible potential of forward movement away from the legacy of the past. At the same time, our perception of whether or not our needs are met is, at least in part, a product of past experiences, as well as the intensity of the experience of wanting to have the need met. Accordingly, in order to be able to disentangle past from present, perception from reality, we need to develop much more capacity to encounter and engage with discomfort.

One of the insights I had early on in my work is that the outcome of discomfort is not pre-determined. Our initial reaction to uncomfortable emotions is a desire to move away from them, which keeps us protected, safer, and with less access to learning and change. If we overcome our aversion to emotions, and we integrate into our psyche the distinction between the original "real" danger of early life and current evaluations of the present situation, discomfort can equally well be a signal for an opportunity to change our relationship with ourselves or with our environment, expanding thereby our emotional strength and options.

Emotional Journeys

It is an integral part of my vision that the process of reclaiming our connection with our emotional life is entirely possible, and I have indeed accompanied hundreds, if not thousands, of people on that kind of journey. Along the way we move from the attempt to *control* our emotions to a state that I experience as *mastery* in relation to our emotions: when we can first tolerate, then inhabit, and finally embrace them. We get there by cultivating the ability to notice what is going on in our inner experience without judgment and to generate compassion for our "self." In my own experience of working in this way, the result has been an exhilarating increase in my sense of self, more freedom to choose, and a much higher degree of compassion towards others, which emerges, as it were, without effort.

Such a journey rests on a willingness to use our emotions for learning about ourselves instead of moving away from them if they are not comfortable. One way of achieving that capacity is to choose to take actions regardless of how we feel. Learning to act in new ways, to embrace values, needs, and states of being that are initially uncomfortable, results in a form of what I call "acquired spontaneity."

On the simplest level, the journey towards psychic liberation proceeds through changing our relationship to fear and discomfort. Psychic liberation does not entail not feeling fear; it only entails not being afraid of fear. Fear itself does not create the contraction in self; it is only our aversion to emotions, what I earlier referred to as "affect phobia," which does.

The journey starts from where we are. The combination of the level of cultural injunctions against feelings, our own personal history, and societal feeling rules, including those that are specific to our gender, class, and race, creates a zone of emotional comfort, which is uniquely individual yet usually recognizable within the bounds of our cultural group.

Beyond Emotional Comfort

In any domain, be it emotional, moral, intellectual, political, physical, or spiritual, some possibilities, experiences, and challenges remain completely outside our grasp or action; they are possible ways of being that are clearly outside anything that we could even aspire to embody. As an example, for the vast majority of people, taking actions such as Martin Luther King's, or Mother Teresa's, or learning quantum physics, fall in that area. Conversely, many actions and ways of being are completely effortless. For most people, most of the time, for example, it is really not very difficult to refrain from killing people (although for some people and in some situations it clearly is), or to speak our native language. What interests me in terms of the process I am advocating here is the place of uncertainty, of unknown outcomes, which is the fuzzy border separating the comfortable and effortless from what lies beyond reach.

Any situation, either externally created or internally motivated, that places us on the edge of our comfort zone is the occasion for experiencing uncomfortable emotions. In fact, such discomfort is a routine part of everyday life, and ordinarily remains in the background. Because it is uncomfortable, we tend to want to back off from the situation that created it and retreat back into emotional comfort. Because such situations also involve a value that pulls us to a self we would like to be or become, they are often the occasion for internal struggle. The nature of the struggle is similar for many of us even as the areas of struggle can be vastly different. For someone who wants to stand up to another's anger when afraid of it, this is her zone of struggle: her fear pulls her to continue to placate the other person, and her desire to be honest and act in integrity propels her towards confrontation. For another person, such a situation may seem effortless, and she would, without much contemplation, proceed forward despite the fear. For yet another it would be beyond her reach to even imagine it.

What would place us on the edge of discomfort varies tremendously. It could be minor irritations in the supermarket or watching a parent mistreat a child and wanting to intervene; listening to a friend in distress or choosing to reveal our own vulnerabilities; wondering whether or not to eat ice cream now, or major inner conflict around our values; facing charges of racism, or wondering whether to call someone else on acts of racism. Whatever the situation, it is the experience of being right on the edge of comfort that I want to focus on.

The existence of such an edge is unavoidable. How conscious we are of its existence, and what we choose to do with it is what varies radically from person to person. The key to successful movement towards psychic liberation is a unique and precise type of discipline, which requires a conscious relationship and choice in exactly that place. It entails viewing the edge as an opportunity. I call it "strategic discomfort."

Choosing the Edge

What makes discomfort strategic is the choice to use it in a conscious direction. Because these experiences involve a struggle between protection of the self and some other value, strategic use of the inevitable discomfort involves choosing to embrace emotions which likely raise fear in us. It is a concrete way of attempting to overcome "affect phobia" in order to eventually expand our comfort zone, and make more and more elements of our life, including emotional, moral, political, spiritual, and even physical and intellectual ones, effortless. This by no means implies that the zone of struggle will be eliminated in some eventuality. It only expands the particular band where the struggle occurs. Perhaps the difference between a conscious and an unconscious life is not so much the amount of struggle we have in our life, but whether the struggle is expansive or paralyzing.

A number of years ago I spent about ten minutes working with a woman on timidity. I symbolically invited her to overcome her timidity by projecting her voice loudly in a room full of people, a proposal which brought her immediately to the edge of her discomfort. While she didn't actually cross it in that instance, she stayed *at* the edge for the whole time. To this day she claims that those ten minutes changed her life. Subsequent to this experience, she started going against decades of timidity and passivity. She found the option of choosing to challenge people in authority positions and forming alliances with others to increase her sphere of influence. Although the experience of challenging others remains uncomfortable for her, she continues to do it, taking on more and more challenging situations, and progressively expanding the band of her discomfort.

One more element that makes it so difficult to embark on the process of enlarging the self is fear of our own needs and desires, and of their satisfaction. Why do so many of us have this fear? My own experience of working with people has led me to conjecture that the root of the fear lies in early experiences of needs being thwarted. Such fear makes the journey more difficult, in that navigating the discomfort I describe here is likely to take us closer to our needs than staying within our comfort zone does. Dissolving the shell of protection that so many of us have erected around our needs, the protection that comes from not allowing ourselves to want, can, indeed, evoke a great deal of fear, even terror, if we associated experiencing our needs with more pain and disappointment than repressing the needs.

Conditions for Success

Consciously choosing to step outside the comfort zone forces us to confront internal and external barriers of all kinds, barriers which constitute the hidden basis for the maintenance of the status-quo. The tendency to slide into our emotional comfort zone is part of what keeps the social order in place. The willingness to persist through the discomfort is the essence of the emotional journey I am advocating. At any point in the journey, we are likely to experience both internal discomfort and external resistance. In the early stages, what we risk is emotional exhaustion and potential disapproval within our immediate circle, or losing a job. Sooner or later, however, such a journey brings us to an edge that threatens the smooth functioning of the social order, and hence may be met with increasing societal sanctions, even to the point of being hospitalized, incarcerated, or even killed.

On the other hand the journey becomes easier as we progress, and the rewards are often enormous: renewed vitality, expanding horizons, growing confidence, growing ability to contribute, enhanced compassion, and greater clarity. Perhaps because I myself have not completed the journey to my satisfaction yet, several important questions remain open for me: What are the conditions which are likely to inspire such a journey? Can it arise in isolation or only through inspiration from others? What is the role of a supportive community of shared values in facilitating such a journey? How far can it go before radical consciousness must be born? Is it possible for an individual to complete it within a social order at odds with need satisfaction?

I don't have any definitive answers to these questions. I don't believe the research necessary to answer them has been done. What I know is based only on my own experience and immediate observations, and I offer it with humility. The conditions that spark the beginning of such a journey are often experiences of crisis, such as profound loss, illness, trauma, or significant transitions, as well as inspirational contact with others who have been on such a journey already. Although some distance can be traversed individually, either alone, or, more commonly, through some form of psychotherapy, beyond a certain point the support of a community is required, especially the more our expansion places us in direct antagonism to social norms and institutions. In addition, certain kinds of consciousness are not likely to arise for as long as we remain entirely in our social context; a community of others who share the journey may be indispensable to the very ability to cultivate awareness of our emotional state. On our own, it is much less likely that we would develop and sustain radical consciousness, which I see as the capacity to step outside of the normative story of the society into which we were born. When radical consciousness emerges, the horizon of our needs expands beyond simple individual satisfaction and healing, and collective action may become indispensable for achieving larger goals.

For this kind of journey to be successful, what is required is not only an increased capacity to experience our emotions, but also, and perhaps more significantly, the ability to become aware of the needs that are giving rise to the emotions we experience. Becoming aware of our needs, at a much deeper layer than the surface wishes and action strategies, makes it more possible and likely to reach need satisfaction. As we proceed on the journey, we expand beyond becoming aware of our needs alone. Because so many of our needs require and involve other people, what is called for is also cultivating the ability to become aware of others' needs and emotions, and to engage in meaningful dialogue with them. The ability to engage with others intimately under conditions which make conflicts likely, essential for attaining psychic liberation, also calls for the development of empathy, the key to recognizing both sameness and difference, and hence to mutual recognition itself.

Mastering Difficult Emotions

When we make the choice to undo our socialization, to stand up to the legacy of our personal and social conditioning, and to reclaim our full sense of self, we embark on a long journey of learning to engage with our emotions in an entirely new way. The first step in this journey is to identify for ourselves emotions we are so committed to not having that we block our own freedom. Shame is often one such emotion that is so intolerable for many of us that we go great distances to avoid it. If, as is often the case, shame about who we are and what we want has been instilled in us from early on, we learn to hide ourselves. If we cannot tolerate shame, we will then remain in hiding. Despair is another emotion that many of us find unbearable. If that is the case, we have a great incentive to tune out and become numb to any experiences or information that bring up despair, and maintain a surface layer of pleasant feelings without a true sense of connection with self or others.

Emotions, Needs, and Thoughts

All emotions have the signal function of letting us know the status of our needs. One of the reasons to befriend our emotions is so that we can listen to the signal and make contact with our needs, so that we can attend to them.

Some emotions are associated with the direct experience of having needs met or unmet, such as joy, sadness, surprise, and many others. Some other emotions arise in relation to the anticipation of having needs be met or unmet, such as excitement or fear. In addition to all these emotions, I want to call specific attention to three emotions – anger, guilt, and shame – which have a unique relationship with needs and values. In addition to the basic and ongoing inner assessment of whether or not our needs are being met, these emotions generally tend to point to a quality of thinking that focuses on what *should* happen, not only what we *want*. This distinction between what we want and what we believe should happen is foundational in terms of what we end up experiencing. The pure experience of having unmet needs does not in and of itself give rise to these particular emotions. Although this is a subtle distinction, its ramifications are at times enormous, and can amount to whether or not we can get our needs met in the situation. If our attention is focused on the "*should*" evaluation, we are not likely to be attentive to our needs, let alone the needs of others. For example, we may be filled with a desire for revenge when we are angry with someone, and not have full connection to the real underlying need, which could be for recognition of our pain, to be heard, or for some hope for change. Since we are not connected with and acting from the underlying need, even if we manage to get revenge, the need will remain unmet, because the revenge provides satisfaction to an impulse that is not directly related to the need.

Reaching freedom in relation to these and related should-based emotions requires learning to notice the thoughts that lead to the emotions, and choosing to embrace higher levels of vulnerability than those with which we are already familiar and comfortable. Part of the challenge resides in our lack of familiarity with our needs, even more so than emotions. With should-based emotions, more often than not the path to freedom includes a transformation of our thinking so that we can learn to connect with our underlying needs and use them as a guide to action.

Walking towards Emotions

Which emotions are difficult for us varies from person to person. When I started this journey, for example, I learned that I was challenged by four different emotions: pain, shame, fear, and helplessness. Unlike many others, anger has never been a significant challenge for me (although fear of others' anger most definitely has). My journey is an ongoing process, and continues to this day.

So far, I have mastered my emotional pain in full. This means, to me, that I am able to be completely in flow when I am in pain. I no longer try to suppress my pain or hide it. I am not even working hard to not have pain. I recognize, with ease and peace, that my visionary passion and my physical and emotional sensitivities create many situations in which many needs of mine are not met, and that such pain is likely to continue. This recognition no longer takes away from my ability to be present for life fully and enjoy what I enjoy.

As to shame, I am well on my way. I have a clear desire to reach a state of being 100% shameless, which for me means being able to do what I want from the depth of my being without hiding, without giving my power away to others to decide what is or isn't acceptable, and without holding back. I am not talking here about specific shame about specific acts. I am talking about the kind of background shame that the overwhelming majority of people I work with experience: shame about being who we are, shame about looking the way we look, shame about having the needs we have. Even the project of writing this book would not be possible without the immense work I have done over years and years of walking towards shame, again and again. Without this practice, I would simply be too consumed with fear about how I will be received to be able to put myself out there, especially about my vision and my personal life, to the extent I am doing in this book. Each time I walk towards my shame, I discover that some of it burns off and I am freer and lighter at the end. I didn't anticipate this before I started. I learned it over time. Whereas the level of pain in my daily life hasn't subsided much, the level of shame I experience is almost non-existent at this point, and what I do experience almost never stops me.

My journey with fear has not gone as far as either of those. I am still struggling, sometimes, to even notice and be aware that I am afraid. I am still acting on habitual unconscious fear, especially fear of people being angry or upset with me, or judging me, or walking away on connection. These experiences rarely happen, certainly nowhere near as often as I am afraid of them. And still, likely because of experiences I've had in the past, I am often afraid. I have made some strides. More and more I can choose my response even when I am afraid. Also, the time interval until I can notice that I am acting on fear is shorter, and I am able to re-choose and change course.

My most difficult emotion is helplessness. I wonder sometimes if this is only me or if this is a bigger human theme. Perhaps because I am still so early on in this particular journey I don't have as much insight as I have about other emotions. Intuitively, I sense that helplessness is excruciating for many of us because of the memory of infantile helplessness, when we really and truly were unable to fend for ourselves or do anything to get our needs met, and were completely at the mercy of others. I know that helplessness immediately leads me to scramble to find something to do just so that I can step out of this experience. What I have been able to do so far on this journey is to begin to notice when I feel helpless, and what the consequences are to me and others. When I am helpless is when I am most likely to forget my many years of practice in

Nonviolent Communication and to respond abruptly. Others around me often experience me in those moments as angry even though I hardly ever feel angry. What's new and exciting for me is that I have the ability to shift course sometimes and find space within the helplessness to make choice.

If you want to embark on this journey, take an inventory of your own difficult emotions to see which ones block you. The pages that follow contain some combination of personal story and other thoughts about some key emotions that may be blocking you. Perhaps fear is not at all an issue for you, and you are able to have freedom even when afraid. Perhaps you easily lose yourself in anger when your needs are not met. Knowing what your challenges are can be a first step in working with them. Even if the specific emotions or situations described here – which are by no means meant to be exhaustive – are different from your experiences, you may be able to gain some insight about the process by which you can reach mastery and, through it, freedom.

Why Be Afraid?

A few months ago, during a conference call with some colleagues, I found myself, for the millionth time at least, debilitated by fear of judgment. I knew on some *intellectual* level that there was no reason to be afraid. The other people on the call, only four of them, were close colleagues, all former students, all but one Nonviolent Communication (NVC) trainers, who were there because they trust what I have to offer and who I am. That didn't help. Although I was able to talk about the fear in the moment, and I was even able, to a significant extent, to make choices despite it, I remained *emotionally* consumed by fear.

Fortunately for me, I managed to take advantage of the presence of trusted colleagues even as I remained afraid of their potential judgments. I made a leap in my experience, and confronted a new question: Why, in those moments, do I generate fear in myself? (And why do any of us do this? I didn't for a moment think this was unique to me). For the first time, I was able to consider consciously that fear, like every other human state, is a *choice* that our organism makes based on some internal process of considering what would most meet needs in the moment. This process usually remains out of our awareness. I had such excitement at bringing this process to awareness and investigating what could be the internal mechanisms that generate the fear.

Engaging fully with a challenging emotional state, beyond where our own comfort level ends, beyond what we can even see clearly, is a process that usually requires the active participation, beyond mere support, of others. Active empathic presence is an ongoing collaborative attempt to discern what is going on, so self-knowledge combines with the outside insight of a loving witness to recognize truth. This is interdependence in action. Knowing this, I brought this question to a conversation with my beloved empathy buddy, Francois Beausoleil. As we explored this question I learned much more about fear.

The Purpose of Fear

The core insight that Francois and I arrived at is that the purpose of fear, the reason the organism mobilizes it, the need that it attempts to meet, is that of awareness and choice. Usually fear gets mobilized around essential needs, which either are now or have been at some point in the past completely intertwined with survival. The purpose of the awareness is to ensure that we act with care, that we make choices that recognize the needs and manage carefully the level of risk-taking involved with such high-stakes needs.

Given that so often the survival issue is in the past, and the present doesn't actually pose a threat to our survival (as was the case for me on the conference call in question), how can we work with the fear to increase capacity for present-based choice?

Expanding Limits, Embracing Risk

In the past I had only one response to this question. I would always choose the path I have been on for so many years now, the path of vulnerability. This path entails openness to risk, stretching my wings, recognizing my resilience and my capacity to survive that of which I am afraid. Being on this path sometimes invites us to use the specific strategy of imagining worst case scenarios and seeing that we *can*, indeed, survive them. In addition to imagining them, strength on this path also builds on success, on the actual *experience* of surviving, beyond pure imagination. This path, to me, is a core element of what it means to live nonviolently, since nonviolence rests on changing our relationship with fear.

Up until that morning, the only alternative that I could imagine to this consistent and never-ending stretching towards fullness despite fear was to choose *not* to do what I would be afraid of doing. I didn't like that option, because it seemed like giving in to fear, and I treasure my freedom so much that this image was completely unbearable to me. Which is not to say I never gave in. I have done it much more often than I ever would want. I simply couldn't imagine *choosing* it consciously. Whenever I have acted out of fear I would experience a sense of defeat and choicelessness, and would be scrambling to find my way out of the fear.

Tenderness towards Self, Acceptance of Limits

To my great excitement, on that morning with Francois, I discovered a whole new direction for working with fear – a path full of tenderness and acceptance. This path is fully consistent with all I have been teaching for years, just that I had never brought it to bear on fear. Fear was always, for me, something to overcome. What does tenderness look like when it comes to fear? This kind of tenderness is *different* from simply not doing what we are afraid of doing. It's all too easy to remain within the confines of the fear, to give in to the contraction and intensity of protection. Bringing tenderness is about connecting with the underlying longing that the fear is calling us to make choices about.

Choosing this gentleness requires us, first and foremost, to be able to be with the fear instead of either overriding it or giving in. Just being with fear changes our inner experience. Breathing and making space counters, even on the physiological level, the sense of contraction that is so quintessentially familiar to me about fear (so much so that I often don't even know I am afraid). Noticing we are afraid and choosing to be present is a huge step on the path to inner freedom. Only then can we truly put our attention on the longing that is underneath the fear. If we are consumed with the fear we cannot find the need. Unless we can live with the fear long enough to know why we are afraid, what need we are so committed to protecting, we won't be able to make true choice. This is most important when we are talking about fear that is not *in the present* actually related to physical survival. Rather than automatically jumping to protection, or, like me, automatically attempting to override the fear, we can then choose, recognizing the limits of our tender hearts as well as our desire to grow and learn, how far we want to stretch in relation to the fear. This kind of choice is the very foundation of freedom.

Making room for my fear of judgment, I opened up to what it's calling me to notice. Perhaps it's about how much I want to belong. Maybe it's about wanting the deepest freedom to be myself. Or maybe it's about wanting peace and ease. Or all of the above. Bringing tenderness means opening my heart; holding those longings with utmost care; allowing myself, in full, to feel the depth of the longing, separate from what will or will not happen. This builds a different kind of strength that is soft and gentle. I want that strength, for me and for others. I want to grow in my ability to settle into this softness, so I can do what the fear ultimately wants me to do: be mindful and clear about my options when these needs are at stake in any given moment, and have full choice.

Burning through Shame

I started writing about shame in response to an email I received from a blog reader: "Where does shame come from…? How can we approach it so we can eventually free ourselves from it? What works for you? What did you see working for others? Anything alive in you around this topic that might serve other readers as well?"

I don't really *know* where shame comes from, so I can only share my opinions and conjectures about it (and I tend to have those about almost anything). My sense about shame is that it's a primary mode of punishment, a way that adults instill forms of behavior in children who then internalize it and grow up carrying enormous amounts of shame in them. If you look at the language, adults will often say, most literally: "Shame on you." In Israel, where I grew up, the equivalent expression translates into: "Be ashamed of yourself." In both cases, the adult is commanding the child to *experience* shame as a way of expressing their unhappiness with how the child acted.

Shame and Love

Shame is in the category of what are called social emotions, and is deeply connected to our sense of belonging and being loved. If we are shamed often and deeply enough, we end up feeling shame about our very desire to be loved and accepted. Shame is endemic in this culture, and has consequences beyond the pain that it brings to those who feel it.

As James Gilligan so lovingly reminds us in his book *Violence: Our Deadly Epidemic and Its Causes*, apparently an astonishing majority of incarcerated violent offenders are full of profound shame and untold rates of self-loathing. At the heart of their shame he uncovers precisely the longing to be loved, so deeply unfulfilled as to create shame for even having the desire. Their hearts, in other words, are just as vulnerable as mine and yours. They defend their hearts to such a degree that the result is violence towards others. If Gilligan is accurate in his understanding of violence, then overcoming shame goes beyond feeling better – it may well be an essential condition for a violence-free society.

I have already alluded to cross-cultural studies about the correlates of violence (see pages 111-2), which show that the single

most powerful predictor of a violence-free culture is the length of
time that babies are carried in arms. Here I want to highlight another
key finding from such studies. The other key predictor of lack of
violence in any given culture is the degree to which teenagers are
allowed free sexual play.[40] I see both of these findings as pointing to
our freedom to love and be loved, both in our infancy and when our
sexuality wakes up. The pain of not being allowed to show love and
ask for love is so extreme it can lead to violence.

Walking towards Shame

So how *do* we overcome shame? How I have worked with my shame
is by walking directly into it. I have been doing it for many years now,
and I am delighted to say that I have burned through most of my
shame. It takes immense discipline and courage. Often when I have
done it I felt totally spent afterwards. It means going against
everything I was ever told is wrong about me, doing what I was
repeatedly told is shameful, and setting myself up for potential
ridicule and shunning. Perhaps it's been relatively easy for me
because I have suffered so much ostracism in my life that the
prospect of it is not so frightening any longer. I often think that the
best way to experience deep safety is by being thrown into what we
are afraid of and seeing that we can survive it. One tool that helps
with gathering up the courage is finding my own inner acceptance,
which can then nourish and protect me if others don't. My practice
helps me find the acceptance through connecting to the shining light
of the core human need or longing that is at the heart of whatever it
is that I feel shame about. In my case it's almost always about love:
wanting love, wanting to show love, or trusting love or people.

The biggest singular moment of transformation occurred one day
in a therapy session, in 2004. I had just had an experience of losing
trust in two people at once that was so extreme and unexpected that
I had a knot in my stomach that lasted for an entire week. I was
physically uncomfortable and an emotional wreck when I entered my
therapist's office. I was telling her about the circumstances and the
knot in my stomach when I suddenly felt an enormous longing to
have her sit next to me and put her hand on the knot to soothe my
experience. This was entirely unexpected and unfamiliar. My

---

[40] See James W. Prescott, "The Origins of Human Love and Violence".

relationship with my therapist, for almost the entire six years that I worked with her, was difficult. Towards the end of our time together in the summer of 2006, I learned that all along she had a challenge in fully opening her heart to me, something I had sensed all along and never found a way to settle about. So asking her to come sit next to me and put her hand on my stomach was quite beyond the pale. Instead, I just said that I had a request that I was uncomfortable making. To her great credit, she responded with great skill and care. Instead of telling me to push through and ask, or let go of asking, she engaged with the discomfort, trying to understand all that prevented me from asking. Step by step, with gentle questions from her, we discovered a lot: that I didn't trust my request would be received with care; that I didn't trust she would have the presence to check in with herself authentically; that I didn't trust she would find a genuine "yes"; that she wouldn't be able to communicate the "yes" in a way I would trust; that I wouldn't be able to hear it and take it in; that she wouldn't be able to deliver even if she said "yes"; and that I wouldn't be able to relax into receiving the gift if she were able to give it. All this without ever telling her what it was! Then she asked what would happen if I did trust all these things, and I did ask her, and she did say "yes," and I was able to open to receiving what I wanted. The words that came out of my mouth, before I had any time to examine them and make a choice, were: "then I wouldn't want you to ever leave." We were both stunned. The experience I had was as if something opened up from under me and I fell, no longer able to hold myself, forced to entrust myself to life.

Next, I felt a wave of fury directed at no less than the field of psychology, for having coined the term "separation anxiety." This term implies that separation is the expected goal, and the anxiety is an inevitable part of what life is about. Instead, I knew then, without a shred of doubt, that baby knows best. Baby knows that there is absolutely nothing better than being in close proximity with someone we love. Of course it's not always humanly possible to give baby this experience. It is, however, entirely and completely possible to let baby know there is nothing wrong with wanting it even when it's impossible.

I understood in that moment that the entire structure of shame and humiliation that had lived in me for so many years was based on one single point: I had shame about wanting love.

These are all familiar themes: longing for human connection, yearning for support for our heart and sadness, aching for love. We all want so, so very much to give and receive love. We all do. When will we, collectively, lift the taboo on tenderness so we can release the shame that plagues us and live and love freely?

Staying with Helplessness

I sometimes wonder if my difficulty with tolerating helplessness is a personal idiosyncrasy or a more common human affliction. I have enough intuitive sense that it's at least a modern Western challenge because of our early experiences of infancy. It's hard for me to truly imagine what life can be like for people whose early experience is one of stable and ongoing attention to their needs. I am reminded of Jane Goodall's astonishing story about the child she raised among the chimpanzees. She copied their ways, she said, and her son hardly ever cried. I am also reminded of Jean Liedloff's account of the indigenous people she lived with, people who held their infants in someone's arms 24 hours a day for months until the babies asked to crawl and explore on their own.[41] That society had no violence – not between children, and not between adults.

I can't imagine what it's like to have this experience, to have the trust that when I am in need a human being who cares is right there with me to notice and attend to me. I can imagine even less the lifelong effects of this experience. What would life look like if such deep and intrinsic trust was the basic experience we all had? How would we relate to each other? What would then be our theories of human nature? How would we then relate to our children? This way of being, like any, would naturally tend to reproduce itself through generations.

And this is not the experience I am familiar with, not from my own life, not from what I still see that infants, babies, toddlers, and small children have.

Some years ago I visited some friends who had out-of-town guests with two small children – one who was two, and one who was four. At some point, the parents decided it was time for the two-year-old to go to bed. She, of course, had other ideas. Why would she want to go to sleep when everyone else is having fun? Why would she want to be in a room by herself, in the dark, when life continues in another room? After some minutes, the father came back to the room, and the little girl was wailing and screaming. He came back to the adult conversation. The screaming went on for a while. Whether it's a blessing or a curse, I've never forgotten the visceral experience

---

[41] Jean Liedloff, *The Continuum Concept*.

of being a child. In every situation that involves a struggle between an adult and a child, I know in some deep, clear way the experience of the child. I find witnessing such moments, however common and frequent they are, to be utterly unbearable. I tried to persuade him to consider her needs, listen to her pain, respond to her. He was adamant that he was doing what was necessary.

Unlike the children Liedloff describes, this girl's experience was familiar.

There was no question in my mind that this girl knew what she needed. "It's perfectly clear," says Jean Liedloff, "that the millions of babies, who are crying at this very moment, want unanimously to be next to a live body. Do you really think they're all wrong? Theirs is the voice of nature. This is the clear, pure voice of nature."[42] And yet this girl couldn't create the conditions to get her needs met. Her father was trained, as most of us are, to ignore the pure expression of *need* from a child in favor of an *idea* about what is right. What did he have to do inside himself to overcome his heart's natural and immediate desire to respond, to love, to stroke, to attend to his daughter, to understand that her crying is an indication of suffering?

This is the quintessential primal experience of helplessness as I know it: being in need and being at the mercy of others who are not attending to our needs. I am well aware that on the side of the parents the experience can be equally excruciating. Modern life, for example, creates conditions that make it challenging, nearly impossible at times, for parents to find strategies to attend to their infants' needs and still function in the adult world. This is the kind of tragedy that keeps pulling me towards changing social structures instead of thinking everything can be changed by individuals in their personal lives. I am not emphasizing this point here, however, because my interest is in the outcome for the infant, not so much the reason for why this happens in the first place. From baby's perspective, it's not important why its caregivers are not responding.

Responding to Helplessness

Despite being an able-bodied adult with ample access to resources, I still regularly have the internal experience of helplessness. My usual response to helplessness is a knee-jerk habitual attempt to try to *do*

---

[42] Interview with Jean Liedloff, continuum-concept.org/reading/human-nature.html.

something about it. I have gotten far enough in my explorations of helplessness to know that the attempt to do something is a strategy designed to relieve me of the acute discomfort of helplessness. The irony, of course, is that attempting to do something in a situation in which my efforts to get my needs met don't work increases the experience of helplessness. I remain stuck in an attempt to work my way out of stuckness.

So what is the alternative? I want to be able to tolerate helplessness sufficiently to be able to stop and breathe, so I can create enough room inside me to choose how I want to respond to the situation. This is what mastery means to me.

In the moment, consumed by the experience, I can scarcely even be conscious of what's happening inside me. After the fact, I can look back and see the agitation increase in my body in certain situations. In the moment, I am in survival mode and don't *notice* what I later can so clearly see. My voice gets more intense, sometimes almost shrill, and monotonous at the same time. My body contracts. My breathing gets shallower. My actions and my words become abrupt. I know I am unpleasant to be around in those moments.

So far I have discovered two forms of practice that have increased my ability to remain present with helplessness.

The first happens, of all places, on the acupuncture table, when I have needles in my body and get an itch somewhere. Unable to move because of the needles, and with a persistent itch, all I can *do* is essentially nothing. Those are my best moments of practice. The helplessness is not overwhelming, and yet I can feel it, and I use it to gain comfort with the discomfort. In that way, I am already choosing.

The other practice entails bringing more awareness to hearing my voice, noticing the agitation, and learning to interpret the signals consciously as helplessness as early as possible. My deeply ingrained habit is to figure out how to function even when I am not at my best, even when I am challenged or stressed. Even when my well-being deteriorates, my functioning remains constant. Many times others around me don't even know I am straining. The more challenged I am, the more effort it takes to continue functioning. I haven't learned how to degrade my functioning gracefully, to notice my limits before I reach them, at which point (which is not frequent) I no longer manage to function at all. I have, by habit, very little in between. This is what I am attempting to learn. As soon as I notice any of the telltale signals, I now know to name it to myself as helplessness, and slow down enough to regain choice.

Mastery of a difficult emotion is about being able to be present and tolerate the emotion, so we neither shut down nor spiral into more and more intensity. Just as much as attempting to *do* something about helplessness intensifies it, regaining a sense of choice changes the experience dramatically. I may still have no ability to affect the original situation. I do, however, now have the ability to affect my inner experience, and with this shift in focus I can have a sense of choice, the most profound antidote to helplessness.

Experiencing Despair

Penny Spawforth, one of my blog readers, asked me in a comment: "I would love to hear how you transform the despair you feel about where the world is heading and your helplessness about contributing sufficiently as I daily experience and feel a sense of helplessness that creates despair and minimal action (no action seems large enough to be of use). What I see as my tiny contribution to the world I want to help create just doesn't feel 'enough.'"

Before discovering my current passion for Nonviolent Communication, I was in exactly the kind of place that Penny describes. I saw no way that I could support movement towards what I wanted to see in the world. I was debilitated by this thought.

The first step of movement happened when I realized that having a calling, knowing what we are to do in our life, is a form of privilege. It provides clarity and focus, eliminates or drastically diminishes certain forms of struggle, and provides a sense of meaning, and energy for action. Knowing this provided a modicum of relief even though I still had no idea.

Today I still often fall into pits of profound despair. What helps is that I now know what I am called to do, and do it to the best of my ability. Then I think of all the people who, like me years ago, *don't* have a clear sense of what they can do to contribute, and I remember how wrenching and helpless this experience can be. I want to offer some tips and milestones about how to be with despair, and how, ultimately, to mobilize the energy inherent in it to create action.

Opening to Despair

The first thing I learned was to embrace my despair. This was no easy task. Many times over I shut down instead of feeling the despair. Over time I found ways of keeping my heart open to the pain and anguish that live in me. They're still there. What's changed is my ability to keep breathing, thinking, moving, and connecting with myself and others when the despair is present.

How did this happen? I had the good fortune of encountering the work of Joanna Macy. Starting in the 1980s she developed and deepened the insights and practices that have helped many people shift their relationship with despair. Her primary thesis, as I understand it, is that despair is not the problem. It is only our resistance to *feeling* the despair that keeps us shut down or stuck in anger. Once we allow ourselves to experience despair without shying away from it, something melts and we discover there is no reason to be afraid of despair, because it's simply a manifestation of care. The more despair we feel, the more care we know is there.

Touching the core of care that lives in any of us unleashes enormous energy, a sense of empowerment, and a longing for active participation in shaping the future. This continues to happen to me, again and again, as I open to deeper and deeper levels of feelings in me.

Along the way I came to realize and accept fully that I am likely to die in a world not dramatically closer to what I want than the one I live in now. I derive relief and patience from realizing that I am not able to control the outcome no matter how hard I try. As a result, I keep moving closer and closer to doing what I am doing because it's the only thing I could be doing. While I have truly no idea about the long-term effects of anything that I am doing, *in the moment* I experience more effectiveness when I am able to be present and connected instead of fueled by the frantic energy of urgency, itself born out of despair that I haven't metabolized. Mastering despair, for me, has meant dipping into it, alone and with others, as often as possible, so I can reconnect with the care and with the un-knowing, so I can let go and only act based on the burning passion of my care and vision. Whether or not I create what I want in the world, I want to die knowing that I lived with the integrity of trying.

Transforming Our Experience of Anger

Anger is a peculiar feeling in at least two ways. One is that we have "anger management" classes alongside the contrary injunction to feel and express our anger. The other is that I have yet to meet someone who relishes others' expression of anger, and yet so many of us want, even expect, others to be available to our own expressions of anger towards them. These paradoxes intrigue me, and lead me to believe that we know very little about how to relate to anger in a way that supports ourselves and others.

While anger has not been a major obstacle for me in my life, I have worked with many individuals and with groups on the topic, and have learned enough about it in this way that I hope my thinking can be a gift, even if it doesn't come from my own direct experience. I also want to express my appreciation to Marshall Rosenberg for giving me initial insights about anger that have served to frame my investigations for years and years.

The core insight I have come to have about anger is that most of the time we either stuff our anger or run with it, and that we hardly, if ever, give ourselves the opportunity to use it well as information about what is going on, which would allow us to learn from it. I believe changing our relationship with anger to have curiosity and space instead of constriction and urgency is key to mastering and transforming our experience of anger.

Understanding Anger

It goes without saying that anger only comes up when our needs are not met. The question remains, however, about why in some situations our response is anger and in others our response is hurt, anguish, or helplessness. What is it that makes our organism move in the direction of anger?

If everything we do and all of our reactions are attempts to meet needs, then anger is no exception. The more intense our anger, the more it points to important needs we are attempting to meet by mobilizing it. Anger is a feeling, and it may appear odd to think of it as something we *do* or *choose*. Still, take a moment to reflect on a time when you were angry. Can you see now what you were hoping (usually unconsciously) that the anger would give you? Sometimes, we mobilize anger as a strategy to ensure that we will take care of our needs. At other times, we mobilize it as a strategy to be heard by others. What was it for you? Now think of other times when you were angry. Can you identify what led you to mobilize anger?

Anger and Evaluation

If you keep asking yourself why you are angry in a particular situation, you are likely to hear yourself say something like: "Because s/he didn't do what s/he said s/he would do." This kind of expression – the idea that someone else can *make* us feel a certain way – shows a strong lack of sense of power. Indeed, I have come to believe that we are extremely unlikely to feel anger at a time when we feel powerful. We are much more likely to feel anger when we feel powerless.

If you really want to understand your anger, keep asking the question again and again. Why would you get angry when someone doesn't do what s/he said s/he would do? This is where the question starts becoming strange, because it seems self-evident. I have found many times that unpacking the self-evident provides astonishing opportunities for learning. I have found, many times, that persisting with this kind of question uncovers, somewhere, a belief that the other person *should* act differently. It is this belief and the implicit moral evaluation, rather than the action itself, which lead to anger.

Needs Leading to Anger

Having identified that anger stems from thoughts about what someone should do, we can ask again why our organism chooses to think in terms of what someone should do. Clearly, some of it is deep habits in our culture. However, I have found many times over that if I can identify the active need instead of attributing choices to habit, I have more of a chance of making full connection.

I want to illustrate the variety of needs that may be at the heart of the kind of thinking that generates anger with a real-life example.

Fred[43] regularly got into fits of rage in his relationship with his partner, and wanted very much to get a handle on what was going on

---

[43] Not his real name

and what he could do differently. In order to support him more effectively, we focused on one specific incident. Fred started by sharing his initial inner reaction that led to the rage: "I can't believe she would do something like that! She asks for more kisses and hugs, and, when I do it, she spits on it. What a bitch! I hate her!" With deeper exploration, we discovered together that the needs at the heart of the conflict for him were respect and dignity. Then we looked more closely at why he chose anger. Why would he need to mobilize anger to ensure that he took care of his needs? Three themes emerged.

One was that he had an inner struggle about owning his need for respect. On the one hand, he was holding really tightly to wanting respect, with an intensity of "having to" have this need met. On the other hand, he was working double-time to make the need go away so that he would not have to deal with having a need that wasn't acceptable to him. The more he tried to make the need go away, the more desperate he became about meeting it. Finally, he unconsciously mobilized the anger to ensure he would attend to his need for respect, however unskillfully. In this way, the anger served to "win" his inner battle, while also protecting him from feeling shame about having the need, because the anger put the blame on her, not on him.

The second theme was that he had no picture of how he could attend to his needs and hold his partner's needs with care at the same time. Once again, Fred finds himself in an either/or mindset: either he cares for himself at the expense of his care for his partner, or he cares for his partner and gives up on his needs. The anger then ends up giving more weight to his needs compared to his care for his partner's needs.

Lastly, the exploration uncovered the fact that respect, immediately underneath which was consideration, was a surface layer. For Fred, both of these needs signify reassurance that he is loved and cared for, which he immediately realized was much more vulnerable than respect or consideration. The anger, then, served the purpose of protecting and hiding the vulnerability of wanting reassurance about love.

With these three themes, each one of which was keeping Fred tight inside, it was no wonder that he mobilized so much anger in those moments. His anger was the only means that he knew and could imagine would give him sufficient power to attend to these desperate needs that were hidden from him.

Mastering Anger through Vulnerability

Protecting our vulnerability often *appears* to others as if we are aggressive even when we don't feel it. Anger is the quintessential emotion that masks vulnerability, shame, fear, and helplessness. Especially when we are vulnerable, sometimes the only way our system can recognize that we are taking ourselves seriously, that we matter, at least to ourselves, is through anger. For as long as we haven't made the deep choice to embrace vulnerability, anger is also a likely strategy for power. In addition, for many of us anger is a major path towards aliveness, being "drunk with fury" as one workshop participant put it. Anger often comes with intensity and pleasure even when we are judging it. It's as if we rejoice inside about doing something for ourselves, something that supports a sense of mattering.

We rarely experience the expression of vulnerability as a path to getting such needs met. How likely are you to experience the sharing of your vulnerability as a powerful way to express yourself? How likely are you to imagine that your vulnerable expression will be heard by others? Can you easily imagine that a vulnerable expression of what you want and feel will matter to others? Does it seem plausible that you will experience aliveness when sharing vulnerably? Suppose Fred said to his wife, when he recognized his growing anger, "I'm so scared you won't love me." Until we recognize vulnerability as a viable different path – for power, for mattering, for aliveness, or for being heard – we are likely to keep going to anger.

When you add to our great fear of vulnerability the fact that most of us tend to judge ourselves for our anger, we are unlikely to release ourselves from the grip of anger even though we know all too well that the way we express anger doesn't create the kind of connection we want.

For as long as we judge our anger, it stays, because the anger is there for a reason, and when we berate ourselves for it we are not making room for it to speak to us about that reason. We give in to anger, or we suppress it, but we don't listen to it most of the time. And since the other person we are talking with doesn't listen to the anger either (When was the last time you expressed yourself angrily to someone and received in response something like, "Honey, darling, I so want to give you what you want"?), we never learn from what the anger has to teach us. It is only through making a different choice – to listen to our anger, to uncover the vulnerability that it hides, to prioritize our needs – that we can transform the dynamics of anger.

After our conversation, Fred took it upon himself to share his vulnerability with his partner. This was not an overnight task, and required letting go of many cherished notions of fairness and ideas of what a relationship "should" look like. Slowly, over the course of about two years, Fred learned to express and ask for what he wants; to say "no" when he would otherwise develop resentment; and to bring his most tender feelings to his partner even when she herself was not most receptive to it. The result was nothing short of a miracle. After quite a number of years of distance and alienation between them, Fred now regularly speaks of the grace and beauty they now share. From repeated and frequent experiences of rage, he has shifted to extremely rare expressions of anger that stand out and are then used for further learning. He also delights in his own internal transformation, which affects other areas of his life as well as his relationship.

When our practice of vulnerability is integrated and embraced, we can recognize vulnerability as an alternate source of strength and power that comes from within, which then diminishes the appeal of anger as a strategy for power. We literally need to *learn* how to express our truth vulnerably and still experience a sense of power, mattering, and aliveness.

Recommitting in the Face of Grief

I consider it amazing good fortune that I was able to tap into some areas in my life where I carry with me a lot of pain and anguish. I feel blessed by what happened. I imagine that the idea that experiencing grief can be a positive experience may be puzzling to some and possibly inspiring to others.

In order to be understood clearly, I want to start by distinguishing between grieving and hopelessness. I believe that hopelessness still contains in it a resistance to the experience (some attachment to having a different experience). In grieving, on the other hand, we surrender completely into the truth of what is, with complete acceptance and heartbreak. As you read below, the specific experiences of what brought up such pain for me may be foreign to you. Please bear in mind, though, that the stories I share about me here are simply an illustration of a key insight. What the sources of pain are for each of us varies, and yet we all have our own sensitivities, and I trust the experience of pain and grief is familiar to all.

I am reminded of a line that inspired me many years ago, from R.D. Laing: "There is a great deal of pain in life and perhaps the only pain that can be avoided is the pain that comes from trying to avoid pain." Although I have long accepted pain as an integral part of life, my organism still habitually resists embracing the experience of pain. Not much. Just enough so that when I succeed in opening my heart up in full to the wrenching experience, whatever it may be, I feel the difference and the relief of being aligned with life again.

Below I describe experiences of grieving that took place one week in the fall of 2010.

The Gift of Trust

For myself, and I know it's not necessarily so for everyone, the only reliable way to release that last little closing of my heart is to be in the company of others whose love and presence I trust, either globally or at least in the moment. So the first blessing was having had the experience of trusting another's presence so much and being able to rest in that trust sufficiently to release the last threads of tightness and contraction in my heart around my grief.

I was most conscious of that gift in the first instance of touching grief. It was about my experience of feeling so alone in the world. I've been blessed with much that I want to offer, and I am receiving more and more encouragement from others that the gifts are wanted. I have many people who are passionate about supporting me and I know I wouldn't be able to do what I do without the ongoing flow of support I receive. At the same time, at the very core level, I lack a sense of anchor in the world, support in the day-to-day of my life, the kind of support that people share with each other when they are in a primary relationship or in a tight-knit community. When this first came up, the person I was with attempted to offer me suggestions for what I could do to structure life in a way that would result in more support for me. I engaged with that conversation without touching the grief that was there. I didn't experience the suggestions as full presence with *me*. When I remarked on this to my friend, and when the energy shifted and I experienced her full presence, I was able to relax and in that trust found my way to the grief.

The Gift of Truth and Acceptance

In each of these encounters I came to more clarity about something in my life that I don't see a way of changing for the moment. In opening to the pain I am opening to acceptance. It's as if the resistance to the pain comes from the unconscious idea that by not accepting it I can have more hope of changing it. Not so. In the acceptance I find peace, alignment, and the recognition that my choice is internal.

This gift was most pronounced in the second instance of grieving. I was able to share with another friend the pain of having had many significant and close friends exit the friendship, sometimes even disconnecting altogether, by their choice. In certain moments I found the pain so excruciating that it took a certain kind of effort to keep breathing. There was no accusation of others for having left, no self-blaming for not knowing how to show up in ways that people can relate to with sufficient ease over time. Just clean grief. I cannot change what happened, nor the fact that it may well continue to happen again and again. If I find acceptance, I can have more choice about how to meet my life. This has happened about 30 times in my adult life. The only chance I see for continuing to choose, again and again, to show up and keep my heart open to the possibility of being so attached and affected in a new friendship, comes from accepting that all this has happened to me, and letting myself grieve it.

The Gift of Energy and Freedom

And so comes the third blessing. By finding a way to release the residue of visceral resistance to experiencing the pain, I lose my fear of the pain, and I gain back the energy, at times immense energy, that it takes to keep the pain at bay. Losing the fear means more choice, more freedom to be and live as I wish.

The last example of dipping into grief was the clearest to me in this regard. This time I connected with the familiarity and frequency of times of conflict in which I find capacity in me to stretch and open my heart to another until they experience themselves fully heard. And then, when I try to express my experience of the same conflict, the other person doesn't find a way to be with me and hear me. This one comes to the heart of what nonviolence means to me: the willingness to keep showing up and acting in the world in integrity with who I want to be regardless of how others act. I need all the energy in the world to keep this commitment again and again despite all the disappointments. Grieving, letting myself cry and cry and rip my heart open without blaming, without grasping for change, and without contracting, frees up enough energy that I can keep my heart open.

This energy allows me to re-commit, freshly each time, and without reservations, to keep my passion for my work and plunge without knowing if there will ever be enough support or anchoring; to make myself available to love and be loved without knowing if anyone will ever stay; and to show up with compassion and integrity without knowing if I will ever be received in the way I long for. That, in a nutshell, is the power of grieving.

Embracing Life

Except in rare circumstances of physical damage or severe early abuse, most infants and even toddlers have no difficulty knowing what they want. This doesn't surprise me, because they are still connected to life and to their own self, even if without conscious awareness.

I have been on the journey of reclaiming inner freedom for at least 15 years. What I see as the main goal for me is to be able to choose freely how I want to respond to each moment in life. The more I have been on this journey the clearer I get that the essential quality of this freedom is to know, both on the largest scale and moment by moment, what's most important to me, and to be able to choose how to act without fear of consequences.

Beyond knowing what we need, moment by moment, and acting with inner integrity, embracing life also means doing all we can to nourish our soul, to provide food to support our resilience, so we can keep doing what we do with joy and wholeheartedly.

Awareness of Needs

The forces that operate against the cultivation of needs-awareness have been entrenched for several thousand years in the majority of the cultures in the world. The journey of reclaiming our capacity to engage with our needs and live from within them faces real and persistent obstacles. I nonetheless feel confident and optimistic, based on my experience with myself and of working with people, that we can move toward greater and greater capacity in this area. If I look at myself, for example, when I started this journey, most of the time I had no concept of what I wanted in each moment. The question itself would have seemed strange to me. Now I can hardly think of a time when I wouldn't be able to immediately know what was important to me. I still am challenged many times to translate my connection with my needs into action that honors them fully. I trust the process enough to anticipate that my capacity in this direction will continue to grow. Meanwhile, I have recovered so much sense of freedom and self-acceptance that my life is dramatically different from what I remember it being only a few years ago.

Overcoming Obstacles to Connecting with Needs

The goal of embracing our needs puts us at odds with the culture even more than mastering our emotions does. After all, an entire industry of therapy has been around for long enough to make the goal of "being in touch with our feelings" absolutely acceptable. Needs, on the other hand, continue to be equated with weakness, dependence, and lack on the one hand, and with selfishness on the other hand. As I have already touched on earlier, having needs is one key source of shame for many of us. Instead of accepting our fundamental human vulnerability, we learn – often at high cost to ourselves – to ignore, deny, override, or in some other way to suppress our needs.

In order to know what our needs are, let alone embrace and own them, we have to overcome these obstacles when the culture surrounding us continues to downplay the importance of needs.

Wanting Fully
Without Attachment

The origin of suffering is attachment.

– The Buddha

The Talmud tells us that in the world to come, everyone will be called to account for all the desires they might have fulfilled in this world but chose not to. The things we desire – the desires themselves – are sacred. Who put them in our hearts if not God? But we have been taught to be ashamed of what we want; our desires become horribly distorted and cause us to do terribly hurtful things.

– Alan Lew, *This is Real and You are Completely Unprepared*

One of the key obstacles to becoming aware of and embracing our needs is the fear of being consumed by our needs. In particular, within a number of spiritual traditions, the idea of no-attachment has come to such prominence, that the idea of cultivating our needs as a path to freedom may seem strange at best[44].

But what does it take to let go of attachment? What exactly does that mean and what can we do to get there? Is letting go of wanting the only way to let go of attachment, or is it possible to want what we want with full passion and, at the same time, to remain genuinely relaxed about whether or not we get what we want?

The main challenge arises when we experience tension between what we want and what is, or what seems possible. We then frequently respond in one of two ways. Externally, we might try to force what is to conform to what we want by outright coercion and threats, or by using more subtle forms of demand. Internally, we might try to suppress or give up on what we want. In both cases we are forcing others or ourselves instead of being in a dialogic relationship. Neither of these strategies engages with life openly, and both lead to suffering.

---

[44] This piece is excerpted and adapted from a much fuller version that is a chapter in a future book I am writing with my sister Arnina: *The Power of Inner Freedom: Using the Gift of Needs to Make Real Choice Possible.* An earlier version of this piece was published in *Tikkun* magazine:
(tikkun.org/article.php/jan10_wanting).

The alternative is to build openness to the humanity of our own needs, to release our attachment to outcome without giving up on what we want, and to strengthen our ability to maintain dignity, connection, open-heartedness, and acceptance in the face of situations we cannot transform.

This requires us to grasp experientially and become comfortable with the radical notion that needs are a deep expression of life rather than a "problem" to eliminate. We cannot turn off our needs any more than we can turn off being alive. We can only choose how we relate to them. When we "fight" our needs, they are more likely to "run" us unconsciously, leaving us with less choice and power. When we own our needs and embrace them fully as core expressions of our humanity and aliveness, we find more self-connection and develop the freedom and strength to attend to our needs as well as to the needs of others.

Owning Our Needs

Part of what's at issue here is the difference between having a need, which is a fact of life, and owning a need, which is a conscious choice. Owning a need means experiencing a relaxed comfort and acceptance about having it. When we own a need, we make no attempt – however subtle – to distance ourselves from the need, pretend we don't have it, be harsh with ourselves for having it, or tell ourselves that we "should" not have it. In fact, when we own a need we hold no negative judgments about ourselves even when we don't like the actions we may take to fulfill it.[45]

Reaching for full inner freedom is an invitation to redefine our notion of need, and to walk through the layers of shame about having needs, about having a particular need, and about possibly having too much or too little of that need in relation to what we believe we "should" have. Only then can we live in peace with whatever needs we have in the exact form that we have them. Think about it: If you are not going to be you, who will?

---

[45] Most everyone sees, intuitively, why negative judgments, of self or other, interfere with compassion and connection. Just as much as rewards have similar, sometimes more devastating consequences to punishments, I see positive judgments as also contributing to separation. This happens both because of the static nature of the judgments compared to specific observations, as well as the comparison with the negative that is implicit in them.

This new connection with ourselves then leads to almost pure magic: as we uncover and embrace our full humanity, we discover that our needs also provide a way of connecting with people. Because all human beings without exception have the same set of basic needs, whenever we experience a need, we have an opportunity to be in unity with the rest of humanity. The experience of having the need itself is common and similar to all of us even if we choose different strategies to meet it.

On a deeper level, needs can be understood as the basic unit of life itself. When we can tune in to needs as pure movement of and toward life, sometimes we can experience a larger unity with life itself – a melting into the spaciousness of all that is. If wanting is life, then any attempt to give up on wanting, even if motivated by the attempt to cultivate non-attachment, is a form of interfering with life.

Opening to life in the form of wanting creates a deep and intimate bond with ourselves. Being grounded in the truth that lives inside of us then becomes a profound internal resource that is crucial in our quest for inner freedom.

Working toward inner freedom and full acceptance of our humanity moves us beyond the notion of needs as equal to narrow self-interest and invites us to redefine and expand what we mean by need to include our passions and visions for the world. The Talmudic rabbis said: "More than the calf wants to suck, the cow wants to suckle." We all know the deep satisfaction of giving without expecting anything in return, of supporting and nurturing others in need, of embracing our dreams for the world, and of working toward a cause larger than ourselves. Caring and giving are deep, core human needs that transcend our separate, individualized existence even while being individual human needs.

Beware, though, of the "secret hierarchy" of needs. True self-acceptance embraces the full range and variety of our needs, the personal ones as well as the ones more focused on contributing to others. None are more "okay" than others. All of them are equally human.

Accepting Our Needs

The hardest challenge is to open our hearts to full self-acceptance when we don't like the strategies and behaviors we use to meet our needs. In those instances we often employ self-judgment in an unconscious effort to realign ourselves with our values and become more acceptable to ourselves. The tragic mistake is that when we judge the behavior, we fail to realize that the behavior is merely an attempt, a way to meet a need, not "who we are." If, for example, I see myself as "lazy" when I don't do certain chores, I lose sight of my own humanity, which in that moment is manifesting itself as the need for comfort (in the form of "laziness").

Instead of creating the space for the need itself to exist, and then allowing the emergence of another way to meet it, we fight the strategy. We often attempt to change our behavior instead of getting to know and embrace its human roots. And we do this using habitual tactics such as sending "should" and "must" messages and making negative self-judgments about ourselves. Sadly, these tactics rarely support us in creating change in our behavior. We usually believe our own judgments, disconnect from the source of life inside us, and have less and less access to free choice about how to act and react. If, instead, we open to and fully accept the needs that have led us to the strategies that do not work, we create an opportunity to find strategies that meet those needs without cost to our self-connection or other needs.

Transforming Suffering

Wanting fully without attachment requires us to stretch ourselves in two directions: toward wanting and toward non-attachment. Letting go of attachment is, in the end, about changing our relationship to the experience of wanting. There is a kind of wanting that is contracting and grasping, which is about coming to take something from life. And there is a kind of wanting that is expansive and relaxed, which is about coming forward to meet life. Shifting from the former to the latter is what makes it possible to stay comfortably in the wanting. When we let the wanting be, we can experience ourselves as more alive, regardless of outcome.

The first step toward living without attachment is to overcome a deeply ingrained habit of seeing our preferred strategy as indistinguishable from our need. When we manage to let go of a particular strategy as the outcome, we usually see more options in the form of a variety of strategies to meet our needs, and are thus more likely to have what we want. Even if not, we can still experience a release of attachment that is not about giving up and contracting.

Rather, it's about expansion and liberation because we are no longer limited by having only one possibility.

The next step is to inhabit the experience of the need without the almost-invisible but very strong attachment to having it met at all. This may seem confusing. After all, isn't the wish to have a need met the very essence of having a need in the first place? Didn't we just learn how to want? What now?

This confusion is the heart of the paradox of non-attachment. Wanting and attachment are not the same. Non-attachment does not mean giving up on wanting what we want. It only means letting go of attachment to getting what we want.

Becoming aware of which needs are up for us is the first step toward letting go of our attachment to getting them met. The next step toward letting go of attachment is to learn to simply be with the need, releasing all of our stories about it. This is where embracing our needs becomes a spiritual practice in its own right, a form of meditation.

From Need as "Lack" to Need as "Life"

When people begin the practice of connecting with needs, they usually connect with the unmet aspect of the need rather than the need itself. This habit reinforces the experience of need as "lack" which, in turn, reinforces the tendency to distance ourselves from our needs to avoid the undesired association with "neediness." Instead, we can work on increasing our ability to experience pure needs, without any connection to whether or not they can be met, only as the desire itself.[46]

If we want to learn about wanting and understand more clearly the significance of needs, we can look at babies. Babies don't wonder whether it is okay to want or not – they just want. And they are not happy or sad about it – they just want. It seems that the energy of wanting is simply life propelling them forward.

As adults, we can recover some of this original connection with our needs, without the attachment, by increasing our capacity to stay relaxed while wanting. Again, a key part of the practice is to truly uncouple each need from any association with stories, strategies, or the angst of wondering if it will ever be met or not, and to just

[46] These notes are not meant as a substitute for the experiential learning necessary for practice and integration.

embrace the need as an expression of what it means to be human in this moment.

The capacity to simply sit with the need is a key way to touch the ground of non-attachment. In this non-attachment, we can rediscover the beauty of being the human that we are, and of life being just what it is.

Doing this work brings us closer to offering ourselves as a gift. The more we practice, the more we are present and connected with our needs – wanting all we want without attachment and without fear of being judged. Then we can face whatever comes our way. Then there is no more "rejection" because we are able to stand inside so powerfully that we can see the humanity of others, we can hear the "yes" behind their "no," and we can connect with their needs as well as with ours. Such freedom allows us also to transcend other limitations on the path to full liberation.

Gratitude in the Midst of Difficulty

Despite years of knowing that gratitude contributes to life, and suggesting to people in my workshops to start a gratitude practice in their lives, it was only in late 2009 that I was finally able to start my own practice. In the past, using gratitude as a *practice* instead of just when it arose spontaneously just wasn't working for me. But the times were hard enough in my life, and the draw strong enough that I started.

The Basic Practice

I knew I wanted to have a daily practice, because I knew that I would need discipline in order to shift the momentum of the habit of focusing on what's not working. I picked something simple that wouldn't require changing my daily routines, because I know myself all too well. Setting aside time for daily practice simply doesn't happen. I forget, other priorities arise, and I end up not doing it. So I picked bedtime. Whatever else happens, I always get into bed at some point. That was the point in time I chose.

The practice consisted of lying in bed, breathing fully and slowly, and reviewing my day, looking for everything that could possibly be a source of gratitude. Not as a check list, but really pausing with each one, putting my attention again and again on the mystery, wonder, magic, and awe that is the experience of whatever happened, whoever contributed to it. My primary focus was on the people who contribute to my life.

Early Months

The first few months took place during a period that included some of the most challenging times in many years. I was intent on finding the gratitude despite the immense challenges I was living through. I was equally open to something really small and something extensive that someone did to contribute to my life. Regardless, I focused my attention and my heart on really taking in that there was no reason for this person to do what they did, they didn't really have to do it, they only did it because they are human and we humans do things for each other, sometimes without even intending to. On a few occasions my focus was on people I don't even know, who produced something I was consuming that day.

Slowly, I attempted to open my heart to the person, as if I was trying to *be* that person and feel what it's like to have done what they did that contributed to my life. I still find enormous beauty in doing this. Within a short period of time I found that I could be more peaceful as I went to sleep. And, after only a few short months, my inner experience shifted into more softness and less anguish, despite the fact that the challenges in my life were unchanged.

Early Lessons

My first two lessons were completely surprising. The first was that, exactly like Marshall Rosenberg, creator of Nonviolent Communication has said, gratitude is a kind of fuel. Especially on days when I felt depleted, lacking resources, or particularly stressed, I found the practice to nourish me, give me some energy, and release some of the stress.

The other thing I learned was even more surprising to me. I learned that on the days that were the hardest, I usually had more things that I could be grateful for, more people that contributed to my life on those days. I wondered why that would be. Here's my hypothesis: when we are doing well, we require less support, and we can more easily hold on to the illusion of self-sufficiency. When we are faced with challenges, we become more aware of how much of our life depends on the grace and generosity of others. I find immense comfort and richness in this realization.

A Year of Practice

I maintained this practice with utmost rigor for over a year. I may have missed four or five days in the course of that year. One of the things that started happening was I often found myself looking forward to going to bed, because the practice was so satisfying. (Considering that sleep issues have been a significant presence in my life, looking forward to being in bed was a minor miracle.)

I was quite aware of the enormous benefit I was experiencing. The times remained complex and challenging in a variety of ways, and yet my experience of life was improving. On the face of it, it could clearly be that I was feeling better because, alongside the challenges that continued, I can name – in retrospect, and even while it was happening – more and more needs that were met. My own intuitive sense of matters is different. It appears to me that the deepest effect of my practice was the growing facility with noticing, naming, and celebrating the ways in which my needs were met. For the longest time I had a story that I was living a life in which most of my needs most of the time were not met except for key areas in which they were: connection with my sisters, the privilege of having work that is so meaningful to me, living in line with my values, and having a high degree of self-acceptance. In the course of this year this story started dissolving and transforming into a much more nuanced picture of life.

Given how much I was getting from the practice, I didn't have any urgency to end it. In fact, I was perfectly content to accept gratitude as my daily practice for the duration. I was present, curious, and unattached. Until one day I knew with complete clarity that the daily practice of gratitude was completed. Not because I didn't need gratitude any longer. I was, and have been since, all the more aware of the extraordinary gift of gratitude. Rather, I had a sense of completion because of trusting that I have integrated gratitude into the cellular fiber of my being in a way that didn't need daily tending. If I have a particularly challenging day I call on the practice for that night, and go to sleep more peaceful. Otherwise, I am simply living with more gratitude as a background color. In addition, while I've always been blessed with relatively easy access to spontaneous gratitude, now I am so often awash with waves of gratitude that life truly feels different.

Replenishing Inner Resources

Sometimes I have fallen into the mindset of believing that things are so horrific and painful in the world that it would take heartlessness to have any joy, celebration, or gratitude in the midst of the destruction we are experiencing on a global scale.

I haven't had anything like this orientation in quite a while. I attribute this shift also to seeing the effectiveness of my gratitude practice. The fuel and energy it provided contributed to my resilience. In fact, I believe I now have a little more capacity to be present with and witness what is happening in the world without shutting down. I also have grown in my capacity to trust my contributions, to envision ways of generating resources to do the work I am called to do, and more faith that possibilities will open up as I keep moving forward. I never forget that one child under five years old dies every five seconds (over 18,000 daily!) of malnutrition and related causes, not to mention the effects of wars of all kinds.[47] I am more able to keep my heart open to this horror instead of becoming paralyzed.

When I first became aware of how powerful a source of fuel gratitude had become in my life, I started wondering what other aspects of life also act as fuel. A friend acquainted me with one. She told me she once went to one of her teachers and asked him what he thought was the antidote to despair. Without hesitation the teacher said: beauty. Indeed, many times in my life when I was overcome by anguish and hopelessness I turned to music for support.

Especially if we are going to take on a major piece of work that goes against the grain, either internal work to reclaim our full heart and humanity, or external efforts to create the world of our dreams, we will need to call on tremendous inner resilience and capacity. What else can we call on besides gratitude and beauty?

Without conscious tools to keep our hearts open, many of us do, indeed, shut down and tune out the plight of the children so we can manage to continue with our own personal lives, while others succumb to anger and desperation that can lead to re-creating domination and horror.

---

[47] Beyond digestion as these numbers are, they are actually a huge improvement on a decade ago. See www.who.int/mediacentre/factsheets/fs178/en/index.html.

Until I opened up fully to gratitude as a method for replenishing my resources and nourishing my soul, my primary fuel, for far too long, was always vision. I used vision as a pull, and internal will as the motivation. And I was worn out from the effort. Still, I am grateful to have such easy access to clear vision to pull me forwards. I am well aware that having access to vision is a resource that's not available to everyone, which is part of why I chose to dedicate so much of this book to vision: it's a strength of mine, and a lack in the world, and I want more people to be able to visualize, in detail, what is possible, so they can be moved to act.

My next candidate for a source of ongoing fuel for our work is closely related to vision and to beauty: inspiration. In effect, both vision and beauty can provide inspiration. I also often get inspiration from hearing what other people are able to do (except in those cases where I get into comparison thinking and feel despair about not having done and contributed more than I have). I get inspired by stories of how some people are already raising their children, how others are finding ways to resolve conflicts and restore peace in their workplaces and communities using the principles I am bringing forth in this book. I get inspired most when I hear of people without access to external resources who managed to mobilize their own inner resilience and resources to create collaborations and movements that I simply could not have envisioned were possible.

Last on the list is the experience of love. I find myself quite nourished and replenished when I am able to take in others' love for me. I can rest in the acceptance, the understanding that comes from being fully heard, and the companionship of having people appreciate me or what I do. This kind of resting recharges me to some extent. I get much more recharged from experiences of loving others than from being loved. The experience of loving another or others so completely opens my heart that I literally *feel* the flow of life inside me, and the shift in my awareness that comes as a result.

I am far from believing this is an exhaustive list. Gratitude, beauty, vision, inspiration, and love are only the types of experiences that have worked for me and some others I know to increase resilience and provide more energy. Whatever the source, what seems of vital importance is that we need our inner resources in order to face life with open hearts.

Beyond Submission and Rebellion

I have never been successful at mastering obedience. As a child, often enough it was my attitude toward my father, rather than something in particular that I did, which was the cause of punishment and criticism. Obedience is highly prized in authority-based systems. No surprise, then, that my father was attempting to control my defiant spirit more than my specific actions.

Obedience is a form of submission, of giving our will to another out of fear of consequences. It is almost essential to obedience that no specific rationale be given by the authority for the action it demands. "Do as I tell you" leaves no room for questions. We are not supposed to understand, only to carry out.

My father never managed to break my spirit, as was his clear and explicit intention (my mother regularly tried to dissuade him from this plan, to no avail). My defiance, a deep-seated rebellion of the spirit, became an article of pride for me. More often than not, I did what he insisted I do, simply because I had no particular reason not to. And yet I knew that I wasn't going to let him "get to me," and I know much of his wrath was precisely about that.

Given my inner satisfaction at emerging from childhood with my full defiant self, I was utterly surprised when I first heard Marshall Rosenberg say: "Never give anyone the power to make you submit or rebel." It had never before occurred to me that my rebellion, however successful, left the power in my father's hands. Internally, I was more preoccupied with not giving in than with knowing what I wanted and going for it. I chose my actions reactively, not truly from within. I didn't see what is now so clear to me: that true choice, true freedom, emerges from inner clarity.

I still struggle with this legacy, all these years later. Any time I see someone in a position of authority, be it a police officer, a doctor, or even a therapist, I stiffen a little to protect myself. I recognize that vigilance, that intentionality of protection and defiance, as blocking my soft, open-hearted access to myself, my values, my needs, my feelings, and the choice that emerges clearly from there. Still, often enough I don't have the inner resources to release the protection.

As luck would have it, I also became, myself, an authority figure for hundreds, if not thousands, of people who have studied with me. I have watched the dynamics of submission and rebellion from this side, too. I have seen people defer to me when I didn't ask them to do so, and have felt the pain of separation, the loneliness I experience when people give their power away. I have also seen people respond to me in defiance and rebellion, react to what I didn't say or do, just because I am in power.

I have been studying this now for years. Although I am still learning, I have already figured out some things. I know that much of the challenge revolves around asking for what we want and being asked by others. When power differences exist, which they do most of the time, even in apparently equal relationships, making requests, saying "yes," and saying "no" are not simple matters.

Transcending the paradigm of submission and rebellion means asking for what we want without giving away our own power and without taking away the power of others. Children are usually trained to believe that the power resides with the parents. Accordingly, instead of asking for what they want, they tend to say "can I ...", a form of request that leaves the decision about what will happen with the parent. This is a form of submission. Rebellion, often in teenage years, though sometimes years earlier, takes the form of "I am going to ..." without leaving any room for the parent to have a say. Freedom, for me, resides in the dialogic stance. "I would like to ... and I want to know how you are about it." Possible at any age.

Moving towards full choice also means being able to receive another's request, however it is couched, in a way that maintains our own dignity, autonomy, and care. I continue to work on being able to say "no" without closing my heart in defiance, and on being able to say "yes" with full generosity and willingness, even when someone is in a position of authority and, from their perspective, there is no room for dialogue. Choice is soft, empowered, intrinsic.

Such choice is at the heart of a radical consciousness that can see and understand without reacting, a consciousness that can stand up to authority without losing love. Radical consciousness means standing outside the authority structures, seeing them fully, understanding the effects they have on us and others, and knowing internally what matters to us. Sometimes what matters to us is at odds with the culture, and sometimes it is entirely within. Sometimes it aligns with what others want, and sometimes it makes us stand out in our naked vulnerability. Either way, we see and know, and choose from within, continuing to liberate ourselves from our own blindness, fear, complicity, and mindlessness, and moving towards freedom and full human aliveness. Nothing can stop us when we reach this state.

Recognizing Our Interdependence

Each of us lives in and through an immense movement of the hands of other people. The hands of other people lift us from the womb. The hands of other people grow the food we eat, weave the clothes we wear, and build the shelters we inhabit. The hands of other people give pleasure to our bodies in moments of passion, and aid and comfort in times of affliction and distress. It is in and through the hands of other people that the commonwealth of nature is appropriated and accommodated to the needs and pleasures of our separate, individual lives. And, at the end, it is the hands of other people that lower us into the Earth.

– Jim Stockinger[48]

In recent times I have seen more and more evidence of a growing awareness in our society and culture of the fundamental interconnectedness of all life, the web of which we humans are a part. I see less evidence of an awareness that this interconnection also exists within the human realm, that our lives, and those of people near and far, are intertwined.

I am not surprised. I believe that cultivating awareness of our interdependence is one of the biggest challenges that we could present to the modern sensibility of industrialized countries, where our dependence on each other is invisible, and where the values of self-sufficiency and autonomy are so paramount. One of the ironies that our way of living creates is that in actual fact we are less and less able to be self-sufficient at the same time as striving for more and more self-sufficiency. Fewer and fewer of us even know how to grow the food we eat, weave and make the clothes we wear, build the houses we live in, or find water anywhere other than in the faucet.

On the material plane we mask our dependence on others through the medium of money. Collectively, we uphold the illusion that if we only have enough money we don't depend on anyone, without realizing that we use the money to pay for something we are unable to do on our own, which effectively means we *are* relying on others, not just ourselves, for surviving. In addition to masking our

---

[48] James William Stockinger, Locke and Rousseau: Human Nature, Human Citizenship and Human Work.

dependence, we also pretend that we don't have an effect on others. The result is that collectively we operate, in the U.S., without any sense that we matter, and live reckless lives without much concern for the cost to others and nature.

On the emotional plane we mask our dependence on others through pretending to be OK even when we are not, and maintaining a stiff upper lip. The result is living in profound isolation, which is likely one of the causes of the high rate of depressed people in the U.S.

This particular aspect of isolation begins early in life. Ask yourself a simple question: What is a good baby? If you have been raised in a Western culture, chances are you know the answer right away (whether or not you agree with it): A good baby is one that doesn't cry! The training against the vulnerable exposure of our inner life starts very early in life.

I have already alluded to the ways of being raised in Western societies with regards to the sources of violence. There is no accident here that the same practices are at the core of masking our dependence on each other. In fact, the injunction to hide our dependence is one of the keys to understanding the level of shame I discussed earlier. So many people I work with will go to great lengths, even to harming themselves (e.g. by carrying weight that's too heavy for their bodies), just to ensure they don't ask for help. Countless times I have been in situations where I offered help to people, especially parents of small children who were struggling to get their shopping done, and have invariably been politely declined. As I work with people on opening up to receiving support, to reaching out, to knowing that we matter enough to get our needs met, I learn of the depth and persistence of those messages. They are internalized so deeply that even when they are questioned they continue to be passed on. Reclaiming the truth of our fundamental dependence on other people, and, even more significantly, our ability to take action based on this awareness, require enormous strength and perseverance, as this insidious form of separation keeps us from being able to band together, reach out for support, form communities, and create the conditions for all of our thriving.

Cultivating Radical Consciousness

I used to believe that it was enough to do sufficient personal healing in order to come to question the fundamental beliefs on which the social order stands. I used to believe that we would automatically come to see the social dimension of how we come to be who we are and how things are kept in place. After observing my own path to liberation, and accompanying many others on theirs, I now believe that radical consciousness – which I defined above as the capacity to step outside of the normative story of the society into which we were born – requires a proactive practice just as much as personal healing and liberation does. One does not imply the other, and practices exist for both.

Crisis, Empathy, and Community

Crisis is often an initial stimulus for embarking on an emotional journey that takes us outside our comfort zone. At the same time, not all crises, and not even all emotional journeys, result in opening up to life and embracing a radical consciousness. In the absence of empathic support in the context of a community, such crises can just as easily result in closing down by receding, shutting down, numbing out, or entering the world of despair, all without any change in our perspective. I know this possibility well from my own life.

I grew up in Israel, where war was a persistent and formative part of my life. Like most Israelis, I identified with the story of a persecuted people defending itself. I saw us as being misunderstood by the world and having only our ingenuity to protect us from annihilation. The Six-Day War took place when I was eleven, in 1967. By 1973, when the Yom Kippur War broke out, I had barely begun to see war as a choice rather than a painful, choice-less reality. I was 17. This was my third war.

I was not prepared for the intensity of my reactions to the war, which definitely served as a crisis point in terms of my own path to openness. I couldn't bear to hear anything about the war, which everyone else was talking about all the time. In order to remove myself from the pain I went for some days to a remote village, with minimal access to the media (that was still possible in those days in Israel), and volunteered to support the harvest of tomatoes.

After I came back I remember vividly how stunningly beautiful the sky was, completely clear and blue, with a warm and friendly sun quite past its blazing summer intensity. This beauty took place only 150 miles away from where war was raging. All I could think about was this: under this same blue sky people are killing one another. I wasn't thinking "Israelis" or "Palestinians" or "Arabs." I was thinking "people." I was aware of this, and knew this meant I was already outside the common story.

This was a time during which I had a very close association with a friend who provided immense support and inspiration. She understood what I was going through because she had already had her own departure from the social norms. She went much further than I did, because she managed to get herself out of the draft by claiming psychiatric disability. It was an almost-unheard-of step at the time for people to dodge the draft. The level of national unity and alignment around the necessity of full draft was almost unanimous. This friend was a trailblazer in Israel, and her support was something I could lean on to feel less alone.

I also got support from another unexpected source, my mother, who also had an opening at about the same time and embraced my challenges wholeheartedly. Having support from my mother, who was an adult and an authority figure in my life, meant the world to me at the time, and allowed me to keep walking on that path until I was ready to leave the mainstream way of thinking about the situation. I slowly released the old story of Israel being the pure victim suffering at the hands of hostile nations that refused to accept and welcome us. Something else was going on, and I was just learning what it was.

I passionately didn't want to go to the army. For starters, I knew my personal sensitivities, and intuited that being in the army would be devastating to my soul. I was also objecting to the whole idea of armies and war, though the full clarity about this emerged later in life. I was busily reading *Catch 22* and buttressing my defiance, which sat perfectly well on top of my overall approach to life and authority.

Despite all this awakening, the support I received was not enough to stick with my plans for getting out of being drafted. Despite her earlier support of me, my mother joined forces with my father to oppose my plans to enter a fictitious marriage, which, being female, would have automatically freed me from army service. I didn't have enough support and internal resilience to face their staunch battle to get me to change my mind. And so I caved in, closed down within a numb shell, and joined the army. It took me ten years to emerge from the loss.

The Role of Community

When Freud started his work with individuals, in 1895-1896, he was deeply shaken by their stories of child abuse. He was ready to depart from the conventional wisdom of his time, and developed what later came to be known as the "seduction theory." All of his groundbreaking insights emerged during that period and along with them he also held a significantly more radical and open view of human life than later in his life. He was so strongly affected by and open to what he heard from his clients, that he proposed, in a letter to a friend, that the motto of psychoanalysis be a line from Goethe: "What have they done to you, poor child?" During this same time he also maintained a compassionate perspective on clients and respect for the importance of emotions, arguing that the truth of patients' stories of early abuse could be ascertained from the emotions which accompanied the telling.

Freud held on to this view for only a short time, and soon turned around 180 degrees to claim, for the rest of his life, that it was fantasies and internal conflicts that resulted in neuroses rather than actual traumas. Why did he do that? We will likely never know, and yet some traces of his struggle give some credence to my sense of the enormous challenge. He was beginning to be shunned by colleagues, and certainly had no active support. He experienced, and described, extreme isolation and exhaustion. How could a young professional hold on to a view that had such difficult consequences? Lacking tools for working with his own legacy of suffering as a child, Freud ultimately sided with the adult, the authority, and the social order rather than with the child and the expression of emotion. No surprise that for the centerpiece of his work he picked a myth in which a father, Laius, consciously attempts to kill his son, Oedipus, who is saved by the kindness of a stranger. While Oedipus does, indeed, kill his father, this was the result of accident and provocation, not intention. The attempted and deliberate intention to murder is forgotten, erased from consciousness as unimportant. In the end, Freud justified what mistreatment he observed and rationalized it as appropriate given what he saw as the inner reality of the child's own drives.

This about-face robbed psychoanalysis of its potential role in the critique and possible transformation of the existing social order. The potential radical knowledge got lost in the process. There is no way to overestimate the monumental consequences of this failure to remain true to his original findings. What would have happened had he encountered a community of support, people he could turn to when the going got rough, a place to rest and feel at ease? Would that have led to greater strength in him that would have led him to trust his original findings?

A community can not only protect and support us by providing a safe haven; community is also a place where radical consciousness can be born and nurtured. This is what happened in the consciousness-raising groups of the 1960s and '70s, which were a core part of the women's movement. When women came together to share with each other, they discovered through the empathic support they received that they were not alone. Over time, and with effort and willingness to face and experience difficult emotions, women learned that what they thought were personal failings were instead shared experiences of the conditions of being women in a world where men had more access to resources and where men and women were socialized and treated differently throughout their life cycle. This is the quintessential experience of radicalizing consciousness: women in these groups transformed their story of who they were and what kind of world they lived in. They were then, many of them, no longer willing to accept the conditions of their life, and were catapulted into action to create change.

Sometimes such transformation happens in response to specific and acute conditions. A particularly instructive example of the role of community in that way was what happened during a protracted strike in Clinton, Iowa, in the 1990s.[49] As I read about this strike, what stood out for me was the gradual and persistent process of radicalization that the strikers underwent. Over time, the scope and depth of their analysis increased beyond the specific corporation they were fighting to encompass more fundamental questions about the nature of capitalism. The experience of going through the struggle together made it possible for the workers to transform their perspective.

I'm not surprised that community is so critical to this kind of transformation. In effect, developing a radical consciousness means an intentional choice to move away from accepted norms and perspectives. It means being willing to live with the consequences of possibly less social acceptance. It means having the strength to hold on to a vision that may be ridiculed or judged by others. Very few of us can do that without the support of a community, a place to come back to and have our sanity affirmed, our vision shared, our suffering understood, and our passion reflected back to us by others.

Gandhi himself had a core group of about 70 people who worked with him, who joined in his "experiments in truth" and lived together in his Ashram. Even without being mobilized to create change in the world, simply to live a life that rests on love, courage,

---

[49] Rick Fantasia, *Cultures of Solidarity*, Chapter 5.

care, and service, we need each other so we can keep going. We cannot go against the grain alone.

A Personal Practice of Liberation

Even when we embark on an emotional journey, and even if we persist, there is no guarantee of full freedom. Experiencing our emotions, even connecting with our needs, can equally well lead elsewhere.

One of the exercises I have often used in workshops is a practice of re-evaluating actions that we believe we "have to" do and don't want to; actions we do without an intrinsic motivation, only because of things like fear of consequences, or conventions, or internal pressure.

The practice is quite simple. Here are the questions participants are asked to answer. I am including them here so that you can have your own experience to reflect on when you read my comments later. As I mentioned earlier, this is *not* a self-help book, and the purpose of including this activity is only because it illustrates a deeper point I am trying to make about the experience of freedom. I invite you to take an example from your life and respond to these questions before reading my commentary.

1. Write down an action that you are telling yourself you have to do or that you think you have no choice about.
2. What are the consequences you are trying to avoid by taking this action?
3. What are the needs you are trying to meet by taking this action? Take a moment to connect in full with each need you discover before proceeding to another need. In particular, separate each need from the specific strategy of avoiding consequences, and from whether or not the need is ultimately met by the action you are taking. Simply connect with each need you are *attempting* to meet.
4. What needs are not met by taking this action? Again, take a moment to connect in full with each need you discover before proceeding to another need, and separate it from the action you are taking. You may discover some of the same needs as in question 3, since the attempt to meet some needs may not be successful.

5. Bring your awareness to *all* the needs you identified in the previous two questions, independently of whether or not they are met. How are you feeling when you focus on all the needs? Stay with this until you reach full connection with yourself in relation to all the needs you identified.
6. Check in with yourself: do you want to choose to keep taking the original action? If yes, write down what needs you would be attending to by continuing to take the action. If no, do you have other strategies that you believe might meet your needs better?
7. How are you feeling at this moment and what needs are you aware of?

The intention of this practice is to increase a sense of choice. When I first started using this exercise, I had anticipated that at least some of the time people would choose *not* to continue with the action and to find other strategies to meet their needs. I still remember hearing the story of Marshall Rosenberg, the man who created the methodology of Nonviolent Communication, talking about what happened decades ago when he first stumbled on this radical notion of making choices based on needs rather than on notions of "have to," "should," or anything else. He immediately applied this to writing clinical reports in his psychotherapy practice. As he unpacked his choice, he realized that he was only doing it because he wanted to ensure his financial sustainability. When he weighed that need alongside how much he never wanted to write another clinical report, he decided to stop writing them. Sure enough, he lost his position in the practice, and went through some years of struggle during which he did various and sundry jobs including driving a taxicab. Although he doesn't make this connection himself, I'd like to believe that this choice was part of what got him started on teaching workshops instead of having a private practice. Perhaps his gift to the world would not have happened had he continued in his practice.

Despite this radical possibility of freedom from the "have to," I've been sad and concerned about the results of using this practice. In years of using it, during which many participants have found it very moving, deeply connecting, and clarifying, I have rarely encountered anyone who, at the end of this journey, decided not to continue to take the action. Almost to the one, people re-choose the action and manage to release the "have to" energy. Why am I concerned? Because I want more of us to be able to make choices that are at odds with society's norms and injunctions, so that the change I long for is more likely to happen.

Full, uncompromising freedom is elusive even when reaching full self-connection (assuming that people indeed slow down enough to achieve it, and I would have to believe that at least some do). Recovering this freedom requires, in addition to self-connection, the willingness to break away from being embedded in business as usual. It calls us to transform our relationship with life as it currently is, with our fears, habits, and patterns; with our responses to others' expectations and pressure; with our internalization of norms that may or may not work for us or anyone else.

Our early experiences and our continued exposure to pain and suffering leave us with profound marks and traces that structure our responses to everything. Especially given the prevalence of early childhood trauma, how can we learn to understand and transcend our societal and personal legacy of the past? What is required so that we can use our experiences, our emotional journeys, our crises, and the support available to us in ways likely to expand our consciousness? How can we avoid submitting even further and adjusting to a social order at odds with meeting our needs? Where do we find our human agency to choose a life for ourselves?

I don't know how it is that some of us are never fully socialized, and never forget what we knew as children. I don't know how it is that some of us never turn around and inflict on others the suffering we have endured. I also don't know what it is that allows some parents and some families to operate in ways that support the flourishing of the human spirit. If enough empathy were present for starters, we probably wouldn't need a major process of recovery. Most of us have not had such remarkable experiences in life, and we must excavate ourselves back into full life knowing that we are embedded in the existing social order.

How many of us have had strong reactions to what happens around us and suppressed them in order to belong? I have some inkling of this phenomenon by virtue of being almost unable not to speak up when I am concerned about something. When I was a graduate student, for example, I regularly had the experience of questioning many practices I found deeply frightening, even something as basic as writing in language that most people would not be able to understand, and makes the insights inaccessible to many who are in deep need of support. Sometimes I felt so alone and vulnerable I would cry in my graduate seminars. No one would join me. Not once. Often I encountered either silence or reiteration of accepted arguments. And yet after class I would invariably be approached by several classmates, almost always women, who expressed to me that they felt similarly and didn't have the courage to speak up. What would it take for more of us to honor our emotions as a source of wisdom?

These and other experiences have taught me that, for a lone individual, feeling, and especially expressing, emotions that are outside the norm is not particularly effectual. Publicly admitting to such emotions can easily be experienced as a personal deficiency. However, such experiences become significant when we are connected with a community that shares our own perceptions and operates on different norms and values. When they are thus shared, such emotions can be mobilized for envisioning an alternative way of living. At such a time they can contribute to the possibility of social change. Here is one way in which the practice of mastering emotions can be helpful in noticing, honoring, and acting on emotions that remind us of our critical perspective on the world. It is precisely at this point that the practice of strategic discomfort allows movement and opening instead of shutting down.

Radical Consciousness through Mind and Heart

So far I have followed two threads. I have looked at the journey of what I called psychic liberation, recovering our capacity to connect with our emotions and our needs and the freedom that comes with embracing discomfort. I have also examined the challenges surrounding the process of acquiring a critical perspective on the world in which we live. Here I want to interweave these two strands into more explicit interconnection by following, schematically, the process that may lead to the cultivation of radical consciousness.

Imagine someone who has always accepted without much questioning the received story about life. Imagine, for example, what it would be like for such a person one day to wake up and realize that people are poor not because they are lazy. How destabilizing and unsettling it would be, for example, to find out that companies continue to sell toxic products knowing they are toxic and saying they are not. Or the shock to our imaginary person to begin to wonder about her or his role in society, the privilege or lack thereof that she or he has access to, and the effect of her or his choices and actions on other people near and far. Coming to terms with our position within a complex multi-layered system of differential access to power can be utterly overwhelming.

Most of us accept the status quo without much challenge, though our acceptance is often based on repression, even if early and unconscious. Because what is repressed is not entirely gone, in it resides the seed of hope. The possibility of seeing in new ways, of developing a moral and political perception that questions authority and domination is never completely destroyed.

Because socialization is such an integral part of the smooth functioning of society, and because we are socialized into a world that is not set up to meet human needs, socialization is almost invariably traumatic. As a result, often enough our first clue for embarking on any process of liberation is our own personal suffering.

Once we start questioning, the process of undoing the socialization is often lengthy and painful. Much of what we believe is our own individual personal identity becomes suspect. Our very consciousness, we find slowly, is structured by systems and processes we never chose. We have been exposed for our entire life to messages that affect who we become. How can we find enough strength to undo this entire structure to begin to find what is truly ours, what is the legacy of the past, both familial and social, and what the possibilities are for the present and the future?

Despite what I just said, this is neither a linear process, nor purely, or even primarily, a cognitive one. Along the way we learn that no matter where we are in the social matrix we have painful facts to discover about ourselves, not just about others. There are hardly any guides for this process, because self-help books so often speak from the perspective of what was done to us, and from a purely individual lens. For true liberation, true radical consciousness, to occur, we will need to also learn the ways in which we are the ones at whose hands, directly or indirectly, others are suffering.

Where is the book that will tell us how to recover our full humanity, and have complete compassion for what we discover along the way? This is one of the main reasons why this process is so intensely difficult, and so easily abandoned in discouragement once started: the pain of our complicity with a system we oppose may be unbearable.

In a remarkable conversation several years ago a male friend described to me the bottomless pit he encountered inside himself when he tried to incorporate emotionally the implications of the feminist theory he was avidly reading. In attempting this he realized that his entire sense of self as a man was resting on the oppression of women, and he could hardly imagine who he would be, at that deep level, or how he could get there without experiencing depths of anguish that he admitted were beyond his reach. Instead, he chose to abandon his pursuit of feminist literature. He closed the books he was reading, and took a long break. It was many years before he could confront these issues again.

What would enable him and others to remain open to what we learn? My own experience, based on my personal journey and on working with others, is that if we are committed to a personal practice of opening our hearts to our emotions, we can learn from the wisdom of our emotions, and the pain becomes an opportunity to rethink our morality, our perception of reality, our understanding of social relations, and the choices that emerge from such understandings. Once again, as we continue to walk *towards* rather than away from our emotions, our freedom and consciousness expand.

Personal change is always limited within any social structure, especially one that is at odds with human thriving. There is only so far we can go before we reach the limits of what society presents to us. No matter how clearly I am aligned with a vision of a gift economy, I cannot fully create that kind of life for myself or others for as long as the world around me continues to operate on the basis of exchange. The tight loop that exists in sustaining the culture also operates in attempts to create change: the personal and the systemic are mutually reinforcing, either hindering change or, once we get the ball rolling in the other direction, enabling it. Beyond a certain point, if any of us wants to become a fully free human being, we will need to engage together in changing the social structures that hinder full freedom. At the same time, it is impossible to wait for another social reality before embarking on the personal journey. If we attempt social transformation without creating a deep change within ourselves, we are likely to re-create the very structures we oppose. It is no accident that Gandhi always spoke of his work as an expression of his personal practice.

Facing Privilege

Since privilege masks certain aspects of reality, having privilege tends to create one more layer of difficulty on the path to radical consciousness. We are less able to see the effect of our actions, and are usually very afraid of losing the privilege. What is it that makes us so attached to privilege when we have it? I have seen a lot of polarity in discussions about privilege, with people who have little access to class, race or gender privilege often having disparaging views about those who do have such access, while those who do have the privilege often feel confused, ashamed or guilty, but are nonetheless unable to make a decisive stand on it in terms of their own lives.

In 1994 I was part of a group of people who were very committed to a shared vision of a transformed society, similar in many respects to the vision that I am working towards these days. At one point in one gathering of the group, the person who was facilitating the gathering asked the people present what would get in their way of committing a significant portion of their income or savings to the joint project. As people responded to the question, I noticed the very vivid level of fear about having nothing left that leaked out of them. I understood then that the key to making sense of the difficulty lay in understanding the nature of the fear.

What is it that makes giving up privilege so frightening? The question seems even more pressing today, because our very survival as a species, it seems to me, depends on being able to reduce our consumption of resources dramatically. Because I am completely committed to doing so without coercion, I am called to find the root of the issue, so that letting go of privileged access to resources will be seen as attractive rather than a sacrifice.

Privilege and Needs

Taking seriously the centrality of human needs provides me with an entry into understanding that we are attached to privilege because it acts as a substitute for meeting real needs. While I don't believe that any explicit conversations take place about this with children, I have a sense that an implicit process takes place in which we are first cut off from the hope that we can get our real needs met. We are made terrified and hopeless, and actually give up any belief in getting our real needs met, often to the point of losing track of what those needs might be. This gets reinforced later by theories (such as Freud's) that tell us that our true, unconscious drives are insatiable and can never be fulfilled. I know how often I meet people who dismiss the idea of the real possibility of having their needs met.

Then privilege is offered to some of us as something we can have. Although privilege is a very meager substitute for our real needs, it becomes the only thing possible to have. This is how I currently understand the sometimes desperate clinging to privilege: it looks to us as if giving up the privilege would amount to giving up everything, since the real needs cannot even be experienced. The fear of the void and the nothingness is so strong that oftentimes it can obscure our own clarity of vision about how we want the world to be.

With this framework in mind, I have set out to identify pairs consisting of a real need and the privilege that's offered as a substitute for it. In each case, the privilege end of the pair supports the existing structure of society. I also like to believe that if more and more of us reconnected and reclaimed fully the needs that we gave up when we accepted privilege as a substitute, by necessity this would make us subversive, agents of change. I see comfort as the cement that holds it all in place. Comfort when we have privilege, and comfort in the familiarity of the numbness and craving for it that we have when we lack it and are also living, like so, so many people in this country and everywhere, without our real needs being met. This understanding provides some relief, some tenderness, lots of compassion for why change is so hard.

What is it that we are taught we can't have, and what is it that we are encouraged to pursue instead? Here are the pairs I have come up with so far. Can you think of any others?

Convenience/Joy: We live in a society that provides a huge amount of convenience to those who can afford it. So much that makes life so much more convenient is available at the push of a button. Yet none of these things provide much joy. It is becoming more and more apparent that this level of convenience is numbing, and that many societies and groups, both outside the U.S. and within some groups in the U.S. (not the dominant group), have significantly less convenience in their life, yet display, in many instances, a lot more joy despite the oppressive conditions.

Security/Community: Both individuals and groups try to establish for themselves a sense of security, both physical and economic. Although the trappings of security are often successful, I am repeatedly struck by how much people with significant access to resources are not feeling secure, and continue to be obsessed about having more in order to feel secure about the future. Yet societies exist in the world, or neighborhoods, where a different ethos is the norm. Without in any way romanticizing poverty, in the U.S. or elsewhere, when people have a sense of community, they often have a different relationship with security. There are still places where doors are unlocked, where people know that whatever resources exist in the community will be shared, and that security lies within a community, not in amassing fortresses and savings.

Predictability/Trust: Privilege, in the form of ease of access to material resources, provides the illusion of predictability. In truth, if we ever pause to think about it, we don't know anything about what will happen, not even in two minutes. The deeper alternative to the elusive pursuit of predictability is the fundamental sense of trust in the flow of life, including the cycles of growth and decay, birth and death.

Success/Purpose. In this society, and to a lesser extent in others, people are usually considered "successful" when they achieve a level of financial well-being, or social prominence. In their pursuit of such worldly success, many sacrifice years of their lives working hard in order to reach that elusive goal, and only a minority attain it. Meanwhile, for so many people, the deep need for a sense of purpose in life is not at all addressed, no matter how "successful" they become. At the same time, more and more people discover the possibility of experiencing a life away from the material striving, which is at the same time filled with a sense of purpose.

Productivity/Contribution: Technology has made every aspect of our lives more efficient and productive, and that is offered to us as a substitute for exercising our creativity and being able to contribute our gifts in full to others and to life. We speed up to get things done, and we have more and more gadgets and "time-saving" devices, and yet fewer and fewer of us have a sense of meaning on a daily basis, or experience that we make a difference in the world.

Money/Freedom: The drive to accumulate money is fueled by the assumption that having a lot of money means being free to do what we please. And yet the true sense of freedom eludes most of us. No amount of money can buy internal peace, the ability to respond to situations freshly, and the transformation of debilitating internal messages and external pressures into clarity about what we want and how we want to move towards it.

Earning/Mattering: The fierce sense of independence and not needing anyone contains within it the illusion that we can "earn" all we need to satisfy our needs and therefore will not depend on other people's goodwill and generosity. Although it's impossible to say with any clarity, I have a deep intuitive sense that nowadays we also have less trust in other people's natural interest in our well-being, which only increases our isolation. Instead, if we can let go of the illusion of separation, we can find the vast ground of our knowing that our existence and our needs matter, and that in an interdependent world people will naturally want to provide for and support each other outside of an exchange-based paradigm.

Control/Power: Finally, having given up on the hope that we will have the power to have our life be the way we want it and have our real needs met, we seek instead to have control over resources and other human beings. Time and again it becomes evident that people's sense of power does not increase with the amount of control they are able to exercise over others. In fact, there is reason to believe that at least some of the time people's sense of power actually decreases with more access to resources and is replaced by fear and isolation, which drive people to exercise even more control.

If you find it hard to imagine that we could have a functioning society in which we do away with privilege and function in a truly interdependent fashion to respond and attend to everyone's needs, I invite you to look at my book *Reweaving Our Human Fabric*, in part of which (Wisdom Tales from the Future) I describe in detail a possible society in which meeting human needs on a global scale is the core operating principle. We need vision in order to be able to see outside of what we have been told is the only possibility that exists.

What Do We Know?

If one sees the relations between the sexes in a somewhat crass manner as that between masters and slaves, then it will be realized that it is the master's privilege not to have to think continuously about the fact that he is the master. In contrast, the position of the slave is such that it never allows the latter to forget it. There is no doubt that women much more rarely lose their sense of being women than men lose their sense of being men.

– Georg Simmel, writing in the early 20th Century[50]

I have read and heard dozens of people say that radical consciousness (the capacity to step outside of the normative story of the society into which we were born) is much easier to attain for people who have no privilege. There is an intuitive appeal to this claim. It makes complete and immediate sense that the position of privilege blinds us both to our own privilege and to social reality more generally, while when we are in disenfranchised, subjugated, or otherwise powerless positions we cannot escape that reality.

Despite the appeal, this is not what happens in reality. People in oppressed groups do not all have radical consciousness; nor is it totally absent in people of privilege. I have come to believe that any position we have in society obscures our vision. What differs is which parts of reality are obscured, and what is the cost of lifting the veil. Radical consciousness is always an achievement, never a natural state. It is not trivial to ask how people can exit the material consequences of their social location and see into reality. Unless we come up with a way of explaining how anyone can reach radical consciousness, it will continue to be a marginal and relatively rare state.

I have seen myself and others struggle to achieve, maintain, and share radical consciousness. This experience has taught me some things. I learned that strategic discomfort and psychic liberation are stepping stones on the road to radical consciousness. If we remain on the path, sooner or later we are likely to reach an experience that philosopher Alisdair MacIntyre calls an "epistemological crisis:"[51] a

---

[50] Lewis Coser, "Georg Simmel's Neglected Contributions to the Sociology of Women," p. 872, emphasis in the original. I find it utterly amazing and inspiring that these words were written at the turn of the 20th century, not in the 1970s.

[51] Alasdair MacIntyre, "Epistemological Crises, Dramatic Narrative and the Philosophy of Science."

discovery that our familiar and habitual perception of what's real is suddenly miles away from a newly discovered truth. So much so, that a fundamental restructuring of our belief system is necessary.

The intensity of such a crisis can be extreme, and many of us go to great lengths to avoid it. Because this crisis has a deep emotional component, and because our culture downplays emotions and highlights reasoning, many times we continue to hold on to a belief or theory even after hearing a logical refutation, even after we acknowledge and agree with the opposing view. A particularly striking example of this process is provided by Thomas Kuhn in his analysis of scientific revolutions. Kuhn noted that most often when scientists present new theories they encounter an initial and persistent resistance that can be intense despite the fact that the old theory is no longer capable of explaining many observed phenomena.

Radical consciousness is neither a necessary outcome for oppressed people nor unavailable to others. Whether or not we are members of an oppressed group, coming to have a radical consciousness entails a similar kind of epistemological crisis: we are called to discard received knowledge and question conventional beliefs. For me as a woman to see and question sexism, I had to overcome my internalized sexism, which previously meant to me that we, women, were responsible for our experiences in the world. I had bought into the idea that rape happened in response to our appearance or behavior; that we didn't advance in organizations because we didn't take our work seriously enough; that we were relegated to certain kinds of work because we didn't stand up and insist otherwise. I am painfully embarrassed to admit this on paper, and yet it's true. I had to open up to levels of despair I didn't even know existed in me, as well as to be presented with an image of a different reality, in order to let go of this tendency. All of us must be able to stop believing the myths about men and women that justify the persistence of sexism in order to see through it. What does it take to get there?

The Cost of Radical Knowledge

In order to free our consciousness from its complicity with the existing order of things, we need to be willing to live with the discomfort that comes with challenging accepted views. The discomfort itself is only a precursor to a transformation in consciousness. To actually change our picture of the world requires emotional capacity. The act of facing the discomfort is what enables the transformation, and persistence with it is a requirement for the shift to endure. At some point along the way many of us encounter fear of rejection, loss of community, or even loss of economic survival if we hold on to radical views and/or defy conventional norms in our actions. Or we may experience the pain and anguish attendant on uncovering and coming to terms with a history of devastation. For myself, I had to let go of a deeply ingrained idea that things make sense, that what happens can be explained, and that we have the power, as individuals, to create in full the life we want. Facing powerlessness was excruciating.

The challenge of radical knowledge doesn't end only with inner discomfort. The cost may also involve actual dangers, such as social ostracism or loss of access to work opportunities. In some cases the risks include even more extreme measures such as being locked up or even killed.

What Makes Radical Consciousness Possible

When we are members of an oppressed group we are already familiar with some amount of pain and discomfort that comes as part of being oppressed. The mystification of reality, to the extent that it exists, serves to numb us to a fuller experience of being shut out of power and privilege. Such numbing, paradoxically, may even be the only way to hold on to any semblance of hope. Ann Berlak, a university professor who wrote about her persistent attempts to invite critical engagement from her students, documented with astonishing clarity how the facts about oppression in and of themselves fell flat and were strongly resisted by her students who tended to be members of oppressed groups. One of her students, a black woman, responded to information about racial discrimination as if the information itself was racist and untrue, because she wanted to believe, in her own words, that she could, if she wanted, become the president of a Fortune 500 company.[52] This is similar to my rejection of the reality of sexism because I wanted to believe that I could have a full life despite being a woman. Despite this initial block, the journey eventually becomes easier. Once we overcome the initial resistance to seeing a different reality, there is much less

---

[52] Berlak, "Teaching for Outrage and Empathy," 70.

difficulty for any member of an oppressed group because we have no real stake in maintaining the status quo, given that its benefits are questionable when seen with a radical needs-based perspective, and at any rate, are not available to us.

However, if we have a lot at stake in terms of privilege, or the prospect of potential privilege, stepping outside the "taken-for-granted" requires two steps that are fraught with difficulty. One is the willingness to forego potential privilege. The other, and perhaps even more demanding, is coming to terms with our own implication in inflicting pain on others. The level of discomfort many of us experience when attempting to open to this reality is immense and not many are willing to embrace discomfort to such a degree. This is how I understand the failure of much of the "Men's Movement" to have any impact in reducing sexism in our society. They examined their own deprivation, but not their role in perpetuating the oppression against women. Thus, their emerging picture of reality is not based on a wide enough challenge to the existing system of thinking.

Needless to say, reality is more complex. Especially in contemporary Western societies, we don't come packaged neatly into oppressor and oppressed. Almost all of us in such societies have schizoid experiences in that regard, being members of many criss-crossing categories. For almost all of us, embarking on this journey entails coming to terms with what has happened to us as well as with our complicity in systems of oppression. We also need to understand the link and overlap between the two. While the specific emotional experiences may be radically different, there is no essential difference in the kind of courage necessary to disentangle our implicit alliance with systems of oppression, exploitation, and degradation.

In 1994 filmmaker Lee Mun Wah gathered eight men for a weekend workshop about racism: two Black men, two Asian-American men, two Latino men, and two white men. The result of this weekend was the movie *The Color of Fear*. One of the persistent dynamics shown in the movie is the frustration Victor, a black man, felt in relation to David, a white man. Regardless of what Victor and others were describing about the meaning and experiences of being a person of color in contemporary U.S., David deflected. He kept individualizing and trivializing their concerns.

In a pivotal moment in the interaction, director Lee Mun Wah turns to David and asks him to entertain the possibility, however briefly, that maybe everything that Victor is saying is simply true. What ensues is dramatic and striking. David's face, previously rather expressionless, gets contorted with visible anguish, and he responds by saying that this would simply be too sad. David expresses his utter horror at trying to imagine why anyone would want to inflict such pain on another. Because David was able, finally, to face the painful truths, his understanding of the world was shattered and reconstructed. Because he had the support of the other men in digesting his experience, he did not retreat into comfort or complacency. Two years later, when the eight men were invited to participate in an Oprah show, David described the cascade of events and changes that followed that weekend, including in particular the loss of friends who did not join his journey and were offended by his insistence on bringing up the topic of race. With new knowledge of this kind, his life could not continue as it was. It was, specifically, overcoming his fear of the intense anguish he subsequently had to endure that made it possible for David to acquire knowledge about the world that he previously could not contain.

Learning about Privilege

I continue to grapple with the question of how to support learning about access to resources and privilege without guilt or shame. I do not pretend to know the answer. I only have some preliminary thoughts about this immense task. It's clear to me that love is essential, so the landing into reality is cushioned, not harsh. I also imagine that rekindling the hope in having our real needs matter makes it more likely that we can open up to experiencing the longings we have. My goal, for myself and for others, is not to "give up" privilege. My hope is that each of us can wake up to the deepest goals and dreams that we have for ourselves and everyone else. When we can accept and celebrate both our needs and our resources, we can learn to use resources with conscious choice. That is my vision of true responsible freedom.

Minnie Bruce Pratt, a white, southern, Christian woman, set out to learn about and undo the history of racism and domination into which she was born. She chronicles[53], painstakingly, without sparing herself, without guilt or shame, and without any pretense, her feelings and thoughts in the process of coming to terms with her acquiescence. Because of her naked honesty and thoroughness, I learned so much from her about what is actually entailed in such rigorous self-liberation and about coming face to face with what it means to have been raised racist and privileged as she tries to overcome the effects of such upbringing.

As she began looking at her life and its meaning, Pratt discovered fear and terror in herself. Initially, the nature of this fear was unknown to her. Over time, she became clearer: "I have learned that my fear is kin to a terror that has been in my birth culture for years, for centuries: the terror of a people who have set themselves apart and above, who have wronged others, and feel they are about to be found out and punished."

She discovered that this fear, and with it the breakdown of connectedness, led her to the denial of others' existence as human beings, and to being utterly lonely, caught within herself without finding a way out. Eventually she became acquainted with Black history and learned the extent of the damage done in her name, at which point it became almost impossible for her to hold on to her sense of self. The struggle she came to have in recognizing that she was implicated in the injustice done to others was unbearable.

This phase may be one of the most painful steps in the process of psychic liberation. Although on some level she knew that she could survive and the struggle wouldn't destroy her, this knowledge didn't mitigate the fear that after stripping away every form of deceit there would be nothing positive at the core. Because what she was discovering about her heritage was so painful, it was difficult for her to maintain a sense of respect for herself.

Once she recovered some sense of pride and self-respect based on new grounds and values, she had to come to terms with yet one more loss. She could no longer maintain connection with those of her heritage who did not participate in the same journey.

With all the pain of the journey, Pratt knew the rewards were also significant. She discovered her own strength and a renewed source of vitality.

---

[53] Minnie Bruce Pratt. "Identity: Skin, Blood, Heart".

The dangers are not imaginary. The process of stripping away our false identity and recovering our self is often excruciating, even if it is also exhilarating. It entails facing all the fears and dangers that we are spared when we conform, and losing the comfort of the familiar. Domination is kept in place in large part by many people doing what's comfortable. Through reading Pratt's story I developed much more compassion for the stubborn resistance to change on the part of the "privileged." It's painfully clear to me now why people do not engage in this journey en masse.

Despair, Vision, and Love

Facts and information in and of themselves do not usually create radical consciousness. I have heard from and about so many people who see through the cultural messages. They may be fully aware of the cost of existing systems without achieving radical consciousness. An oppositional consciousness is not the same as radical consciousness. The hallmark of radical consciousness as I understand it includes embracing life and moving from anger and despair to love and vision. Gandhi and Martin Luther King made that move. Kafka didn't He, like many others, saw with great clarity what the modern world created, and remained, in my understanding of him, wrapped up in despair and absurdity. I haven't seen redemption in his stories. The characters remain locked in the utter meaninglessness of the modern world. No vision of possibility emerges. I don't even get the sense that he loved any of his characters.

Despair does not provide fuel for change. Anger may provide fuel for an uprising, even a revolution, without changing the fundamental logic of separation that is at the root of violence and destruction in the world. Love is needed for that.

I often wonder about what this love is, and what we can do to cultivate it.

To make sense of what I am trying to grapple with, it helps me to think about what it takes to transform an individual relationship. It's clear to me that when both people are committed to honoring both their needs within a relationship, and have the skills for translating their commitment into practical steps, then it takes half the skill and half the love from each of them. I tend to believe that almost all of us are born with sufficient automatic inner resources to participate in this game if everybody else were to participate in it. Almost all of us have enough love and enough skill under such circumstances. By extension, then, I would imagine that almost all of us could care about our own and others' needs if others did, too.

If, however, only one party to a relationship is committed to the vision of everyone's needs mattering, it takes them double the love and double the skill because they have to compensate for the fact that the other person is not bringing that much love and skill into it. It's not undoable; it's just that much harder. You would have to do the loving for both of you. You would have to do the skills for both of you. And that requires more love and more skill than if it were mutual because you would have to bring in additional love to support the other person's mistrust. Most of us don't have it.

And that is, in sweeping generalizations, the situation into which almost all of us were born. We came into a world where most people are not framing the conflicts between them as dilemmas they are holding together. In those conditions it takes exceptional skill and capacity and love and resilience to try to live the love in a world that doesn't.

This is, for me, the dilemma of world transformation: can we find and cultivate enough love and skill to do the work, to do the loving towards and on behalf of those who don't have access to their love? Can a sufficient number of us develop enough capacity and resilience and skills to stand tall in the midst of mistrust, judgment, and even violence from others and maintain our stance of love? This deep capacity is the essence of what I mean by radical consciousness: seeing through what is happening, and seeing it with and from a place of love.

I have faith in that. It's definitely tough. I still have faith.

I see more and more people drawn to becoming agents of love in the world without any sense of a fairness calculus, without any sense of what's "right" and what's "wrong," without expectations. Instead, our love can be motivated by a sense of being so privileged and blessed to have been given the gift of radical consciousness, and by wanting to share the gift with others, to fill in the holes and the voids of love until other people can do it for themselves – and all this without giving up on ourselves.

That last point is key to me. A love that is at the expense of ourselves is not true love. When we open up to a love so big we can be tempted to give up on ourselves. We can get into an endless cycle of empathizing with others, hearing them, attending to their needs, and becoming depleted and resentful. I don't see that as true love. For me, true love includes respecting the other person sufficiently to trust that somewhere in them is the capacity to love back, and inviting that love in our direction when the moment is right, no matter how far gone the other person is. Inviting other people to open up, to hear us, to rise to the occasion is every bit as important as hearing them and supporting them. Every time we give up on another person and say they can't do it we compromise the love, because in the loving I want to love the person into their best being.

I know that I'm making a really tall order. I just don't want to compromise on the vision of what's possible. I want us to be completely tender and self-accepting for wherever we are in terms of our own skill and capacity without thereby thinking that nothing can be done more than what I am able to do now. I want to accept myself where I am, and keep my heart and longing open to grow more and more towards taking on more and more of the loving – until there is enough to turn things around.

Radical Consciousness, Reason, and Emotions

Radical consciousness is different from a momentary peak experience or conceptual political awareness. Radical consciousness amounts to a permanent shift in our consciousness: an integration, on the deepest level, of a different perspective. Integration means embodying such consciousness to the point that it affects our habits of action and even our emotional responses in addition to our beliefs. Gains can only be temporary as long as they remain purely cognitive. Even when a social revolution radically transforms social institutions,[54] the initial enthusiasm some people may experience is likely to crash on the walls of emotional conservatism.

This kind of emotional conservatism showed up in a study of heterosexual couples and their coping strategies for dealing with housework and childcare. In all the couples in the study both spouses participated in paid labor. Several of the men in the study professed an egalitarian ideology, and yet their contribution to the household was markedly smaller than their wives'.[55] Their cognitive

---

[54] And often the transformation is much more superficial than hoped for, as evidenced by the many remarkable continuities between Czarist Russia and the Soviet Union.
[55] Arlie Hochschild, *The Second Shift*.

understanding about women's oppression, even with a cognitive commitment to egalitarianism, was unsustainable without the deep emotional work required to restructure their consciousness at its core through liberating themselves from the legacy of their past and of society's influence. Recall the conversation with my friend I talked about earlier ("A Personal Practice of Liberation," page 189)

Certain forms of knowledge can only be acquired by deliberately transcending impartiality and dispassionate detachment, and allowing emotionally-laden information to interact with our own emotions to create new connections and open previously closed avenues of experience. If this is true, then the very process of dispassionate impartiality *obscures* rather than reveals certain forms of knowledge about the world. David would not have learned about the realities of racism by being provided with statistics and other such information. My friend could not face sexism fully because of emotional blocks, even though he was fully aware of the challenges women face. The facts themselves do almost nothing to create change in perspective.

Because radical consciousness as a fully integrated mind and heart transformation is still so rare, I see it as immensely important, a radical act in itself, to describe the personal experience of reaching it. There is something unique and irreducible about the process that allows any of us to transcend accepted forms of thought and create novel ones. Our accepted practices of writing, which exclude discussions of the self, leave that process invisible. We are presented with a final product. For readers who desire to expand their own ability to move beyond the known and accepted, the text offers nothing. This practice, instead, adds to the mystification of knowledge and to the prevalence of idolizing creators of new ideas. It makes it appear as though some of us belong to a different category of intelligence, which others must resign themselves never to attain. This practice never assists anyone in becoming a critical innovator as opposed to a follower of a critical tradition. This is particularly evident, for me, in the following of Marx and Freud, both of whom engendered many more followers than new theoretical breakthroughs.

I long to see many accounts from individuals who have developed a radical consciousness describing, personally, what their experiences have been of enduring oppression, being complicit in structures of domination, and, especially, learning to overcome fear and discomfort to fully inhabit their new way of being. The absence of such accounts reduces the chances that others would be able to make full use of the results of such knowledge. It is my belief that radicalization and expansion are possible for large numbers of human beings provided they get guidance in the process. I also believe that one crucial form of guidance is models: concrete details about how the process worked for another human being. Had Marx, for example, included his own process of arriving at his ideas together with the ideas themselves, his followers might have become innovators and theoreticians rather than followers who "apply" a theory to changing conditions.

I want to question the accepted custom of hiding the self, a custom that is itself rooted in the glorification of reason. I want to write about myself in a transparent voice, because I hope to support others' ability to embark on their own emotional and intellectual journeys towards radical consciousness. The level of courage necessary for doing this was not available to me when I was working on a doctoral dissertation some years ago. I ultimately "submitted" and wrote my dissertation in a much more detached manner than I had longed to do. Here, in this book, I am reclaiming much of what I wrote there, and putting myself at the center despite my fears, despite accepted norms, and despite doubting that others would find it of interest. To the extent that I make my process available to you, the readers of my work, I thereby contribute to the possibility that you, too, may engage with analogous processes and arrive at new theoretical and political insights and positions. This is not a prescription, but an example of what's possible. I create possibilities for those who want to and can follow them. This, then, becomes one more indirect way in which I can contribute to the kind of changes I believe are necessary in this world.

Finding Me Finding Vision

I am still somewhat captive to the heavy weight of the injunction to prove everything, and find it challenging and vulnerable to own and express my faith, which by necessity is unprovable. In this case, the faith that our souls aim for healing. Maybe it's not even just faith, maybe I have had enough experience to see it in others as well. Despite all that happened to me, all the early hardships, all the coercion and crushing of my soul, and the level of numbness and cynicism I acquired in protection, something never gave up. When the opportunity arose through my encounter with feminism followed by an abortion, I started a journey that still continues. Towards wholeness, healing, integration. Towards embracing life. Towards reclaiming my faith that a different life was possible. For me. For all of humanity.

Life-Changing Choice

Although my journey of self-recovery didn't start until I was in my 30s, an early seed of it was planted when I was fourteen. My family had just moved back to Israel after living in Mexico for two years. I now know, in retrospect, that those years abroad enabled my parents to purchase an apartment in a new part of town and make a partial upward mobility move. Only partial, because my father remained a teacher and his salary didn't provide the possibility for the levels of consumption that most of our new neighbors enjoyed. [56]

Being entirely new to the neighborhood, I engaged in an experiment. I joined a group of kids my age with the explicit intention to "be like everyone else." This was quite a stretch, because these kids were more like the ones I had met in Mexico than like the kids I had known back in my old neighborhood. I had not changed. Despite the two years of misery in Mexico that I described in "Forced Exile" (page 80), I maintained my original viewpoint and beliefs. And yet I was so tired of being a social outcast, I had such a deep need to belong, that I decided to try it out, just so I could be part of some group, any group. Or so I thought.

This experiment lasted about two months. During this period I was regularly invited to parties, an experience which hadn't happened before. When I went to parties, I was asked to dance. I was neither at the center of popularity nor in the sidelines. I was matter-of-factly included.

At the end of two months I left this group. I was acutely aware of the cost of belonging to the group – to me, to my integrity, to my sense of meaning, to my dignity and authenticity. I couldn't fathom developing an interest in the general chitchat of the parties, which consisted of gossip about things and people without any core engagement with life, depth of relationship, or a sense of purpose.

I was never again invited to parties for the rest of my years in high school and for many years thereafter. For the most part I still am not. The loneliness has at times been quite agonizing, especially on the weekends in high school and during my 20s. I never once looked back on my choice. I feel lucky to have been in this position,

---

[56] These were the times in which a major transformation occurred in Israel, shifting from a glorification of "labor values" such as simplicity and some forms of communalism to an embracing of the consumer society values. Our family moved into a neighborhood marked by the new values.

despite the pain. I'd like to believe that I can find ways to have authenticity and belonging at the same time. In fact, I have more and more of both every year as my journey and my practice deepen. At the same time, if I am ever in a place where I don't see a way to have both, I have the experience of choosing authenticity and losing belonging, and being able to survive. I feel lucky to have known that I can survive this kind of discomfort so early on. It may well have served as the foundation of my later willingness to choose to embrace more discomfort in order to achieve more inner freedom.

Feminism as Personal Healing

For many decades my relationship to being a woman was reactive without my knowing it. I experienced myself as different from many women, if not most. I wasn't interested in being attractive, I was drawn to science, including advanced math, and later worked as a computer programmer, and I felt strong and able to fend for myself. I find it painful to admit that I had some contempt for many women, and held women accountable for some of the effects of what I now see as systemic sexism. I was completely committed to equality with men. I just saw it as my responsibility to create it for myself, and was blind to the structural obstacles I now see.

One particularly intense example of this lack of awareness on my part took place in my twenties, when I became involved in a relationship with a man who had very specific and intense expectations that I would be the one to do the housework even though we both worked full time jobs, I saw it through the lens of him making a personal choice to do this *to* me because he knew it would be offensive to me, rather than interpreting it accurately to mean that this is how he was raised and what he saw around him, and therefore expected without ever questioning.

Discovering Feminism and Hope

In the spring of 1986, when I was thirty and living alone in Manhattan, I visited my younger sister Inbal's apartment in San Francisco, where she lived with three women friends. I arrived there at the tail end of a two-week trip with a man with whom I was in relationship at the time, during which we struggled mightily over simple things. I remember the relief, the ease, the joy, the immediate understanding, the affinity I felt with these three women I hadn't met before. For the first time I became conscious in a poignant way of the particular qualities of friendship among women, and how much I missed that in my life. I went home determined to have more women in my life.

Some months before that I had started therapy. In keeping with my fierce ethic of personal strength, and despite the fact that life was primarily challenging for me, I had said to myself that I would only go to seek support if I felt completely stuck. For as long as there was any movement, however slow, I wanted to do it myself. Looking back at myself, I see the social influence of an ethic of personal strength and willingness to endure and even sacrifice. Originally installed in relation to a larger cause – the establishment of a Jewish homeland – that ethic then became a personal yardstick for generations, including my own.

I had no idea that my therapist, Alexandra Symonds, was a feminist, the founder of the Association of Women Psychiatrists, and a key pioneer in bringing women's issues to the foreground in the practice of therapy. What I did know was that on the most personal level she became the first authority figure in my life to convey to me that it was simply OK to be who I was. I hadn't gotten that message from anyone to that degree of fullness until I was twenty-three, and that was from a peer. No authority figure had accepted me throughout my childhood and early adulthood until that moment.

My therapist's even bigger and most lasting contribution to my life was a short book she gave me to read one day, the most unlikely book I could imagine a therapist giving to a client. It was Ruth Bleier's *Science and Gender*. This book was the explosion of feminism into my life, and the beginning of a transformation beyond anything I could have ever dreamed about. From being a scientifically-inclined intellectual with extreme challenges in social interactions, numb and often depressed, my journey took me to embracing myself and ultimately life, assuming positions of leadership in the world, and dedicating my life to a large vision that centers on transforming how we relate to ourselves, each other, and the world.

Ruth Bleier's book achieved for me the first step in the direction of change: understanding the existing conditions. For the first time I could really see the fundamental way our thinking about being human and being female is entirely shaped by pervasive forms of bias. That was the beginning of freedom.

The second step in creating change is to see an alternative reality. This, too, came to me in the form of a book. Remembering my longing to have more women in my life that I found when visiting San Francisco, and having just discovered the wealth of information out there to explore about women and feminism, I organized my first women's group, which was going to be a book reading group. Someone proposed Marilyn French's *Beyond Power*. Everything I had ever believed about why life was the way it was turned around. I became acquainted with a history that included earlier times when social organization was entirely different, and where women and men lived together harmoniously. I also learned about the many hundreds of years that it took to extinguish the remaining pockets of ancient wisdom and practices until finally put out during the witch hunts. I was exposed to horrors that had happened and were continuing to happen against women on a large scale, ranging from the physical treatment of women all the way to how intellectual life was structured. The pain of reading this was made bearable by having a group of women to engage with, mourn with, get inspired with, and be together with. I remember everything opening up when I finally grasped beyond a shred of doubt that the world we lived in was not the inevitable result of human nature. It was a world created by specific conditions and actions. Once I knew that another reality was possible and had existed, and how much concerted effort it took to squash it, I found hope, for the very, very first time ever that I can remember, that another world is possible, as the World Social Forum activists chant all over the globe these days.

Because I can trace my opening up so directly to these books, I have a deep awareness of the very specific and direct social context and social influence on my personal life. My healing and transformation started as a direct result of being exposed to the women's movement. Because of my personal characteristics, books and ideas more generally would, indeed, be the likely avenue for me to be affected by the massive changes that women were attempting to create in so many different forms at that time.

The Courage to Feel

Two years after my journey started, I still hadn't taken it into myself and my cells. My heart was still shut off, still a survival mechanism that seemed clearly, though unconsciously, essential. While I recovered an abstract sense of vision and possibility for the world, I had none of it, still, for myself. I still never cried except in extreme moments of acute and severe humiliation, almost against my will.

All this changed when I had an abortion in the summer of 1988. Having never wanted children since I was seventeen, my image of an abortion was of a physical procedure I had to go through in order to get rid of a nuisance. I had painted myself into a corner in which many feminists find themselves: because of wanting choice about reproduction to be available to me and other women, I had downplayed the significance of having an abortion. I was completely alienated from any other meaning it might have: hormonally, emotionally, or spiritually. Three weeks later I experienced the most intense depression I remember, in which I connected with an experience of profound abandonment and felt lonely beyond words. My feelings were so intense that I cried at any display of kindness towards me, however minimal. It still took a friend to point out to me the connection between my feelings and having had an abortion. I learned that my depression was a reaction to the letting go of a potential life that was starting to grow in me. It was my abandonment of this new life, I now believe, that brought forth my feelings about what had happened to me in my own life.

I knew that to move forward I would have to invite this pain into my conscious experience, engage with it, embrace it, allow it to be, and learn from it. This awareness was the third step of change: trusting in the possibility of movement, and of enough resources to make it happen.

This is what I proceeded to do next. I undertook a proactive willingness to experience emotions. On a personal level, my willingness to step outside my emotional comfort zone resulted in expanding my sense of self, increasing my experience of inner freedom, and recovering and deepening my commitment to work toward social transformation. Along the way my views about human nature were transformed, including my perspective on human needs and emotions.

Now, all these years later, when I have full awareness of paradox about abortion, knowing that it is, indeed, an ending of a life, and also knowing that killing is essential to living, at so many levels (if nothing else, our immune system kills all the time), I regularly feel gratitude to the little being who never came to be, for giving me the initial push into my personal journey of healing and empowerment that brought me to where I am now.

Permission to Be Powerful

It was one thing to have clarity about my next step and to know I wanted to embrace my pain and despair; it was a whole other thing to know how to go about it. The therapy I had done never touched the depth of my pain. I remained guarded despite my therapist's care and support. I didn't trust I would know how to transform that relationship sufficiently to have the opportunity to do the work I knew I needed to do. It was time to look elsewhere.

Within weeks I joined a co-counseling class led by Peter Hoffman, who subsequently went on to become a renowned chef and restaurant owner in New York City. I participated in co-counseling activities for six years, one in New York and five after I moved to California. In those six years I received three profound gifts that I still carry with me.

The first was moments of healing for my personal experiences of trauma. Those came through the loving presence of people who were peers, and who were able to be with me in a relaxed manner while I experienced very challenging emotions. I learned that the present was different from the past, and that I can embrace and make room for my most intense feelings without getting permanently lost in them. I have never again been afraid of allowing pain and despair to surface all the way and never again felt the urge to suppress them. I have never regretted the consequences, even in the many occasions when I wasn't received with the love I wanted. I am stronger, more available to life, and more capable of experiencing hope and joy as a result.

The second gift was the exposure to a social analysis that made sense of my own and others' suffering. It was the first time I was truly able to make the connection I have since been exploring and learning more about: the effect of having gender roles, class differences, racial barriers, and other social cleavages. These insights found fertile ground in me following my earlier exposure to feminism and supported me in changing my view of human nature. My choice of research focus in my doctoral studies was deeply influenced by the mind-and-heart-opening experiences of learning in my years in co-counseling.

The third gift, the one I am perhaps most grateful for, is the discovery of my own power to be of service to others. To some extent this was an immediate effect of learning to be relaxed about my own intense feelings, and through that experience gaining the capacity for relaxed presence with others' intense emotions. To some extent this was the result of specific training we received about being present and relaxed with others.

Still, the true moment of discovering my power was beyond all of that. In one of the sessions we were practicing the tools we had been learning for some weeks. One by one, we did a mini-session with one other person that everyone else observed and about which they then provided feedback. I remember my turn arriving, and the woman I was to counsel started speaking about what she was struggling with at that time in her life. She paused at one point, and it was clearly my turn to say something to support her process, to provide the container that would allow her to experience her feelings more fully. Suddenly I had an experience I had never had before in my entire life. I felt myself connected to a larger whole. Words showed up internally to be said, words I had not figured out or thought through. Words I couldn't entirely say were mine. It was the first time of many that I felt this completely intuitive inner wisdom and clarity and experienced myself more as a conduit than the source of such wisdom. Not even knowing for sure why these words would work, I chose to trust them. When I said them to the woman I was counseling, it was like magic had just happened. She burst out crying, having been touched exactly where she wanted to be touched to enable her anguish to be released.

I had never before had any inkling that I had the power to touch other people's hearts. That moment, in a very real way, was the precursor to all that I do now. It was also the first experience in my life that I would name spiritual. Ever since that day I have felt open, and more and more so over the years, to the possibility that non-material aspects of life have a reality to them.

Despite these astonishing gifts, my years in co-counseling were more challenging than rewarding, and I ultimately chose to leave. Three factors combined to make this decision. One was difficulties in my relationships with people who were challenged when it was their turn to be counselor to me, even though they loved my counseling of them. A second was painful experiences with leaders within the community that I found no way to transform or even understand and integrate. The third, and ultimately most important, was my increasing difficulty with the functioning of the formal organization.

Despite the critique of existing forms of power within society, my own encounters with the organization led me to believe that it operated without transparency, with unilateral decisions made from the top, and without mechanisms in place for people who were unhappy with decisions to be able to bring their concerns to leaders and have them addressed in collaborative ways. With my growing desire to trust that organizations that work for social change can model the future they want to create, and without trust that I had a say in how the organization would function, I could not stay with any sense of integrity. I am happy to have arrived at such clear vision about how an organization can operate, even in our world as it exists, in conscious commitment to maximize everyone's access to the power to meet needs.[57]

---

[57] You can find out more on how I imagine such organizations in my book *Reweaving Our Human Fabric*.

Writing in Community

Growing up in Israel meant war was a persistent and formative part of my life. I experienced four distinct wars, not to mention the ongoing state of hostility with neighboring countries. Like most Israelis, I fully identified with the story of a persecuted people defending itself. I saw us as being misunderstood by the world and having only our ingenuity to protect us from annihilation. I believed the official story that Israel was ready for peace and there was no one to talk with. As I mentioned before ("Crisis, Empathy and Community," page 184), in 1973, when the Yom Kippur War broke out and I was seventeen, I began to see war as a choice and to envision other options for dealing with conflict. Finally, in 1983, when I was twenty-seven, I left Israel, unwilling to support the violence being done in my name. I no longer believed that the government of Israel was genuinely interested in peace. I came to the U.S., believing it to be a stronghold of democracy.

Although I began my journey of healing in 1988, and was working steadily to heal the traumas of my life on the personal, familial, and social levels, it took six more years before I approached the havoc wreaked in my soul because of serving in the Israeli army for two years when I was eighteen, and before I started to explore what it means to be from Israel in terms of the politics of it all.

In 1994, I heard a reading of the Veterans Writing Group[58] at Cody's Books in Berkeley, and I knew I wanted to join them. I sensed that this would be a place I could dig deep into my fears, longings, and unhealed experiences related to my army experience and beyond.

This group has been social healing at its best. We heal by sitting together and meditating. We heal by writing in community, in silence, for about ninety minutes each time we meet, now four times a year. We heal by sharing our lives with each other when we open the circle. Perhaps more than any other aspect of this group, hearing each other's stories has been the most profound experience for me. Discovering other people's humanity, whether similar to or different from my own, allows me more and more compassion for everyone.

---

[58] To learn more about the group and about the anthology we put together – *Veterans of War, Veterans of Peace*, visit vowvop.org.

Many of the people in the group are Vietnam veterans, whose stories move me deeply, time after time. Reading out loud, many of us cry while we read, and at other times we cry as we listen. It all makes our pain and our hopes more bearable, because they are held in community. I wish this experience for anyone who's suffered trauma, especially collective trauma of any kind.

Of the many dozens of pieces I wrote in this group, I am including three in this book. One of them, the one below, I am only including parts of with present commentary. It was written in 2002, and much has changed for me since. I had intended to include it as it was, until I asked a new Palestinian friend for his feedback, just days before the final copy was finalized. What I learned from our exchange is priceless. I learned that even after years of practice and learning, when it comes to a political struggle I am personally immersed in, engaging with others changes me. I hadn't seen what he pointed out. Just the process of meeting him while teaching in the West Bank recently was a profound experience of finding true and deep companionship about nonviolence. At the time of writing this piece, a true commitment to nonviolence was the very thing I had been afraid didn't exist in Palestine at all. This piece, and the continuing journey since, are a direct expression of my willingness to open up and heal these particular wounds. This is clearly still a work in progress.

The original piece was written in the form of a letter to an unspecified Palestinian person. As my friend pointed out, I flattened all the nuances of what I knew and didn't know about Palestinians into one generic character. While I was holding that person with complete and utter compassion and understanding, I was still not seeing fully and acknowledging to myself the full diversity of experience within Palestine. Having recently met those who came to my training in facilitation there, I have some grief about my unconscious continuing of stereotypes, in whatever form they come, such as the words below, the beginning of the original letter.

> "I want to understand the hatred you live in, your hatred of me. I want to know, intimately, how you come to want to kill me. I want to be able to imagine your thoughts when you wake up in the morning to one more day of occupation. I want to know how long you are awake before the hatred seeps back into your

exhausted self. I want to see your dreams at night, look at your smile when you are able to have it, meet your heart when it's full of love, see your face contort in anger when you hear the news."

My primary intention in writing that letter was to understand, to be able to make sense of the experience of people I didn't know. Clearly, the flattening didn't help me.

My second intention was to offer understanding for the suffering I was intuiting.

It was not hard for me to acknowledge what my people have done.

"I speak the language so obstinately revived by a generation of crazy visionaries. They despised your people. They ignored your people. They pretended your people were not here…"

"The soldiers come into your house, scare your children, take away your son. They stop you on the road, you are not free to come and go in your own land. Your land is confiscated, your houses bulldozed, your trees uprooted, the olive trees giving sustenance to your village. You are under curfew, your supplies blockaded."

Somewhere in there, I also had a third intention: to seek understanding for my own experience. For example, as much as I offered acknowledgment, I knew, still know, that "my compassion is strained." For "those who rule my country," and for those who "express their shock" when there are suicide attacks, "thinking to myself, exhausted, that they are fools for not seeing it coming." I also find it hard to have compassion for the attackers and those who delight in the results.

"I still cannot picture what it could be like to want someone's death so much, to take action to kill, to be sitting on a bus, looking at people's faces chattering away innocent of any knowledge of imminent death, to turn off compassion and fear enough to activate a bomb, and stop that chatter forever. What are the last images, the last feelings, the last thoughts, before the trigger is pulled, and after?"

Even while writing this letter and creating this almost two-dimensional image of the person I was writing to, I knew that not everyone was the same. I even included a reference to it, and still I couldn't see, in full, the contradiction: "I picture you struggling to have some stability in your life, desperately trying to feed your family. Perhaps you are not involved. Perhaps you would want to have just a simple existence in peace."

The main experience I had at the time was fear, both of the people ruling Israel, and of the results of their actions. I didn't trust that the person I was imagining could really and truly accept my existence as an Israeli. As I wrote:

> "I am afraid the people ruling my country, our land, will not stop feeding your hatred. ... I am afraid you will not tell me the truth, because the world is listening, and you want to look good, reasonable. ... I am afraid there aren't people on your side committed to peace and nonviolence. ... I am afraid you will not talk with me unless I hate my country. ... I am afraid we won't find a way to make room for each other on this tortured piece of land we both love."

Now, twelve years later, I have a Palestinian friend whose commitment to love and nonviolence I trust to the very last cell of my heart.[59] I am seeing, once again, the profound role of community and relationships in our process of reclaiming our humanity.

---

[59] I wrote about our friendship in one of my blog pieces: baynvc.blogspot.com/2014/01/israel-palestine-home-me-part-ii.html. I cannot think of a deeper act of friendship than giving me the loving, honest feedback I received.

Discovering Empathy

Arnina, my sister who still lives in Israel (Inbal and I live in the Bay Area, these days around the corner from each other), called us one day in 1993 to tell us about Nonviolent Communication (NVC). Next time I was in Israel I went with her to a workshop led by Marshall Rosenberg, creator of the process and vision of NVC. I have boundless gratitude to Marshall for the precious gift he brought to the world, to large numbers of people, and to me. The transformation I experienced and that I see possible on a global scale gives me so much palpable hope in the concrete and practical possibility of making things work.

Initially, however, I was not so taken. I was comparing what I saw Marshall do when he worked with people to the dramatic and intense demonstrations I was accustomed to seeing in co-counseling workshops. Oh, the treacherous waters of comparison. It took some time until I was able to disentangle the level of visible cathartic intensity of the moment from the longer term integration of the moment of change.

Even without getting super enthusiastic, I was still intrigued enough to want to continue to explore and learn. I attended some workshops and an ongoing practice group, and kept coming back, intuiting there was something there, and not quite experiencing it in full.

In the spring of 1995 Marshall came to San Francisco and I went to see him. This being before his book came out in 1999, we had only about thirty-five people in the room. At one point, while we were practicing empathic reflection, I volunteered to connect empathically with the person who organized and coordinated the event. She was completely full of judgments and in visible distress. I don't remember with any detail what she was talking about. What I remember, which was the absolute turning point in my relationship with NVC, was finding words in me, in the exact same way I found them in 1988 when I first discovered power inside me. I said to her something like: "Is it that you want compassion so much that you end up judging those who appear to act without compassion?" The effect, then, and countless times since when I have found my way to such empathic reflection, was instantaneous and visible. Her body shifted, her facial expression relaxed, and she found peace inside again by connecting to her passion for compassion.

I was stunned by the effect. Over the course of the weekend I tried out my newly found facility with empathy several more times, and confirmed for myself the power of empathy. I finally found the power of NVC, and I wanted to learn all I could so I could bring this gift to others and the world. That summer I went for my first intensive training with Marshall. A year later, after my second intensive training, I became certified to teach NVC and made my first experiments with bringing it to others.

The similarity between these two moments intrigues me, especially the focus on what I can bring to others rather than what the process can do for me. With all the years of work already behind me, I was still not fully opening up to life as it was lived inside me.

Embracing Vulnerability

Immediately after my second intensive training with Marshall Rosenberg, I went on a solo camping trip through Michigan to Canada. Nothing prepared me for the moment in which the personal path I am still on fifteen years later found me.

As I was driving towards Indiana, the night before flying home from Chicago, I heard of a major storm, possibly a tornado, approaching the area, and decided to stay in a motel for the night instead of being exposed to the elements far away from anything familiar.

I was reading *Love in the Time of Cholera*, by Gabriel García Márquez. One of the things that I absolutely love about his books is the way he writes about sexuality. More often than not I find writing about sexuality to be demeaning, and feel uncomfortable being witness to it. With Márquez, I am transported into a reality that is rich, vivid, extraordinarily sensual, and so completely spiritually dignified.

I finished the book, closed it gently, as if handling a rare piece of china, put it down on the side table, and discovered that I was silently crying. I had recently turned forty at that time, and crying by myself was far from a habit for me. The moment was very tender and soft. I knew I was crying about what I then thought of as the loss of my youth; that I had never developed sexual relationships that were all I wanted when I still had a chance. This was deep grief for me. I made the connection, then, between sexuality and vulnerability, a connection that at the time felt completely revelatory and profound. If I wanted to have sexual relationships that are satisfying, I would have to reclaim my vulnerability.

Next thing I knew I was having a mini tantrum, all by myself. I was sitting on the bed and banging my fists and knees against it, and crying out loud that I wanted to reclaim my vulnerability, every last ounce of it, the way I had it when I was a child.

And that's when I started my path. For some time I was stymied in my efforts. I had a picture of what full vulnerability would look like, and I was so far from it that I couldn't imagine how I would ever cross the wide expanse of utter discomfort and intolerable exposure to get there. Then I learned what the Chinese knew a long time ago: even the longest journey starts with one step. In each moment I could make a micro-choice. One word could get me closer to vulnerability, one other word could protect me more. If I simply committed to noticing all the moments of choice, and deciding, again and again, to take the ever-so-slightly more vulnerable direction, and kept doing it, then I would get progressively closer to where I wanted to be. Over time, the choices became easier and easier, as I had the repeated experience that despite my fear no real danger to me ever arose. Yes, many times people responded in ways that were painful. So be it. I learned a freedom I wouldn't trade for anything. I found my way to more and more and more and more self-acceptance I had simply never dreamed was possible, because a certain level of self-judgment had seemed like air to me.

This journey is not complete, and is unlikely to ever be complete. Whenever I believe I am "done" or even "done enough," I discover new layers or nuances of holding back that are then available to be worked with, loved into softness, and given to others. I have a playful goal of becoming 100% shameless, and I am happily somewhere in the 90s. I have a no secrets policy about myself which is intertwined with the path of vulnerability.

The biggest surprise came when I felt the deep and profound connection between my personal path of vulnerability and Gandhi's path of transcending and transmuting fear. On the personal plane, complete and total willingness to let go of emotional protection and expose myself to whatever people will do is my deepest understanding of the condition for being able to live nonviolence.

Heaven on Earth

Growing up a secular Jew in Israel in the 1950s and 1960s meant being exposed to a social milieu of disdain for observant Jews and, more remotely, for Christianity. Although in my own family we were exposed to many treasures of wisdom that I appreciated, the overall climate in Israel in those years made it very difficult for any secular Jew to openly engage with the legacy of Judaism, and quite taboo to experience anything positive about Christianity. Any kind of spirituality, even outside organized religion, was suspect in the circles I frequented.

Living outside Israel for so many years created enough of a social distance that I could eventually transform these limitations and begin a tentative process of opening up to non-material aspects of life. I have already described ("Permission to be Powerful," page 218) the first opening that took place in 1988 and that has only deepened and settled since. I describe my discovery of what Jesus stood for (quite separately from the religion that later emerged) in Part Two below ("Loving No Matter What," page 292). For now, I want to highlight the significance within my own life and path of connecting with and taking pleasure in aspects of Judaism that have become profoundly meaningful to me – both as personal nourishment and as inspiration and reinforcement for my capacity to imagine, articulate, and work towards a vision of a different world.

Tikkun Olam

The first core aspect of Judaism I could wholeheartedly embrace is the tradition of healing and repair of the world – *Tikkun Olam*. This tradition goes all the way back to Talmudic times (first few centuries of the Common Era), though the meaning and scope of application have changed considerably over the years.[60] More recently this term has come to connote self-consciously chosen acts in support of creating a world that is more just, humane, and caring for all.

The whole notion of repairing the world is rooted in a profoundly Jewish perspective that sees this world as redeemable, and life as perfectible through human actions. Instead of

---

[60] See the entry in Wikipedia or other resources.

theologically focusing on a personal afterlife (a notion originally foreign to Judaism and eventually imported from Christianity) or an apocalyptic future, Tikkun Olam is about transforming *this* world into a "Garden of Eden."

Even as a small child, I already had dreams of making changes in the world to bring relief to those whose suffering I was then aware of, primarily Jews in countries where they didn't have freedoms, and poor people anywhere. The more inner freedom I have to follow my own inner being and engage with life from within, the more the fire of Tikkun Olam burns in me.

Economic Justice

Among the many detailed instructions that the Torah contains, significant segments are dedicated to a variety of practices designed to alleviate and mitigate poverty and the plight of immigrants. These range from particular and detailed injunctions about how growers of food are supposed to provide for the poor (e.g. leave a certain area of the field unharvested on purpose for the poor to have access to it) to instructions for large-scale land redistribution every fifty years.

Whether or not the most radical of these were ever fully implemented, the very fact that all these laws were conceived of, codified, and preserved for posterity points to a deep commitment to finding ways of creating a community where inequality was minimized and socially-based suffering was alleviated, if not outright eliminated. I am amazed to recognize that the social vision that the Torah writers held was so radical that I still find it relevant and inspiring so many hundreds of years later. The boldness of their programs nourishes me in trusting my own growing vision and conviction.

Practice

From the very beginning, Judaism has been a religion of practice. Even the mythical founding event contains the words, attributed to the people of Israel upon hearing Moses read to them, "we will do and we will listen."[61] The doing comes first, and is in fact mentioned twice before the above line in the book of Exodus. Throughout the

---

[61] Ordinarily translated into English as "be obedient" rather than "listen."

generations, the preponderance of the focus, the entry ticket into membership in the community of Jews, was the practice, not the belief system. Even with my own limited knowledge of the sources, I remember many references to complete leniency about beliefs mixed with a strong intensity about the practice. If someone wants to convert to Judaism, traditionally they would be asked to learn all the practices and rituals more than pledging to a set of beliefs. In this regard, Judaism is more similar to Buddhism and even to Islam than to Christianity.

One of the reasons that Nonviolent Communication (NVC) has appealed to me all the way to the core may well be the historical context of emerging from a religion of practice. Although NVC, as well as Judaism and any other form of practice, is based on certain assumptions about what it means to be human and certain visions about how we want the world to be, neither is significant in terms of participating and benefiting from the practice. I never settle in my teaching of any element of NVC until I am able to give it a completely practical and concrete form that can be practiced immediately. Anything that is purely an idea can be limited in effecting change.

Not against the Body

Unlike dominant forms of Christianity and the Greek tradition from which it arose, especially the neo-Platonism that was prevalent when Christianity started to flourish, Judaism was never based on a mind/body split. Judaism has no monastic tradition, and a strong injunction exists that any who want to enter the raging waters of the mystical tradition be firmly situated in a practical life, including having a wife. (It was, indeed, essentially a male privilege to be able to engage in study and practice both of the Talmud and the mystical traditions.)

Judaism is a householder religion that sanctifies family and community, blesses the many functions of the body, and views sexuality as a practical and integral part of life. In later centuries, as Judaism was affected by the Christian context in which it continued to evolve, notions of a split between mind and body entered Judaism even though they are not original to it.

Descending from such a tradition allowed me to embark on the radical vision of integration on all levels without being saddled with and having to overcome centuries of contempt for the body and by extension everything that is not "mind."

Human Fallibility

Whenever I look through the Hebrew Bible, I am struck again by the deep wisdom of showing the mythical heroes as being imperfect. Even the biggest leaders of the Bible, including in particular Moses, are described, in the most direct terms, in their full, complex humanity. Some of what they did exposes fear, lack of faith, or even meanness. In this way, this tradition averted the worshipping of individuals. There is no Jewish Holiday that is dedicated to a person, only to collectively meaningful events; no Jewish equivalent of saints.

In addition, I like to believe that knowing that all of our ancestral leaders have been imperfect human beings can encourage more people to be willing to step into leadership without waiting to be perfect first. I didn't wait, and it's likely that the absence of idols served as some subtle support or role modeling.

Life Is Redeemable

When I was a young girl in Israel, in the early sixties, one of my favorite days of the year was Yom Kippur.[62] For a full twenty-five hours a great silence descended on the Jewish parts of Israel. No traffic, radio, or commercial activity of any kind took place. For many families, including mine, this was the one time a year we went to synagogue. In the silence I could hear everyone's footsteps echoing in the empty streets. That silence was my young idea of the sacred.

Even within my ambivalent-at-best relationship with the legacy of Jewish observance, Yom Kippur continues to be meaningful to me. I love being part of a tradition that sets aside regular time every year for self-reflection, consideration of our actions, and re-dedication to a life of meaning and value.

Part and parcel of this tradition is a fundamental premise of Judaism: the possibility of choosing again, of changing patterns, of

[62] en.wikipedia.org/wiki/Yom_Kippur

coming back to what's important to us, of transforming habits, and reclaiming life.

The practice of NVC has at its core an ongoing invitation to shift out of notions of right and wrong, the very foundation of the world I was raised into. How could I reconcile the notions of "sin" and "repentance," so central to the traditional meaning of Yom Kippur, with the expansive spirit of nonduality captured so precisely in Rumi's oft-quoted poem?

> Out beyond ideas of wrong-doing and right-doing,
> there is a field.
> I'll meet you there.
>
> When the soul lies down in that grass,
> the world is too full to talk about.
> Ideas, language, even the phrase
> each other
> doesn't make any sense.

Transcending ideas of wrong-doing and right-doing has been an act of immense faith in human beings – in our capacity for care and consciousness, in our ability to learn and grow, and in our fundamental interest in our own and others' well-being. As part of this journey I have found it meaningful and enriching to reframe the meaning of Yom Kippur in a way that speaks to that faith.

In a world without God, the only available yardstick is internal. "Sin," a word I am quite reluctant to use, could only mean acting in a way that is not aligned with a source of life that is deep inside me. Indeed, the root for the Hebrew word for "sin" is the same as that of "missing the mark." Sin in Hebrew could be seen as being distant from the core, which is more compatible with a nondual perspective like Rumi's or the practice of NVC. "Repentance," equally problematic for me, then means coming closer to the deeper truth of who I am, to the flow of life in me. Again, the word for "repentance" in Hebrew shares a root with the word for "coming back."

No right and no wrong. When I find myself "sinning," meaning acting in ways that don't align with my deepest values, I don't judge my actions. Instead, I "repent" in the form of opening my heart wider and wider to all of myself. I mourn and grieve the needs of mine that I *didn't* meet in taking the action, and I bring compassion for myself by finding the needs I was *trying* to meet. No matter how far from life the outcome of an action is, I trust I will find life in the form of the human need that gave rise to the action. More connection, and I am more likely to find strategies that speak to more needs.

This is the purest and most loving form of change and choice I can imagine.

Interdependence

Still on the theme of Yom Kippur, I want to pick another aspect that speaks to me deeply. Secular as I am, I still find beauty and peace in the clear notion that God can only forgive transgressions towards God, and transgressions involving other people can only be forgiven and transcended with the other person.

We are interdependent, relational beings. Confronted with the other's suffering I open myself even more deeply to life. My secular, nondual reframing reaffirms what the old sages said: if others are involved in the results of my actions, no amount of inner work is a substitute for the magic of reconciliation. This is not only because of the significance of reconciliation for the other person. It's also because hearing from the person who was affected by our actions is an integral part of our own inner work.

In full reconciliation I don't make myself wrong, and I don't justify or defend to avoid being wrong. Instead, I offer my empathic presence and authentic mourning to whomever was harmed. As my heart expands and heals, too, I can show my own humanity, thereby deepening the healing further. In our relatedness, the other person's ultimate healing and my full coming back to life are intertwined.

The fundamental recognition of our relatedness also extends to many other areas and aspects of Jewish practice. Here are a few more examples. One relates to the core practice of prayer, which Jews are instructed to do three times a day. The form of the prayer changes if done alone or done with others, and the preferred practice is in community, in a group of at least ten people.[63] Another is how many of the holidays are celebrated communally. Yet another is the age-old tradition, which is still available to some degree today, of a global

---

[63] Originally only men.

hospitality within the Jewish community. When Jews travel to an unknown city and visit the synagogue, they can generally rely on there being someone in the community who will host them. A friend, for example, was in Canada for work during Passover, and participated in the Seder of a family of complete strangers.

Even in the strictly secular upbringing I had, mutual aid was interwoven into every aspect of daily living, be it with neighbors, at work, or even with strangers. A sense of fundamental human solidarity and the unquestioned assumption that we, humans, need each other, have never been far from my awareness. It has made it that much easier to embrace in very concrete and specific ways the deep understanding and practice of interdependence.

Questioning Authority

A non-Jewish friend of mine once read the Hebrew Bible and the Christian additions to the Bible back to back, and commented to me on how different the relationship with God is between the two portions of the Bible. In particular, she noticed how many of the main characters in the early narratives stand up to and question God's choices and pronouncements.

Continuing further, the Talmud is primarily made up of a series of recorded conversations between various sages on all matters of life, from the most mundane to the most esoteric and abstract. In many of these conversations people question each other and, even more, senior rabbis. Also astonishing to me is the inclusion, often in great detail, of minority positions that didn't align with the final ruling. I am told that when people study the Talmud, they are expected to be able to argue for the minority position, invited to revere fully those whose opinion has been overruled.

In this way I see the Talmud as embodying a questioning of authority that is both bold and respectful. The antidote to submission is not a knee-jerk rebellion. Rather, it's a fully grounded willingness to follow choice from within with respect and care for all, either as an individual when possible, or by organizing nonviolent resistance when the individual consequences are too overwhelming.

Throughout the generations Jews have had an ongoing dilemma about how to apply rules and regulations from earlier times to the conditions, challenges, and meanings of their own. The most common response to this dilemma has been a continual process of reinterpreting the older texts to find ways of adapting to current life. Jews have been doing this for two thousand years. This understanding of Jewish law as a living tradition is so thoroughly foundational to Judaism that clear and specific instructions exist about how to make meaning of text, how to interpret, how to read into it even radical changes, and still preserve a sense of coherence and integrity.

As has happened to many groups under attack from modernity, when Orthodox Judaism lost its primary leadership in the Jewish community in the early Modern era, a sad new rigidity descended on the communities, and the creativity, flexibility, and courage that used to flourish have been lost.

In Summary

In writing this section, I am deeply aware of how complex my relationship with Judaism continues to be. I continue to have profound dislike of rituals of any kind, and since Judaism, being a religion of practice, is integrally full of rituals, I continue to have an ongoing aversion to it. This is most pronounced in relation to the liturgy. Although I have an intellectual understanding that interpretation, reframing, and even radical change in meaning are core to Judaism, I find the words and the imagery narrowly nationalistic, intensely limiting of women's options and of how they are seen, and altogether rigid to the point that I simply cannot find a home for myself in what is, ultimately, the sine qua non of Judaism as I understand it: the daily practice of Mitzvot (usually translated as the commandments or precept of Jewish law).

In addition, I hold enough discomfort about the acts of both the State of Israel and many individuals within Israel and the Jewish community in the U.S., that I have actual fear of being associated with Judaism and therefore not being taken seriously in what I say overall. I recognize this kind of fear as internalized anti-Semitism, and feel a fair amount of grief over this. I long for the inner freedom to embrace what I love about Judaism and let go of what doesn't speak to me, and to take my place in the time-honored tradition of wrestling with the practices and texts that we have inherited.

Looping back to where I started, it has never been a surprise to me that Jews, as individual human beings, have been so over-represented in movements for social justice wherever they have lived.

I feel honored to see myself as participating in a rich tradition of personal and group empowerment to imagine and work towards significant change in how human life is structured.

Integrations

Since embarking on this journey, I've seen in myself a steady movement towards integration, towards becoming whole in multiple dimensions, and with it an increase in my capacity to clarify vision and be an effective agent of bringing integration to the world.

Head and Heart

One reaction to the heavy weight of the focus on rationality I see is a disturbing trend of anti-intellectual bias which often shows up in the form of a judgment: "You're in your head." Conversely, in the academic subculture I used to be part of, as well as in many business cultures, I experience, often, an active denigration of emotionality.

My own longing and practice is to connect the two faculties so that they become interdependent. I want my mind to be in the service of my heart, supporting it by gathering information, making logical inferences, and thinking through strategies. I want my heart to be in the service of my mind, providing emotional context, clarity of purpose, and a moral compass.

Theory and Practice

As a former academic, I am aware of what I see as an artificial split, where theoreticians distance themselves from the practical implications and applications of their work while social activists often have a disdain for theory.

My own aim is to remain deeply rooted in theoretical depth and understanding, allowing theory to inform and drive my choices as practitioner. At the same time, I keep learning from my practice and that of others, and want to keep expanding and refining my theoretical understanding of the world in an organic manner that emerges from my practice.

Process and Action

In my work I have often heard people refer to themselves or others as process-oriented or action-oriented. I have also often seen people become impatient or frustrated with those whose interest is in more or less process or action than they themselves want.

My own work continues to be bringing the two together. Key to this integration is an understanding I developed about focusing on the amount of connection and process necessary for the purpose at hand. I have enjoyed developing language and frames of references that allow this principle to be put into practice. I fully trust in the growing possibility, as we release anxiety and fear of scarcity, of working with each other in ways that make process and connection essential without ever losing sight of goals and efficiency.

I also strive, in a similar manner, to grow in my ability to make things happen on the material plane and cultivate technical skills in parallel with being savvy in how to be in relationship and have emotional wisdom and presence for intensity.

Visionary Passion and Practical Wisdom

Our stereotypes often depict visionaries as hopelessly impractical. I continue to work on seeing the biggest, most radical vision possible without compromise while at the very same time being able to work in the real and material world that exists now, and show concrete steps that people can take, in all contexts and situations, to make their lives more livable, and contribute to peace and movement around them.

I am particularly happy to have come to a place where I see a vision of a world operating on profoundly different principles and, at the same time, I work with people within current organizations, and am able to support them concretely and without judgment, even when I have concerns about what their organizations are doing.

Personal and Political

In writing about myself as part of a book that is about the world and people, I am in part making a statement. The claim I am staking in writing this portion of the book has been made before many times, and I doubt I need to make the arguments again. Suffice it to say that I am hoping, as I imagine do all the women who revealed their vulnerabilities in writing during the current long wave of feminism, that hearing about me could be an integral part of others' movement toward liberation and wholeness. My struggles, my early challenges, and the path I have taken to creating healing and to empowering myself to call out my vision without holding back an iota of it, are both completely unique and idiosyncratic as well as essentially human and universal. I am no longer able to experience the two as separate.

Mending the Tear

None of us can heal fully by ourselves. We are not designed in this way, and when our fundamental sense of self has been eroded and we don't feel fully welcome in this world, we can only go so far on our own. We need other people and the magic of empathy to experience sufficient transformation.

Early on in our journey, empathy can provide us relief. Just being heard, just the presence of another human with us, can release tension and expand our capacity to breathe. Relief, however, can often be temporary. Unless we reach deeper understanding, open ourselves to the full experience that lives in us, and understand our deeper needs, our sensitivities remain and we can lose the opening that comes with being heard.

Empathy for healing, as I describe it below, is a further stage, helping us to reach a level of self-understanding that enables longer-lasting shifts.

If, however, we wish for full transformation of our experience, such that the contraction that comes from painful experiences can be permanently undone, we need to recover others' humanity, not only our own: we need to stretch into empathy for those who have harmed us. Such transformation in reframing traumatic incidents frees our spirit more fully and allows us to reclaim the trusting joy we had before life's challenges affected us. This section contains two real-life stories of such attempts at transformation. I call this section "Mending the Tear" because I see such enormous potential in this practice of healing and reconciliation to support people across enormous divides in seeing their shared humanity. Our world is torn in innumerable places. We will need this practice on a massive scale to be able to live together on our precious and finite planet.

The Healing Power of Empathy

The capacity to give one's attention to a sufferer is a very rare and difficult thing; it is almost a miracle; it is a miracle. Nearly all those who think they have the capacity do not possess it.[64]

– Simone Weil

Although the fundamental capacity for empathy, which is part and parcel of mutual recognition, is an innate human feature, we need to receive sufficient empathy early in life to be able to attain and maintain true mutuality as well as empathic connection with ourselves and others.

Most of us have not had sufficient empathy early in life, and for many of us this means that our capacity for empathy gets stunted, both towards others and towards ourselves. The healing force that allows us to recover our lost capacity to connect is, once again, empathy. Empathic connection with another is an almost indispensable condition of psychic liberation. Although some individuals are able to choose strategic discomfort on their own, for the most part, the challenges of the journey are such that they require the presence of empathic others to sustain it. Without empathy, the likelihood of retreat into our comfort zone increases. With it, we are more capable of opening up to the discomfort and the painful emotions that await us on the journey.

That empathy per se is healing has become progressively more accepted. Being heard, in full, is one of the most profound experiences we humans can have, and has a transformative effect that more often than not we don't anticipate. Even a few minutes of this experience can sometimes transform seemingly intractable situations. Even after years of practicing and teaching empathy, I still find myself astonished at the immense power of it. In moments of intense conflict with someone, for example, I can still forget that the entire conflict can be dissolved in a few empathic exchanges, as has so often been the case.

For the purpose of psychic liberation specifically, the purpose of empathy is to support us in moving towards embracing aspects of

---

[64] Quoted without a citation in Rosenberg, *Nonviolent Communication*, 78.

our experience that are particularly challenging. Beyond connection with feelings and emotions, the biggest healing potential of empathy arises from focusing on tuning into needs in addition to feelings. If the essence of empathic presence is the ability to decode and understand others' emotional state in full, then needs are absolutely integral to that understanding. If emotions arise in response to an assessment of how well needs are met in a given situation, then full empathy must include an understanding of those needs in addition to the emotions themselves.

For as long as empathy is focused only on feelings, it can still provide the kind of momentary relief that comes simply from being understood, but without the forward movement that can come from becoming aware of our needs, from peeling away layers of defenses, surface desires and fears in order to encounter our deeper hopes, longings and values. Ultimately, psychic liberation includes an openness to our full human experience.

Paradoxically, the possibility of attaining and sustaining full empathic connection with another is also one of the important achievements of psychic liberation. Our own capacity to exhibit and engage in empathic connection with others is one measure of our healing and freedom. Moreover, I have often had the experience of recovering from hurt through opening my heart to the other person's experience. Entering empathic space with another calls on my own human essence to such a degree that I find more freedom in my heart. Ultimately, empathy is both a condition for and an expression of our psychic liberation.

Finding Unexpected Humanity

When Rose (fictitious name) was eight she experienced unwanted sexual touch at the hands of a carpenter who did some work on her parents' house. In her mid-30s I accompanied her on a journey of healing from the effects of this experience.

As facilitator of this process, without the option of locating and bringing in the carpenter, I took on his role. This meant I had to *become* the carpenter, to dig deep into what it could be like to be him, so I could support Rose in claiming more of herself back.

Rose carried this pain, alone, for years. She needed to be heard, to know that she was gotten, in order to experience relief. So I sat in front of her, imagining being the carpenter, imagining Rose at eight. Looking at her eyes, I took in her pain and allowed my heart to absorb her loss of trust in herself, her pull to contract from showing her full self, her habit of hiding her vulnerability. I listened, as the carpenter, and I reflected until Rose felt fully heard, and was calmer and lighter.

Being heard is not enough. Rose also needed to know that she mattered. As I sat with her, I overcame my reluctance, as the carpenter, to face what happened. I expanded my heart to allow my body and spirit to touch the horror of knowing that what I had done directly affected Rose's life to this degree. I shared my grief and let Rose know how much I wanted her to reclaim her full self and be, again, a free spirit. As I shared, Rose could see that her suffering was meaningful, not random. More of her loss surfaced. We digested it together, moving closer towards connection and healing.

The third level of hurt is endlessly subtle, and often invisible. When we are harmed, we often explain the horror to ourselves by making the person whose actions harmed us less than fully human. This protection comes at the cost of separation. We lose some of our own humanity, too. We heal in full by coming back to seeing that person's humanity. That was the gift I was next called to give Rose.

When we started I didn't know how it would unfold. I was tasked with loving life, people, Rose, and the carpenter enough to find his humanity underneath his actions. Being and understanding from within this person who had harmed a trusting girl also required abundant faith and total surrender. Faith to surrender and to trust that life would provide me the visceral solution to the emotional equation my body was trying to solve in being this man, that if I let go of figuring it out I could recognize the emotional truth when it arose.

This is the point when I get tested, again and again, each time I offer healing. Everything in my practice gets tested: my love, my authenticity, my imagination, my care for everyone, and my willingness to trust what arises. Submitting to life, tiny and significant clues appear along the way to decipher the emotional logic of the action.

In my imaginary existence as the carpenter I had formed a bond of exquisite tenderness and special connection with Rose. She was so mature, clear, alive, and real, that she didn't appear to me as eight. I was shocked to understand that the beauty of our friendship was so magical that at some point I lost track of her age. I deluded myself into imagining us to be equal. And then I couldn't see a reason not to engage in sexual touch with her, as a celebration of the connection.[65]

Trusting the gut sense of this unbelievable and unfamiliar truth and offering it to Rose was the ultimate surrender and required inner strength and exacting vulnerability. Even more shocking was the effect on Rose. She had been trying for years to find a human way of making sense of the carpenter's actions. My story provided an answer that felt resonant for her. As we looked in each other's eyes, both of us in tears, I knew the connection had been made. My heart, in real life, grew to include one more human experience, and some part of Rose would now be freer.

---

[65] I want to stress that this was an intuitive understanding that arose from the particulars of Rose's story and is not any kind of attempt at a theory of child sexual abuse. In each situation, the person who harms the child would have their own specific subjective thoughts and experience, which might be very different indeed from the ones I chanced on as this carpenter. What's significant and important to me is that in each case the challenge would be to find what the underlying needs are as a way to rebuild human understanding.

Connecting Across an Abyss

The names, location, time, and any identifying information were changed below to maintain complete anonymity for the people involved.

Marsha contacted me when she was forty-two after years of suffering from extreme nightmares and debilitating daily terror. She had acute, vivid, and detailed memories of severe physical and emotional abuse at the hands of her mother. Marsha left her home town in rural Wisconsin and moved to New York, and had not seen or talked with her mother in twenty years. When I suggested that she could perhaps get some relief from her pain if I facilitated a meeting with her mother, she immediately agreed despite her terror at the prospect of seeing Louisa. When I subsequently approached Louisa, who was seventy-seven, she was in tears. She talked about the pain of being estranged from Marsha, and about her deep wish to understand what had led to her choice to disconnect. Louisa had no recollection of any of the events or feelings that Marsha had shared with me previously. We made arrangements for a meeting in a neutral place.

Even though they both knew that they didn't have a shared reality about Marsha's childhood, I had no idea the reality gap between the two women would be as wide as I found it to be. I had instructed Marsha to be prepared to talk about three incidents from her childhood. I had hopes that such specifics, including names of people who were there, would be the easiest thing for Louisa to hear. I checked again with Louisa that she was really ready to hear whatever Marsha would say. She assured me she was a tough lady and that she wanted to hear the truth, no matter how painful.

Against the backdrop of Marsha's crystal clear memories of abuse and neglect, and her absolute conviction of not being wanted and not being seen for who she was, Louisa started our time together by expressing her gratitude for being with Marsha again, and her grief at not being allowed, in her words, to connect with Marsha or touch her. Marsha expressed how hard it was for her to be with Louisa. In her shattered inner state, she became completely preoccupied with Louisa's feelings. I assured her that I was going to attend to Louisa's feelings so she, Marsha, could be free to express her full truth. I reminded them that our time together was only about hearing and understanding, and not about matching realities. Then I asked Marsha to tell her first story.

Marsha was struggling mightily to remain present, one small step at a time. When she mustered enough inner strength to speak about her experience, the extent of the reality gap became fully apparent. Marsha told of a time when she was four and was completely paralyzed in fear and hence couldn't accept an invitation to go visit a friend's family. I looked over at Louisa, and saw no sign of recognition. Marsha continued, recounting how after the friend's mother left, Louisa hit her with a branch until she bled and screamed in pain. Louisa listened attentively, still without memory of the event. Moreover, she had no memory of ever hitting Marsha, who also remembers being kicked around the house. The closest thing Louisa remembered was spanking Marsha on her buttocks on occasion. She remembered herself as having loved Marsha all along, without any trace of ambivalence.

I chose to hold paradox, to have them both live in me, side by side, trusting them both, refusing to collapse it into the idea that one of them was lying. Marsha, with the absolute devastation of her life, with having had to run away from her family to have any hope of recovering even a basic sense of self, and Louisa, with her anguish of having lost her daughter, who was completely inaccessible to her. Holding both of them was almost beyond my human capacity to make sense of the world, and I kept breathing by leaning on my absolutely laser clarity that only connection was important.

With a gap like this the question of factual truth becomes irrelevant. Who can know? Who can find out? With that much gap, I said to both of them, all we could do was to hold together the existence of the gap, the inability to make sense of the impossibility of both stories being true factually, along with the deep honoring of the clarity with which each of them had her experience and memory.

When Marsha was speaking I was in awe of her plight, of how much effort it took for her to choose to keep going. I figured that with all the destruction, she would need enormous effort to organize herself inside to even speak. In parallel, I was working with Louisa, reminding her to just listen and understand, listen and understand, and focus her attention on Marsha's experience, independent of her own. It didn't matter what she did or didn't do. All we wanted, I kept reminding her, was to give Marsha the experience of being understood. From time to time Louisa's reflection shaded into her own incomprehension, and she used phrases such as "holding on to pain," or "choosing not to let me in." In such moments I invited her, again and again, to hear Marsha's experience from inside, on her terms. Periodically I stopped the process to give Louisa some relief, so she could be heard, too. I reflected to her, repeatedly, my own understanding of her pain of separation and incomprehension, all the while aware of how far she was from being able to grasp Marsha's pain.

This was where our first meeting ended – some relief to both and a huge gap. Full heart connection was still elusive. Our second meeting took place the next day. Although Marsha had prepared a few more concrete incidents, my intuition led me elsewhere. I decided to step into the process myself. With their permission, I "became" Marsha and listened to Louisa. As Marsha, I made contact inside with the daily endless pain of Louisa's longing for me. I had a visceral sense of how devastating her loss was. I felt the sorrow of my own inability to offer her anything else. Louisa felt my understanding more fully. And she had a little bit more peace. With that, I turned my attention to "becoming" Louisa listening to Marsha. My goal was to serve as a thread of human possibility within the gap of impossibly divergent realities.

Tapping into the trust I had in Louisa's authentic care for Marsha, I allowed myself to sink into the grief of Marsha's daily existence of horror, her absolute need to recreate her sense of self by moving away from me. Even with all of my pain as Louisa, I felt complete acceptance of her choice because I understood that was what she needed to do in order to save her life. I knew, as Louisa, that I would be willing to restructure my sense of self to include any horrors I might have done and forgotten about if only I could, so as to be able to provide Marsha with the relief of acknowledgment, of not being so, so alone with her experience, without anyone else present. These words, this heartful sharing, even as surrogate, were reaching Marsha. She *felt* less alone. She was able, she said, to come from complete non-existence as a human being to some modicum of existence, some ability to trust her own reality and have compassion for herself, ever so slightly. What helped was my longing to provide her with acknowledgment, and my curiosity and interest in her experience.

Although I was a surrogate, I was tapping into a deep truth, in both directions. Each of the two women felt heard in full, maybe for the first time. The gap remained the same. Their experiences remained utterly divergent; except that they could now see and feel each other, beyond just intellectual understanding. The acceptance was whole. Marsha received some acknowledgment and care she never even knew existed, and Louisa got to understand why Marsha left, and came to accept it. Would they now have an ongoing easeful relationship? No. Considering the amount of suffering Marsha had experienced, this was unlikely to happen. Was that a failure? Hardly. After decades of painful estrangement they came together, heard each other, cried, and came to acceptance of where things were. As we closed our time together, we all celebrated truth telling, stretching, the power of listening, new insights, healing, and hope. This is the power of reconciliation even in the most extreme of circumstances.

Getting from Here to There: What Comes after Waking Up?

Do we ever heal sufficiently to reclaim the fullness of our humanity? In all honesty, this is an open question for me. I myself have been on this path for about twenty-four years of my fifty-seven, and yet I still recognize in me significant areas in which the cumulative trauma I have experienced continues to limit my freedom. At the same time, I am aware of a degree of freedom to be myself, in more and more and more circumstances, that some years ago would have seemed unimaginable. However far we can go on this path, at some point we cross over into a new place, where we can recognize ourselves as the agents of our lives, where we are able to accompany ourselves on our own journey as well as seek support from others without shame. Perhaps one bold way of saying it is that we can become feral by choice.

Unless we are hermits, or satisfied with a mostly internal life, sooner or later we encounter the reality of being far along on a journey that others may have not chosen to embark on. For example, while I may be completely at ease with my own emotional state and have no qualms about crying in the presence of others, others may be quite uncomfortable with public display of emotions. I may be free of any desire for revenge, while others find a sense of belonging with each other through shared judgment and blame, seeking punitive responses, or are content to view some people as less than human. I may be open to examine my relationship with power and privilege, while others are in wholesale acceptance of the status quo or defensive about their role in it.

Even more pointedly, my own reclaiming of my humanity does absolutely nothing to the systems and social structures within which we all live. No matter how open, loving, human, courageous, or otherwise free I become, the horrors of the world do not change as a result.

How do we then act with integrity, authenticity, and care for self and others within a world that is fundamentally unchanged? The challenges are far from trivial. Any choice that any of us makes that is different from what the norm has created requires some degree of effort. Even something as simple as buying fresh, organic food instead of the "standard America diet" requires varying degrees of effort depending on where in the U.S. we happen to live. For me, living in Northern California, the effort is quite minimal, though the cost most certainly makes it prohibitive for many people. For someone living in a rural area away from the coasts, it can sometimes require extra travel, planning, and research to find sources. The same is true when we operate outside the familiar norms of social interaction. We will not be supported by the visible and invisible structures of society, and we will need to put an effort into bridging the gap. In addition to courage, bridging the gap takes a huge capacity for love and acceptance, so we can truly meet people exactly where they are and do, on our own, the work of creating connection. We also need to tend to ourselves, to continue to nourish our commitment to live the way we want, and to seek support from others so we can rebuild the fabric of interdependence around us.

These are the kinds of core questions that Part Two of this book, "Pioneering a Future of Collaboration," addresses in detail.

Part Two:

Pioneering a Future of Collaboration

Living as if ...

In the fall of 2009 I was gripped by a bout of despair that rendered me almost incapacitated. The downward spiral started during a workshop I was teaching. I was focusing on making the distinction between caring about someone and actually taking action to support their wellbeing. To illustrate the intensity of this distinction I chose the example of the more than 18,000 children under five years old who die daily of malnutrition and related causes.[66] I care about them deeply. I am haunted by them, as a matter of fact; in moments the anguish is unbearable. And yet every day I participate in our collective willingness to let them die, because we can't figure out how to bring food to them. And it feels very personal to me. Not only this, I am not making their plight my top priority. While I knew all of this, including my own choice, I was shattered by taking it in as fully as I did in that moment of making it public in the workshop.

As I was acknowledging that feeding these children was not my highest priority, I was called to focus clearly on what *was* my priority. At first, it seemed easy: my priority is to change the human conditions that make it possible for children to starve and for everything else that troubles me to happen. Those human conditions are both internal and external to each of us. Internally, it's about our ability to live the consciousness of love, interdependence, and choice in how we relate to ourselves and to each other. Externally, it's about setting up governance, economic, educational, and other systems based on the principle of meeting needs.

And so it was that my second humble landing, within a week of the first, also happened at a workshop. I was suddenly hit by the enormity of change from the habitual ways of being that any of us would be called upon to make. What was I asking of these people who had come to my workshop thinking they were learning about empathy in the workplace? And, on the heels of that, immediately, the harsher question: Who was I kidding? I started wondering how many of the thousands of people who had attended my workshops, listened to me on the radio, or read my articles had truly embraced the fullness of the radical shift. And how many of them have also

[66] While the estimates of this number vary widely, there is currently widespread agreement that the trend has been going down (see footnote on page 176). The details of attempting to make sense of this finding are far beyond the scope of this current project.

joined me in passing it on in its fullness? This was far from an idle curiosity question. If I am in the consciousness transformation business, then the question of how many actually make this shift is the measure of my effectiveness. And my effectiveness is not about my satisfaction. It's about seeing if the work that I do is actually contributing, at least over time, to transforming the conditions that sustain hunger, war, environmental degradation and all the host of intractable issues that we are facing as a species.

And so I lay in bed one morning and started counting. I didn't reach ten. Of course there are likely others I don't know about. I didn't imagine those would add up to a significant number. With that realization, I sank into full despair. The equation didn't add up: I didn't have enough of a combination of effectiveness, support, fun, sustainability, and choice in my work to balance the level of effort and intention I tend to put into my work and my life.

I temporarily lost my faith that what I did could have a lasting effect on people's consciousness. I knew, even in the midst of the anguish, that I was deeply privileged to touch people's lives in significant ways on a consistent basis. I also knew that being moved and inspired was not quite the same as the choice to integrate this consciousness into daily living, into the fabric of how we make choices moment by moment, into what our lives are about.

I had an intense pull to quit, resign, and give up, which was strong, and which I knew I wasn't going to heed. Instead, I looked deep and hard to find what I was longing for, what would be truly nourishing, how I would want to work.

That was when I first connected with the fierce and deep longing in me to work with people who are already committed to the consciousness of nonviolence, the consciousness that infuses the choices we make with awareness. I wanted company in embracing the ferocious experience of a life given to the service of consciousness transformation, internally and in the world. Thus was born inside me the dream of a community of dedicated people who continually apply themselves to living the consciousness of nonviolence and passing it on to others.

Against the weight of my crisis I stretched my spirit into envisioning what this truly meant and what it would take to create this full alignment. As a first step in creating such a community, I sat down to write my understanding of what constitutes the consciousness of nonviolence as I understand it. The story of the virtual community I created, and the various metamorphoses it went through before ending its existence after two years, belongs elsewhere. If nothing else, the dream served to create the list of core commitments that have now sparked the imagination of many hundreds of people around the world, more than I even know about.

More than anything, I see these commitments as one form of offering guidance to anyone who embarks on the process of psychic liberation I outlined in the previous part. When we reclaim our full humanity, awareness, and love and embrace life and the radical possibility of living a life of freedom and service, we face some pretty significant questions about how to live, because while we change, the world around us doesn't. I speak about living "as if" and I am deeply aware of the weight of the challenge. How can we live a life of dignity, love, courage, truth, freedom, and connection in a world that isn't living that way? How can we meet others where they are while we are moving towards our dreams? How can we embrace in full the radical teachings of nonviolence, when violence is still an organizing principle of life? How can we keep enjoying life as we open more and more to the suffering in the world?

With these kinds of questions in mind, this part includes three sections.

Core Commitments

I see the commitments I put together as one way of translating Gandhi's principles into concrete guidelines for living. They describe and define a way of relating – to self, to others, or to life – that embodies and sustains the consciousness of nonviolence. Together they form one way of responding to the questions that arise when we try to live "as if," though I most definitely don't intend them to be seen as "the" way. Simply put, each of the commitments provides one lens into how to approach dilemmas of living. Many of them exist in paradoxical relationship to each other.

Practices

Because the commitments require tremendous dedication, I have developed a number of very simple practices that have helped me immensely in integrating these commitments into how I move in the world, on the minutest level. Without imagining this being exhaustive, I offer a range of examples of practices as well as some guidelines for what you can do if you want to create and sustain practices for yourself, so you can continue to inhabit and live the consciousness that *you* want to inhabit in your daily living.

Final Reflections

To conclude this book, I come back to my own personal journey, important parts of which I shared earlier in this book. I want to bring it full circle, to complete it to where it's taken me as of the time of writing. Part of why I have included my journey in such detail is in the hope that you will see how far one person can and can't go.

I end this section, and the book as a whole, with some reflections about how a deep enough personal journey might awaken in us the desire to contribute to others on a significant scale, which would lead us to join forces with others to work towards social transformation. It was important for me to include this here even though this book is not about social transformation per se, because I want to reduce the chances that anyone will read me to mean that personal transformation is all that matters.

Section 1:

Core Commitments

All-in: Fully Committing to a Life of Nonviolence

Gandhi spoke about applying nonviolence in thought, word, and action. I have found that applying nonviolence becomes progressively more difficult the closer it is to thought. Many more people can refrain from physically violent acts than from using the language of judgments, threats, or demands. Similarly, many more people can train their language than can train their mind and heart to hold the commitment to nonviolence. The result is that it is not uncommon to find people who engage in nonviolent direct action, which means they cause no physical harm, including to property, while at the same time harboring hatred toward those in positions of power. The full depth of the commitment to nonviolence is about living through the powerful combination of compassion, fierceness, and courage, with an uncompromising willingness to stand for truth.

Nonviolent Communication (NVC), a process created by Marshall Rosenberg in the 1960s while helping communities to desegregate peacefully, is designed to do just that: to help us integrate as far as possible our commitment to nonviolence all the way into the deepest structures of our thoughts; to speak in ways that carry this commitment forward into all of our relationships; and to apply this consciousness in all our actions, including our participation in the collective enterprise called social structures.

Many of us who share NVC in the world are asked what exactly NVC is. There are probably as many answers as there are people who practice and teach it. In the context of where I am on the trajectory of this book, I am most interested in the aspect of NVC that has to do with consciousness – the specific ways that we can live nonviolence in everyday life. As much as we want to take on the global challenges of our times and move toward transformation, unless we learn, in parallel and at the same time, how to live differently within ourselves and with each other, we run the risk of recreating the very structures we want to transform.

Embracing nonviolence as a deep practice is something many of us find daunting, even after doing some intensive work to liberate ourselves, precisely because we have all internalized the structures of thought, word, and action that have brought us to where we are. To move from where we are to what we want to embrace, we will need to overcome the fear and shame that get in our way of embracing love and truth as core principles of being; to welcome conflict and challenge as a path towards greater wholeness; to examine our assumptions about ourselves and others; and to move closer to the dream of Rumi's field, where we can live beyond thoughts of right-doing and wrong-doing.

This section of the book introduces the seventeen core commitments I put in writing as I was trying to capture what this consciousness exactly means and how it translates into guidelines for living. I have found that they support me and others on our path by providing antidotes to the obstacles that keep us separate, desperate, and powerless. The commitments serve as a compass, a reminder, a scaffolding that can hold us in living by choice. They help us navigate the challenging struggles of everyday living so we can come to more and more integrity in how we live our lives, moving closer and closer to being aligned with our core values of nonviolence, and at the same time finding more and more gentleness toward ourselves when we don't.

At the same time, these commitments are not all there is to nonviolence, and contain two significant and deliberate omissions. One is the absence of a call to take on structural change. The choice to engage in an attempt to create structural changes is one that I hope at least some people who are reading this have already made or will make. Nonetheless, and although others may disagree with me, I continue to believe that we can choose, as individuals, to live the commitment to nonviolence in the contexts in which we find ourselves without also choosing to engage with the larger structures of life with an intention to create change. I would feel a meaningful loss if all such people were not seen as part of the movement of nonviolence. However small the effect of our individual acts might be, living them nonviolently at the very least models to others what is possible.

The second and related omission is the complex question of how we respond to situations in which others act in ways that we see as contributing to harm, on any scale, and in which the option of dialogue is closed off by those very people. This issue invites an entire exploration about how nonviolence is or is not compatible with use of force, a topic I attend to in the book *Reweaving Our*

Human Fabric, which is dedicated to the work of social transformation. For the moment, suffice it to say that the conditions I see for when and how force is compatible with nonviolence are exacting and stringent, and, to my mind, rarely met.

I have not found a word that captures the exact line I want to walk. Commitment may be a bit too strong, and tends to connote "should," thus invoking the non-choiceful energy of obligation and duty. "Intention" is not strong *enough*, in my mind, to carry the unwavering force of staying the course even when the going gets hard. Somewhere I also want to capture the unpredictability of life. These commitments are not a promise, which none of us can give. I have full understanding of how challenging life is, and imagine that no matter how strong the choice, every single one of us at some point or another will not find sufficient inner resources to follow through on these.

In order to soften the intensity of "commitment" without losing the strength, I chose to use the word "want" rather than "commit" in the actual wording of the commitments. Another reason is that I want the words to remind any of us who makes the choice to follow this path of the overarching clarity that this is what we want, that there is no in-principle objection to living life in this way, no matter what anyone else is doing, no matter what the structures of the world look like, no matter what the circumstances are.

This is a tall order. This, to me, is a mobilized life. The commitments serve as a compass, a reminder, a scaffolding that can hold us in living by choice.

While the choice is ours to make, and the invitation is to extend ourselves to life fully without conditions, we need each other to be able to continue to face reality – external and internal – and keep focused on what matters to us most. This is why each of these commitments includes a reference to seeking support. I have already written ("Emotional Journeys," pages 135-9) about how essential community is to embarking on and sustaining an emotional journey. No matter how far we are on the path to wholeness, sustaining where we are continues to be a journey because of the continued challenge of meeting a world that is not designed to meet human needs. This is why I call on all of us to welcome and seek support and reminders for staying on track with these commitments.

Relating to Myself

1. **Openness to Myself:** Even when I act in ways I really don't like, I want to keep my heart open to myself. If I find myself in self-judgment, I want to seek support to reconnect with myself and hold with compassion the needs that motivate my actions.

2. **Openness to the Full Emotional Range:** Even when my feelings are uncomfortable for me, I want to stay present with myself and keep my heart open to the fullness of my emotional experience. If I find myself contracting away from my experience, numb or shut down, I want to seek support to release defendedness and open to what is.

3. **Risking my Significance:** Even when I am full of doubt, I want to offer myself in full to the world. If I find myself thinking that I am not important or that my actions are of no significance, I want to seek support to come back to my knowledge that my presence and my gifts matter.

4. **Responsibility:** Even when overwhelmed with obstacles or difficult emotions, I want to take full responsibility for my feelings, my actions, and my life. If I find myself giving my power away to other people, larger forces, or analytic categories such as my past or any labels I put on myself, I want to seek support to find the core source of choice within me to live as I want and ask for what I want.

5. **Self-Care:** Even when I am stressed, overwhelmed, or in disconnection, I want to maintain my commitments to my well-being, and take actions that nourish my life. If I find myself letting go of strategies that I know contribute to my life (such as exercise, eating as I want, receiving support and empathy as needed, enjoyable activities, or anything else that I know works for me), I want to seek support to ground myself in the preciousness of my own life and my desire to nurture myself.

6. **Balance:** Even when I am drawn to overstretching myself (including towards any of these commitments), I want to remain attentive to the limits of my capacity in any given moment. If I find myself pushing myself, I want to seek support to honor the natural wisdom of my organism and to trust that remaining within my current limits will support me in increasing my capacity over time.

Orienting towards Others

7. **Loving No Matter What:** Even when my needs are seriously unmet, I want to keep my heart open. If I find myself generating judgments, angry, or otherwise triggered, I want to seek support in transforming my judgments and meeting others with love.

8. **Assumption of Innocence:** Even when others' actions or words make no sense to me or frighten me, I want to assume a need-based human intention behind them. If I find myself attributing ulterior motives or analyzing others' actions from the outside, I want to seek support to ground myself in the clarity that every human action is an attempt to meet needs no different from my own.

9. **Empathic Presence:** Even when others are in pain, disconnected from themselves, expressing intensity, or in judgment, I want to maintain a relaxed presence with their experience. If I find myself attempting to fix, offering advice, doing mechanical empathy, or turning my attention elsewhere, I want to seek support to regain my faith in the transformative power and the gift of just being with another.

10. **Generosity:** Even when I am afraid or low-resourced, I want to keep reaching out to offer myself to others and respond to requests. If I find myself contracting in fear and unwilling to give, I want to seek support to release any thoughts of scarcity and embrace opportunities to give.

Interacting with Others

11. **Authenticity and Vulnerability:** Even when I feel scared and unsure of myself, I want to share the truth that lives in me with others while maintaining care and compassion for others and for myself. If I find myself hiding or protecting, I want to seek support to embrace the opportunity to expand my sense of self and transcend shame.

12. **Availability for Feedback:** Even when I want to be seen and accepted, I want to make myself available to receive feedback from others in order to learn and grow. If I find myself being defensive or slipping into self-judgments, I want to seek support to find the beauty and gift in what is being shared with me.

13. **Openness to Dialogue:** Even when I am very attached to a particular outcome, I want to remain open to shifting through dialogue. If I find myself defending a position or arguing someone else out of their position I want to seek support to release the attachment, connect with my needs and the needs of others, and aim for mutually supportive strategies to emerge out of connection with needs.

14. **Resolving Conflicts:** Even when I have many obstacles to connecting with someone, I want to make myself available to work out issues between us with support from others. If I find myself giving up on someone, I want to seek support to remember the magic of dialogue and entrust myself to the process of healing and reconciliation to restore connection.

Relating to Life

15. **Interdependence:** Even when I experience separation or deep isolation, I want to open my heart to the fullness of the interconnectedness of all life and to cultivate awareness of the countless ways that our actions and experiences affect each other. If I find myself retreating into self-sufficiency, separation, or mistrust in my own gifts or those of others, I want to seek support to remember the beauty and relief of resting in interdependence, including the many ways each of our lives depends on the gifts, actions, and efforts of others.

16. **Accepting What Is:** Even when change happens (welcome or unwelcome, small or large), things fall apart, people don't come through, or calamities take place in the world, I want to remain open to life. If I find myself contracting away from life or drawn to ideas about what should happen, I want to seek support to find a sense of peace with unmet needs, and to choose responses and actions from clarity about how I want to interact with and respond to life.

17. **Celebration of Life:** Even when I am faced with difficulties – personal, interpersonal, or global – I want to maintain an attitude of appreciation and gratitude for what life brings me. If I find myself becoming cynical or experiencing only pain and despair, I want to seek support to connect my heart with the beauty and wonder that exists in life even in the most dire circumstances.

Relating to Self

It takes commitment and dedication to reclaim the freedom, authenticity, joy, curiosity, and many other aspects of ourselves that we lose to socialization. The structures – both external and internal – that reinforce the separation, scarcity, and powerlessness that most of us have come to accept as normal life continue to operate, and it takes ongoing effort and consciousness to continue to sustain our liberation. This way of relating to ourselves is both a method and the goal itself. It rests on a foundation of self-acceptance, which allows us to engage with life from a position of self-trust and responsibility, while ensuring that we attend to our own basic needs and hold all of our intentions in balance with each other.

Openness to Myself

1. **Openness to Myself:** *Even when I act in ways I really don't like, I want to keep my heart open to myself. If I find myself in self-judgment, I want to seek support to reconnect with myself and hold with compassion the needs that motivate my actions.*

In a way this commitment could be viewed as the foundation on which the practice of living the commitments stands and a counterpoint to most of the others. Without a solid grounding in being open to ourselves regardless of our actions, the paradoxical relationship with the commitments is likely to collapse, and in its stead we are prone to "should" motivation. Why would that be? And why would it be an issue to motivate ourselves through "should" thinking?

As far as I can tell, it is not humanly possible to live all of these commitments 100% of the time. For one, there are times when different commitments would point to different paths of action in the moment, or to different foci for stretching our emotional and spiritual muscles. More centrally, we are such complex, rich creatures, that the likelihood of being able to do something, *anything*, all the time, is simply too low. So, one way or another, some of the time we won't act in line with this or that commitment. What then?

Unless we explicitly cultivate this openness, unless we have easy access to self-acceptance, we can easily have major bouts of self-judgments in those moments. From what I hear from people, many, many people suffer from debilitating self-judgment and shame about who they are, how they act, what they do. Some people judge and evaluate every bit of action they take, every choice they make.

Since we need connection with others as an essential ingredient of life, we will be very motivated to "correct" our actions to make ourselves acceptable in those moments. This is where "should" thinking is likely to creep in. It is often a strategy designed to support us in closing the gap that makes us unacceptable to ourselves or to others.

As a motivation for action "should" thinking generates stress, anxiety, fear, and displeasure. The harshness of the judgments and the "should" thinking interfere with the easeful flow of energy that comes from desire, longing, love of where we want to go. When under the influence of a "should" the movement towards our goals is extremely unlikely to be fun. And without pleasure and satisfaction, we are very unlikely to stay motivated to continue to do the hard work of changing our habits of thought and action to align with a principle or a goal, no matter how wonderful they sound.

So what to do? This is why this commitment focuses on times when we don't like our actions. More and more I see that nonviolence, as a studied art, is best practiced when things are *not* working for us. It is when our needs are not met that we are called to practice love, acceptance, assumption of innocence and all the other commitments. Systemically, I long for a world and a way of living where many more people have many more needs met much more of the time. Yet I know that we cannot ever eliminate unmet needs from life. So, as a personal practice, I want to focus on how I respond in those situations.

How do I grow in my capacity for nonviolence towards myself? Especially when I don't live up to my own commitments to nonviolence, how can I truly find a way to view myself with kindness? In a way, it's about assuming my own innocence. Concentrating on the human reality of the needs that gave rise to the action I am unhappy with, I sink deeper and deeper into those needs. It takes practice over time to get to a place where I can fully uncouple the action from the need and hold the need tenderly even though so many other needs may have not been met.

Do you reach for a cookie when you are trying to be off sugar? Take the time to open and open and open again to how much you yearn for easy pleasure in your life. Grant yourself the freedom to want that instead of fighting that desire in you. Are you yelling at your children? Open yourself to the intensity of trying to navigate the challenging moments, and to how much you are wishing for flow, cooperation around tasks, or respect. In both these cases and others, the trick is to open to the need and to the human condition we live in. This is not about making the action OK. It's about moving out of assigning right and wrong value to actions altogether, even when some *other* needs are very much not met. It's about coming back to the need that's hard to own, so that you can soften towards yourself and regain a sense of full choice. I have seen, repeatedly, that once self-acceptance is regained, new options for changing the behavior appear, too.

And what about the other commitments? Exactly the same process. Let's say I am working on availability for feedback, and then I find myself being defensive and judging the person giving me the feedback. I could judge myself as weak and wavering in my commitment, or I could touch the pool of longing to be seen, understood, and appreciated for who I am. That pool lives in all of us. Accessing it, bringing tenderness, is an antidote to the shame that keeps us locked in actions we don't like without ever seeking support. Each of the commitments calls on us to seek support. How would we ever seek support without openness to ourselves?

Conditional Self-Acceptance

Very often our self-acceptance is conditional on being a very certain way. It's as if we are telling ourselves: "I will accept myself for as long as I am always impeccable in how I do my work, or for as long as I always care about other people and the effect of my actions on others," or whatever else you can insert there for yourself.

What would it mean to accept ourselves unconditionally, exactly the way we are? Imagine the freedom that can come from complete self-acceptance, without conditions, without having to be any particular way, without the pressure to be perfect. Imagine how much stronger we would become in facing whatever people say when we are not scrambling to hide the truth about ourselves. Working on accepting that which we don't like in ourselves can reduce and ultimately eliminate the exhausting endless inner war in which so many of us live. With honest self-acceptance we come more fully into our place in the human fabric, alongside everyone else who's also human, also glorious, also imperfect, also capable of making mistakes. We become less separate and, by extension, more able to accept others, too.

How do we get there? By applying the core principle that whatever we do is an attempt to meet common human needs shared by all. Even malicious intent, however painful to acknowledge, results from some basic human need. Malicious intent arises when we are so caught in a desperate struggle to meet needs that we simply don't see or experience any other way to proceed. Maybe it's an expression of wanting to assert our existence in a situation of extreme powerlessness; maybe it's an attempt to create justice (as violence expert James Gilligan demonstrates in his book on the topic); or maybe it's an attempt to have our own pain understood in full. However unconscious these motivations may be, we can all understand them in others and in ourselves. The practice of self-acceptance is about identifying and connecting with the underlying needs that lead to any of our actions we are unhappy about. Doing this practice increases our self-acceptance and, by extension, our ability to make free and conscious choices about how to act.

In practical terms, you can begin a practice of picking actions you don't like, and finding the needs that led to those actions. Notice the pull to connect with the needs that the action didn't meet, and refocus your attention on the challenge of finding, understanding, accepting, and embracing fully the needs that led to the action even when you don't like the results. This way you can build a foundation of joy and desire to move closer to the commitments, which is much easier to sustain over time.

Openness to the
Full Emotional Range

2. ***Openness to the Full Emotional Range:*** *Even when my feelings are uncomfortable for me, I want to stay present with myself and keep my heart open to the fullness of my emotional experience. If I find myself contracting away from my experience, numb or shut down, I want to seek support to release defendedness and open to what is.*

This commitment speaks to the essence of what I mean by psychic liberation, the process of liberating ourselves from the legacy of whatever we have inherited from our families and societies. I have already written at length about how I see the willingness to feel our emotions, especially the uncomfortable ones, as a key to freedom.

As such, this commitment is both a goal and a process and practice to get to other goals. I know I want the experience of being fully open to emotions just for its own sake, because I feel more alive, more fully myself, when I allow my emotional experience. I also know that opening to my emotions, overcoming any blocks to my experience, opens me up and makes me more able to reach for whatever other goal I want, because it's more often than not an unwillingness to feel certain things that prevents me from living fully as I want.

No matter where we are on our emotional journey, this remains a demanding practice, an ongoing process of continuing to reach for full openness. Key to our success is knowing how to stretch our limits without overextending ourselves to a degree that will become useless. Especially with regard to emotional experiences, if we overstretch we can reach a state in which our organism cannot function at all. How do we find a way to stretch beyond our comfort zone without getting into the alarm zone?

I also want to distinguish between the overall process of reclaiming ourselves, which I envision as an intensive period of inner work (which I described in detail in Section 4, "Going against the Grain"), and the ongoing practice of refining our relationship with our emotional life as we continue to embrace the other commitments. As we expand our sense of self, as we move closer to forms of functioning that are new and challenging, more emotions may arise.

For myself, I continue to watch myself. I study my emotions, examine and explore what I do and how I respond to different situations and settings. You can do the same. Consider which emotions are easy for you to be open to? Which ones do you get so immersed in that you lose choice? Which ones do you resist and move away from? Openness to the full range implies achieving a degree of relaxation about our internal state that allows us complete choice with regard to our actions, reaching for freedom despite and through whatever fear of emotions we may still carry.

Risking My Significance

3. ***Risking my Significance:*** *Even when I am full of doubt, I want to offer myself in full to the world. If I find myself thinking that I am not important or that my actions are of no significance, I want to seek support to come back to my knowledge that my presence and my gifts matter.*

This commitment is one of several that directly invite us to take different action, beyond the inner work alone. It calls on us to change the foundation of how we relate to others. Imagine a world in which everyone risks their significance. Truly, try to imagine this. What would it look like when we don't hold back, en masse?

This commitment was inspired by a poem, "Wide Open," by Dawna Markova[67] that captures deeply for me the way I am choosing to live and invite others to live. I often read this poem at the beginning of the residential retreats/trainings that I lead:

> I will not die an unlived life.
> I will not live in fear
> of falling or catching fire.
> I choose to inhabit my days,
> to allow my living to open me,
> to make me less afraid,
> more accessible,
> to loosen my heart
> until it becomes a wing,
> a torch, a promise.
> I choose to risk my significance;
> to live so that which came to me as seed
> goes to the next as blossom
> and that which came to me as blossom,
> goes on as fruit.

For so many of us, I imagine the world over, growing up includes being told repeatedly that ultimately we don't matter. Bootstrapping ourselves into an implicit trust in our mattering is likely a lifelong

---

[67] "Wide Open" by Dawna Markova, Ph.D., www.PTPinc.org

stretch. This is the invitation. I remember at the end of one retreats one of the assistant trainers took on a practice of asking himself, as often as he could remember, what he would do in each moment if he trusted that he mattered. Take a moment now to reflect on it. Think of all the moments, large and small, in which you hold back on offering yourself, your beauty and your pain, your gifts and your challenges, with complete abandon. Can you imagine what it would be like to change that habit, to throw yourself into the world in your fullness? This is not about generosity. This is about letting go of some bottom that's holding you in place, safe and alone.

Being significant, mattering, means that your presence matters, your actions matter, your gifts matter (and, yes, you have them), and your human experience matters. Here are some examples to ponder.

Have you ever been part of a group and suddenly noticed that someone had left the group without telling anyone? Or someone said they would come to an event and they don't show up? When that happens to me, there's a slight unease in me. There's something missing, the group is not quite the same without that person. And there's also the small wondering about how the person is, why they left or didn't come in the first place. This is the essential bare mattering. So many of us habitually forget that this applies to us, too. That if we don't show up, or leave early, it makes a difference. Or we imagine the group as being an entity out there that we either join or leave, without truly grasping that our participation changes the group.

I have a deep sense that this habit is related in some ways to the level of harm and violence in our world. Were we to know in every moment how much we matter, and specifically how much our actions and choices affect others, we would be less likely to strike out, harm ourselves or harm others. We would know we are part of the sacredness of life, and honor our place in that.

Risking my significance also means being willing to make a fool of myself – for trusting, for sharing my gifts and bounties, for thinking I can contribute. So many of us, so often, were ridiculed and laughed at, that some of us find it unbearable to offer ourselves unless we know beyond any shred of doubt that what we have to offer is meaningful and will be well received. Waiting for this level of assurance involves no risk. The risk in "risking my significance" is precisely in the possibility that it will not be received. I so long to be joined in this willingness to jump without knowing if I will be caught.

Might you be willing to stretch in this direction? To trust your wisdom, your beauty, your knowledge, your unexplained intuition, your hesitant ideas? In these times waiting may be too much of a luxury.

There's more. It's not just my gifts and ideas, it is also my joy and pain that matter, that I want to risk the significance of. Not only inside me, not just by being open to experiencing them. Stretching to cultivate the trust that someone will care enough to know, to be with me when I express myself. Look at the child who runs to the adult to show the leaf or shell she found. There is complete and total abandon in that, no self-consciousness, no fear – until she is reprimanded again and again and told to curb her exuberance. Can you increase your capacity to celebrate with others? What you find, what you think, the delight you experience, all of it?

Life is not complete without the pain and suffering that arrive at our door. Aside from the internal stretching of being open to the pain instead of waiting for it to be over or running away from it, this commitment is about the external stretching entailed in bringing your pain to others, reaching for the trust that they care, that they could understand, that your suffering matters. Even after again and again not being received in the way you most want. Reaching for it just because you and they matter, just because you, like all of us, are part of the human fabric that holds us all together and that we recreate with our actions.

Responsibility

4. ***Responsibility:*** *Even when overwhelmed with obstacles or difficult emotions, I want to take full responsibility for my feelings, my actions, and my life. If I find myself giving my power away to other people, larger forces, or analytic categories such as my past or any labels I put on myself, I want to seek support to find the core source of choice within me to live as I want and ask for what I want.*

My sister Inbal first opened my eyes to the radical possibility of taking complete responsibility for having the life I want. This capacity to take full responsibility is foundational to our ability to maintain a sense of power in our life. It's about exercising full choice, which, for me, has always been what gives dignity to being human. It is the opposite of being an object of other forces.

Reclaiming Choice

For some years now I have been watching and examining all the ways in which I and others can and do give away our power in the way that we think about our life and in the way that we talk about our experience. Here are some of the ways that we tend to do that:

Feelings

Anyone who begins the study of Nonviolent Communication (NVC) usually encounters early on the idea that neither other people nor forces beyond our control cause our feelings. I have never met anyone who didn't agree with this idea *in principle*. Despite this conceptual clarity, *in practice* many people find it challenging to integrate, especially when they are emotionally charged. Most people find it relatively easy to graduate from saying, "You made me angry." The subtler forms of giving our power away take more conscious effort to integrate. "I am angry because you didn't come home when you said you would," for example, seems so logical and simple, that it takes intentionality to see that this statement makes the other person responsible for the anger. Even "Your coming home later than you said you would didn't meet my need for respect" still leaves the power in the other person's hands. Ultimately, the words cannot get us there. If we want the full, uncompromising responsibility, sooner or later we will be called to *experience* that feeling angry is a choice we are making, however unconsciously we may be doing so, because of the meaning we assign to the other person's actions, not because of the actions themselves.

Taking this responsibility invites us to liberate ourselves from a kind of helplessness, and embrace a freedom that comes from the responsibility itself: if we are responsible, then we have the power to create change in our experience, and are no longer dependent on anything the other person will do.

Actions

Our common language is replete with ways of denying our responsibility for our actions and the choices we make: "I couldn't help it;" "That's the norm;" "Everyone would do the same;" "So and so told me to do it;" "I had to do it;" "I'm not good at making choices;" and so on and so forth. Do you have a favorite one that you often use in this way?

Embracing responsibility for our actions invites us to examine the needs underlying all our choices. Even when we are not aware in the moment of making the choice, we can recover the needs later, when we reflect on the action. Here, again, we can look at this practice as going through layers. Even when we can recover the needs, bringing our attention back to our choice takes a different kind of effort. For example, one of the journals that Inbal and I developed guides people through disentangling an "I do this because I have to" message. The journal invites us to focus on all the needs: those we are trying to meet by making the choice; those that are not met; and those that are met. At the end, after making full emotional contact with all the needs, we are invited to consider our choice and re-make it. Given all the needs, do we want to continue to make the choice with more ownership, or do we want to look for other ways to meet the needs? In my unscientific experimentation, I have rarely found people who made the choice to find other ways of meeting needs than the behavior they had been telling themselves they have to do. More often, people find themselves continuing to make the same choice, with a shift in their inner experience of it. They are connected with the consequences of not engaging in the behavior, and clearly prefer the other option. While understandable, I have a niggling sense that we remain compromised in terms of our actual capacity to make a choice if we always make the same choice. For myself, I am working, in those moments, to truly release the sense of impossibility that is at the heart of "I have to" and find more freedom, even when I fear the consequences.

A word of caution: I have encountered people who took the principle of choice to heart so strongly that they didn't keep in balance their capacity to accept themselves. Making a fully owned and empowered choice is a theoretical human possibility, and a long-term practice. We cannot overnight change the societal circumstances or our inner neural wiring. Both of these will constrain our felt ability to make choices even if our theoretical clarity about owning the choices is there. Here are some examples. The level of courage necessary to take on the potential circumstances of making public statements about harmful practices is one that only a handful of people can truly step into, even though many more people experience the strain on their sense of integrity and a desire to do something about it. While people can, in principle, emerge from extreme poverty and become active agents in their lives enough to change the external circumstances they face, only a few have enough inner resources to do so. Lastly, so many people have a deep desire to overcome trauma and be able to respond to each moment from within the present, and still in the moment of a flashback, choice remains purely academic for most. Embracing this practice requires a great deal of gentleness towards ourselves, especially if we have any history of trauma.

Life

The deepest layer of exploration for embracing responsibility has to do with what our life looks like. All too often we give our power over to circumstances, our stories about life, and our stories about ourselves.

There's nothing like a personal example. One of the core stories that still runs me (meaning I still believe it even as I call it a story!) is that people don't care enough. Time and again I have found myself believing, that in the face of differences with others in terms of preferred strategies, or a disagreement about matters of significance, there is nothing I can do to have an effect. The other person won't care enough or be open enough to shift. And so, despite how powerful I generally appear (to others and even to myself), I crumble and forget to imagine that dialogue is possible. Often! Helplessness takes over, and I either collapse and give in, or I become unpleasantly entrenched and desperate without finding a way to connect and recognize the possibility of shifting.

Things started shifting when I adopted, for a while, a practice of engaging directly with my power. In the morning, as I woke up, I reviewed my day to see where I might anticipate challenges, and imagined how I could respond to them from an empowered place inside me. The results were astonishing. It didn't even take a long time to see them. I started finding ways of showing up in times of great intensity and conflict without collapsing. So much so, that my long-standing stories were challenged and started shifting, bit by bit. I found more ease in connecting, and had a few mini-breakthroughs even in long-standing conflicts. None of this is about becoming a different person (at least not quite yet). Instead, it's about finding a way to work with the person that I am and prepare for difficulties. The practice, when I remember it, is amazingly simple. It only consists of focusing – ahead of time or in the moment – on what I want in a given situation, and what I can do to create it. The progress is slow and incremental, and there's nothing linear about it. I have "lapsed" for months on end, and have, on occasion, appeared to myself to have lost it altogether. Not so. I pick it up, I pick me up, and I keep walking towards full responsibility for having the life I want.

What to Do?

Giving our power away to other forces or people, like all strategies, is an attempt to meet needs. What could those be? Perhaps there is something soothing, some sense of ease, not having to do anything, if in any event we are powerless to do so. Perhaps there is a sense of belonging through the shared experience of powerlessness. Perhaps some other needs are at the core of what keeps you from taking full responsibility.

Whatever these needs are, making the decision to take responsibility can be quite liberating. We no longer wait for anything or anyone to change before life starts for real. We no longer nurse resentments with the hope of one day being heard. The alternative is simple and obviously challenging.

The alternative is to keep translating the thoughts and reactions we have about our feelings, our actions, and our lives. Taking each one of them and bringing our focus, heart, attention, and mind back to our needs. What is it that's really going on? What is it that's most important to us? What is it that we really want? What are the needs underneath the strategies and thoughts?

Last but not least, taking responsibility invites us to make plenty of requests. Some of those will be of ourselves – different ways of responding to stimuli, or different choices we might want to make in certain circumstances. Some of the requests will, by necessity, be of other people. Making all the requests we need to make so our lives can be what we want them to be is, yet again, an aspect of risking our significance. And the dance of the commitments continues.

Resentment Is Not Inevitable

I want to illustrate the power of responsibility with another part of my friend Fred's story (see pages 159-61 for the first part). I was talking with him about why he harbored so much resentment towards his partner and their 13-year-old child. The resentment was so strong, that he sometimes reacted with intense anger to relatively minor snappy expressions. He wanted to free himself from the grip of unconsciously chosen anger, so he could choose how to respond.

Invisible Contracts

As we talked, Fred recognized that it's highly unlikely that he can transcend his reactivity in the moment. It's almost always too late. The moment of true power is earlier, when he makes his own choices about what he will or will not do.

Fred suffers from a common affliction I like to call being "overly nice." Simply put, Fred tends to stretch towards his partner and his child, or say "yes" to what they ask of him. That "yes" often comes with an expectation, usually unconscious, that they will appreciate him later. Then, when they don't show appreciation, he can easily experience it as a breach of an invisible contract they don't even know they signed! No wonder he gets so angry.

Complete Ownership of Our Choices

The first practice Fred decided to adopt was simple: before he says
"yes" he will check to see if he is genuinely able to do so without
expecting anything later. Fred was shocked to discover how often he
would then have to say "no." I then offered him a middle strategy as
well. If he couldn't release his expectation, maybe he could be honest
about it. He could say something like: "I'm willing to do it. I am so
sad to say that I don't have the capacity inside to do it without
building resentment. Would you like me to do it given how much of
a stretch it is for me?"

Asking for What We Want

Fred was excited about how much freedom he could get just from
learning to identify and honor his limits. For greater freedom, he
decided to become equally honest and exacting with himself about
what he wanted from his family and to take explicit action to make it
happen. His continuous willingness to stretch had been hidden from
his family, making it so much easier for them to take his "yes" for
granted. When we talked he decided to be transparent about
stretching so he could be seen.

He also took on letting his family know how much he wanted
appreciation, and to ask them to express appreciation whenever they
noticed it. Working his way towards expressing his need, Fred had
further insight that self-respect is about how he treats himself, and
has very little to do with how others treat him. This allowed him to
glimpse the possibility of expressing to his partner, in full, the pain he
sometimes experiences in their interactions, rather than masking his
vulnerability with anger.

Moving towards Freedom

I talked with Fred again the next day. He told me that 24 hours after
applying his practice he already experienced much more freedom
than before. He said "no" to his child on a number of occasions. He
noticed how much harder it was to say "no" to his partner. Even
without changing all his habits, he experienced growing clarity, self-
honesty, and choice, and reduced resentment.

A year later the shifts in his family life became so profound that
he and his partner were able to make, together, some core decisions

about the nature of their relationship that they had previously been unable to visit for years. This is truly a story with a happy ending.

I like to believe that many of us can increase our sense of power in life if we become more honest about saying "no" when anything less than unattached generosity is motivating our choice, and if we grow in our capacity to ask for what we want.

Self-Care

5. **Self-Care:** *Even when I am stressed, overwhelmed, or in disconnection, I want to maintain my commitments to my well-being, and take actions that nourish my life. If I find myself letting go of strategies that I know contribute to my life (such as exercise, eating as I want, receiving support and empathy as needed, enjoyable activities, or anything else that I know works for me), I want to seek support to ground myself in the preciousness of my own life and my desire to nurture myself.*

Some of the commitments about which I am writing have been part of my practice for some years, and I have a sense of having integrated them deeply into my daily living. This one has been a focus without as much success: my own capacity to provide sufficient self-care is still below what I would like it to be. Perhaps the most self-caring way of approaching it is to tell the truth about where it is for me. Maybe this can be a way of inspiring openness and willingness to look at where we each struggle.

When I started writing this piece some months ago, what was most vivid for me was living the paradox of the endless choices about prioritizing attending to something of significance to me (in this case writing this) vs. attending to self-care. And if you think to yourself something like, "Oh, good, she chose self-care," I wish that were true. It's not. I had actually made the decision to do this instead of doing self-care (the absurdity of *writing* about self-care taking precedence over *doing* self-care is hilarious to me in this moment, and of course sad).

I have been working with an image that I find helpful in appreciating the significance of self-care even more. I was thinking about how, if I were a chef, I would be very committed to keeping my knives very sharp, shiny, well oiled. I could picture myself as chef taking time to check my knives frequently, knowing full well how critical they are to the success of my work. For the work that I do, for the life that I lead, the instrument is myself, my own being, body and soul. If I don't maintain myself well, I will become dull, and less able to offer my gifts to the world. The same would be true for anyone whose instrument of work is themselves, which would include therapists, teachers, and many others.

I am of two minds about this image now that I am writing about it, because there is an implication there that the main or only reason for self-care is because of the potential contribution I could make. I want to be able to access self-care purely because I am a precious being and I am alive. Not for some purpose, and not because of any reason other than that every living being, especially humans, needs care. Look at a cat, for example. They can sit for long, long periods of time licking and grooming themselves. I want to learn to do that, too. Like cats, not all of us struggle with self-care! I have even heard a few people wonder if there is such a thing as "too much" self-care.

Recognizing that I have been putting conscious effort and attention into creating self-care for several years now and am still not where I want to be, I know there is something I haven't fully enough connected with to be able to create the shift I want. I have an understanding of some of the pieces, and that also helps me with supporting other people, even as I am still struggling. So I want to share what I have learned so far from working with myself and with others. Not all the obstacles below are ones I have. Which are relevant to you?

Challenge about Holding our Bodies Sacred

Since so much of self-care connects with the body, in order to prioritize self-care we need to have enough of a sense of valuing our bodies to prioritize self-care. Alas, our culture does not train us to hold our bodies with care. Between the body image myths that circulate in the culture and the Western predilection for seeing the body as a lowly aspect of life only to serve the mind, making our bodies central to our lives is elusive for many of us.

What would it take for us to learn to love our bodies?

Self-care always Seeming Less Important than Something Else

This aspect is similar to the previous one, and different. Even if we have a solid relationship with our bodies it's easy, especially for those of us who care about the world, partners, bosses, employees, children or anything else, to give higher priority to anything else. If we imagine that making our bodies central to our lives means having to let go of something else, it's less like to take priority.

What would it take for us to fully connect with how vital self-care could be for us?

Activities of Self-care Not Appearing to have Intrinsic Meaning

Eating well, getting adequate sleep (especially going to bed early), doing exercise and other self-care activities are often done as a means to an end. Many of us find it difficult to *enjoy* eating healthy food (hence the continual joking in the culture that if it's good for you it can't possibly be tasty); to *look forward to* exercise, etc. Making our bodies central to our lives would be far easier if you could find ways of creating meaning and pleasure around self-care activities. For example, I have walking partners for most days of the week, and that keeps me going because I love the company of my friends (and have made a couple of friends in this way).

What would it take for us to make it a priority to look at what happens to us in this area and learn to enjoy caring for ourselves?

Hard to Prioritize Anything that's not Externally Accountable

Because our lives, for so many of us, are so, so full, so beyond capacity (which brings in the balance commitment), with so many stimulations, commitments, appointments, people, and activities, our schedules can get very booked up. We are more likely to keep our commitments to others because they show up in the calendar, and because someone will likely be upset if we don't show up. Our "appointment" with ourselves is usually not scheduled, and even if scheduled, there isn't anyone external to us who will get upset, or even know if we cancel. This makes the only strength of our self-care our own internal resolve, which is hard to cultivate in a culture that promotes punishment and reward. There is simply no "incentive."

What would it take for us to cultivate the capacity for intrinsic motivation for making choices and priorities in our lives, especially in caring for ourselves?

Scarcity 101

Because I know there are probably other reasons, I wanted to name the basic issue I see here, which is how we make choices when our consciousness is so shaped by ideas of scarcity. I know that in this area I am still completely in the throes of scarcity. I don't see a way for me to contribute as much as I want, have a life that's as full as I want, and care for myself as much as I want. In that kind of context, for many of us, the choice will be elsewhere if we haven't worked our way out of any of the specific above challenges.

What would it take for us to transform our conscious or unconscious beliefs about scarcity, connect with our deepest needs, and provide as much care for ourselves as is necessary for a wholesome life?

Concluding Thoughts

One of the trickiest aspects of self-care is that the habitual motivations we use for taking action – that we "should" do it because it's "good" for us – are particularly challenging and painful with regards to this commitment. Why do we even have it, then? My conjecture is that having a should about self-care is likely rooted in not having sufficient trust in ourselves, dating back to when adults around us didn't trust us. We emerge from childhood not believing that if we are left to our own devices we will take sufficient care of ourselves (or do anything else, for that matter).

Because of all of the above, I have come to see the capacity to prioritize self-care as a tremendous act of modeling the life possible for humans. When we truly practice self-care – exercising when there is much to do, eating well when everyone else eats dessert, going to bed early enough to get a full night's sleep when we have deadlines – we model to our families and friends that living well is possible. When we are part of communities of transformation, our self-care models and reminds people that the future can start now, that we can be a community that shows what is possible and lives it, now.

Balance

6. **Balance:** *Even when I am drawn to overstretching myself (including towards any of these commitments), I want to remain attentive to the limits of my capacity in any given moment. If I find myself pushing myself, I want to seek support to honor the natural wisdom of my organism and to trust that remaining within my current limits will support me in increasing my capacity over time.*

I see this commitment as key to making the entire project of living the commitments work. I have heard from several people that in some moments they experience tension between the different commitments. How does it all fit together? What do we do when we have different pulls from different commitments?

Here are a couple of examples. Let's say someone is expressing to me their unhappiness about my actions. How do I use the commitments to support me? Which one do I focus on? I can stretch into "Availability for Feedback" and attempt to hear the feedback in what the person is saying. I can lean on "Empathic Presence" and open my heart to be with the person's experience about me, independently of this being about me at all. I can recognize in myself a pattern of stretching to meet people beyond my capacity, and focus on "Self-Care." Each of these choices prioritizes one commitment and not others. In some ways they can even appear to be in actual conflict. How can we meet these kinds of challenges? What can we do to use the commitments with intentionality in such moments? Is there a way to harmonize and cohere the commitments into a clear whole?

Beyond the use of the commitments, the larger question of how to balance life has become pivotal for many people, especially in large urban centers, where the level of stimulation far exceeds anyone's ability to navigate life with full mindfulness. I often have the experience of my life as a blanket that's a bit too short. I pull it up to cover my shoulders and it exposes my ankles. Increase exercise, and there's more stress about getting to everything that arrives at my "door" (usually in the form of an email). Choose to limit my intake of new email, and there are relationships to attend to with people who are not happy with my new choice. Attend to those relationships and writing slips away. Focus more on writing, and the hour gets later when I get to bed, which makes it then harder to get up early enough to do exercise.

A number of years ago I had a pivotal moment that put some of this into context. I was lying on an exercise cylinder to stretch my back. I liked that form of exercise, because it combined caring for my body with being in one position for many minutes, which allowed for conscious self-connection. That morning I was reflecting on the impossible question of the balance between attending to my plans for the day and being available to life as it unfolds. I was in quite a bit of agony; it seemed completely untenable. My arms were stretched out for the exercise, and I experienced each of the two directions as a weight on one of my hands, pulling me down, heavy. A little later I had a breakthrough in my experience that I wish to remember more often. I could feel how in each moment I could only do one or the other, and that it was only for that moment. In the next moment I could switch. If I truly made myself completely attentive to the truth inside me, and chose again and again, there would be no conflict. I didn't have to come up with some kind of a general or abstract or permanent solution. The imaginary weights on both my hands dissolved into the endlessness of the present moment.

I don't mean to romanticize this experience to mean that I or anyone else can do it all. I, and all of us, are finite creatures. The picture of infinite growth that has come to dominate the culture through the economic models we live in creates confusion inside us and global destruction around us. I want to learn to honor my inner limits and finitude just as much as I am attentive to the limits of our one and precious planet.

As a partial digression, my thoughts are jumping to the significance of feedback loops, and how much control – of nature, of our inner responses, of symptoms, of people, or anything else – blocks the flow of feedback loops. Collectively we have created a world in which understanding and honoring limits becomes ever more elusive, and certainly not seen as a profoundly essential part of living. This provides some relief inside me, an understanding that even the act of becoming aware of limits is culturally subversive.

I see a rich paradox here. Within the imperative of infinite growth we have a prevalent experience of scarcity. When we honor limits and finitude, as so many cultures have done and few continue to do, the experience of trust in sufficiency seems to increase.

Looping back, I see that honoring limits, trusting sufficiency, and mindfulness in the moment are some of the keys to creating balance. In each moment I can only do exactly one thing. Even when multitasking we don't actually do two things at the same time. In each split-second our minds are attentive to only one thing. The price of multitasking is reduced mindfulness for each of the things we do.

With regards to the commitments, specifically, the act of balancing invites many choices. If I know that I tend to overstretch myself in one direction, I try to increase balance by stretching less, and opening to another option. This requires self-knowing. Over the years I have cultivated access to vulnerable self-expression, and I often wonder about shifting focus and making empathic presence a primary focus for cultivating myself. I have a tendency towards rising to challenges of responsibility, and so now I am working on letting go of responsibility and allowing things not to happen rather than do them if no one else will.

I want to close with the image I got from a friend and colleague when we discussed balance. She had been practicing handstands for many years, and what I got from her description is about how balance is forever dynamic. You lean for too long into one hand and you will fall. You attend fully to noticing the subtleties and shift your weight from one to the other all the time, and you will stay upright even in a precarious environment. Nothing is any one way once and for all.

Orienting towards Others

The love that nonviolence expresses is very specific and uncompromising. Inhabiting this kind of love requires us to open our hearts far wider than most of us have been trained to do, no matter what happens outside or inside of us. That openness of our hearts allows us to see the humanity of everyone, to offer our presence, and to offer everything else we have without reservation. This way of orienting our energy straddles the distinction between self and other because engaging in such openhearted living affects our own inner peace and freedom in addition to affecting how we show up in the world.

Loving No Matter What

7. **Loving No Matter What:** *Even when my needs are seriously unmet, I want to keep my heart open. If I find myself generating judgments, angry, or otherwise triggered, I want to seek support in transforming my judgments and meeting others with love.*

The year was 1991. I was having a fight with a friend during and after a back-packing trip. We were lying on my bed, facing each other, talking, and trying to get to the bottom of what was going on. We weren't getting very far, though we were getting friendlier than before. Then my friend expressed an entirely new piece I hadn't heard before: she was upset with me for not protecting myself at all. It drove her crazy, she said, that all through the trip I continued to reach out to her, extended my love and friendship, and tried to connect. I was distraught, to the core. I started crying; I just couldn't contain my helplessness. I couldn't fathom how someone could be upset with me for loving, for reaching out. In my agony I cried out that I didn't *want* to learn to protect myself. I knew even then, before discovering Nonviolent Communication, that I didn't want to learn to protect myself. And right there, in the midst of crying, I suddenly sat up, agitated and excited. I understood, intuitively, from the inside out, from within the despair, what Jesus was trying to do: he was trying to love no matter what. I felt an enormous sense of kinship with him. Not because I was anywhere near where I sensed he got to. That didn't matter. I was on the same path, and I was not the only one. In that moment, without knowing hardly anything about him, I found peace and inspiration in this way of understanding his life.

The Revolutionary Defiance of Turning the Left Cheek

My second interface with Jesus came years later, when I read Walter Wink's *The Powers That Be* in 2004. Page by page Jesus was being transformed back into what I believe he was: a revolutionary Jew claiming the power of love to transform the world he lived in, and willing to risk everything for truth. I understood the courageous wisdom provided in the Sermon on the Mount, where turning the other cheek thrusts one's full dignity on an anonymous oppressor who would aim to demean by a common practice in Roman times:

delivering a back-handed slap on the right cheek. If you want to hit me, says the man who turns the left cheek, hit me as an equal. There is no way I can do justice to the depth of analytic wisdom and historical scholarship that Wink calls upon to bring to light the message of full empowerment that had been masked as passivity for centuries.

Love and the Consciousness of Nonviolence

The commitment to love no matter what was the very first one that I identified as key to the consciousness of nonviolence. It's been the cornerstone of my own attempts for years and years, both inviting me into the biggest possible vista of human transcendence, and keeping me humble about how far I am from the true capacity for loving in this way. I have no illusion that I have this capacity; I know when I stop loving. I also have no desire to remain trapped in my limitations. My soul knows about loving no matter what, and pulls me forward closer and closer.

I still sometimes think that this commitment by itself can serve as the entire foundation for the consciousness we are seeking. Each of the commitments is either a specific expression of love, or requires this kind of love in order to make it possible, or is a path towards finding the way to open up to love.

This is also, in some ways, the most uncompromising of the commitments: "no matter what" is a tall order. In that way love is intimately linked with courage. That was how I first understood what Jesus was doing in the world. No consequence was going to be too much to risk for keeping his heart open and loving. No pain too much of an obstacle. No action beyond the pale. What a magnificent vision, whether or not he himself, or any other human, was ever able to fully live it.

I find it totally unsurprising, in this context, that both Gandhi and Martin Luther King, Jr. made love a central aspect and core insistence in their practice and writing. Love and courage inextricably form the foundation of nonviolence. This is part of why overcoming fear is such a core aspect of the practice. Engaging with fear on the emotional level supports the possibility of opening our heart even when we are in pain or triggered. The ongoing practice of unprotecting ourselves, combined with increasing our capacity to be relaxed in the face of intense emotions, allows us, in the most literal sense, to relax the physiological contraction that prevents us from opening our hearts. In addition, when we become familiar with and comfortable in the presence of fear, we also develop more spaciousness within which we can make choices and take actions despite the fear.

Aspects of Love

I was well into my adulthood before I could ever name an experience I had as love. This was so painful to me that I dedicated a lot of thought and care to understanding what love was so I could have some hope that I could claim at least some aspects of love as my own.

Commitment: This one has always been the easiest aspect of love for me. Because I have always had a strong capacity to motivate myself to action based on will (not in all areas), this one was clear and simple. I can act from a sense of integrity, from knowledge that I care about someone even when my heart is closed, or from knowing what I want for the long term, and I can keep prioritizing connection, dialogue, and generosity even in very difficult times.

Care: It's only in very extreme situations that I lose my capacity to care. Even in the midst of conflict with someone, even when I have experienced harm in the hands of someone, I continue to care. In this context what I mean by care is the very simple interest in the other person's well-being.

Enjoyment: This is the aspect of love that is about taking pleasure in who the other person is. As I am writing this, I see that the challenge, as always, is how we can love people we don't enjoy. How can we truly open to and behold the radical humanity of another, the awesome wonder of another's existence, even when we are irritated, impatient, or upset with their choices, or when we have an aversion to their smell or choice of clothes?

Entrustment of Vulnerability: This is the hardest aspect of love for me. So much so, that for years I was referring only to this as love. It was only when I started recognizing other forms and aspects of love that I started seeing myself as loving. This, for me, is where courage is most needed in the act of loving, whether physically, by showing my soft belly in the hopes that the other person would be moved to see me as human and therefore less likely to harm me, or emotionally, by choosing to share my unprotected self with another and trust their heart's response to me.

Love and World Transformation

BayNVC, the organization I co-founded, has as its vision a world where everyone's needs matter and people have the skills for making peace. I often think about what it would take to get there. Like others, I am essentially clueless. We all are. Still, I have a deep intuitive sense that a certain amount of love is necessary to create the shift.

We can love fearlessly and remain soft and open enough to respond nonviolently to what we don't like. This is how we can transform the legacy of separation, scarcity, and war we have been given into a future of love, generosity, connectedness, and the possibility of human co-existence with each other and the planet that so lovingly provides for our needs.

Assumption of Innocence

8. ***Assumption of Innocence:*** *Even when others' actions or words make no sense to me or frighten me, I want to assume a need-based human intention behind them. If I find myself attributing ulterior motives or analyzing others' actions from the outside, I want to seek support to ground myself in the clarity that every human action is an attempt to meet needs no different from my own.*

Although an assumption of innocence is theoretically built into the law in most places on the planet, I see so, so many of us habituated to taking things personally, assuming negative intent, or not trusting others' motives. Even when we have taken the path of reclaiming our inner life, working to recover our full sense of self, and cultivating psychic liberation, this particular aspect of the consciousness takes ongoing work to integrate. It's relatively easy to gauge progress on this path simply by watching the persistence of judgments of others when not liking their actions, choices, and expressions.

Assuming innocence is a pretty exacting path which follows from and elaborates the core premise that all human action is an attempt to meet needs.

The assumption of innocence is not to be confused with condoning behavior that's not acceptable to us. I see no contradiction between the assumption of innocence and a clear attempt to intervene in any way possible to stop behavior that we consider harmful. Seeing that someone's action is an expression of needs not different from our own supports non-separation, and helps us keep our hearts open so we can see the humanity of the person whose action we consider harmful. If we believe, however unconsciously, that heart openness means letting everything happen, that belief will likely make it harder to open our hearts, and will continue to pull us towards condemning, judging, and separating. Recognizing the humanity of another would not stop us from acting to stop them. It only creates a foundation for the possibility of acting with love when we step in.

Assuming innocence is also completely consistent with imagining an intention to harm. Specifically, assuming innocence allows us the possibility of recognizing an intention to harm without having to create inner distance. Recognizing an intention to harm makes it possible to see through it so we can open to and understand the underlying experience and needs that would lead someone to want to harm. This has, at times, been especially challenging for me, because I have never acted with an intention to harm, nor have I entertained fantasies of harming. I have come close only twice in my life. For years I used this as a source of nourishing separation in me, seeing myself as completely different, almost a different species. In the last number of years, as I work to transform separation in me, I have shifted towards looking for any shred of intention to harm in me as an opportunity to try to understand others and experience more continuity.

Lastly, assuming innocence doesn't require us to believe that people always will know or recognize their need. It only requires us to be able to imagine fully what the need might be, so that we can see the experience from within instead of from the outside.

On the other hand, assuming innocence, that radical practice of compassion, is different from being able to analyze someone's behavior either in terms of history or in terms of psychological motives. Saying to ourselves something like, "She is only doing this because so much harm was done to her," or, "He is too afraid and can't face intimacy," is only one step towards compassion. The full embrace of the assumption of innocence requires us to imagine ourselves into the experience of another, to really grasp and appreciate from within how a human could make the choice we find so hard to comprehend. Imagination and radical compassion are the two supporters for this commitment. For myself, I leave no stone unturned until I can have a 3-dimensional understanding of another's action. I do not stop at analysis. For example, if I conclude that someone is acting based on shame, which is James Gilligan's primary understanding of what leads people to acts of violence (see his book *Violence: Our Deadly Epidemic and Its Causes*), I continue to seek the need. Gilligan's theory is that violence is an attempt to right a wrong and create justice, however ill-conceived and fantastic the connection may be. I add to it my conviction that the search for dignity is fundamental and core to human beings, and that experiencing such profound levels of shame means that the intensity of the need for dignity can override other needs and lead to extreme actions.

Most of the time when we are challenged around the assumption of innocence the specific situations are not so extreme. Even in our daily life so many of us are challenged to assume innocence when we are upset about others' actions, sometimes especially in relation to people near and dear to us. In attempting to excavate the humanity through finding the needs and experiencing the other from within, my inner experience is one of holding myself very tightly to a deeply exacting practice of not giving in to any convenience that could come from writing off the person or the action. As soon as I get lulled into such a path, I bring myself back to the fundamental "no" in me about concluding the inhumanity of another. And then I bring my awareness and attention back to my search, unwilling to give up on anyone for any reason. To loop back, this doesn't mean I would necessarily choose to engage with, befriend or support the other person. It only means that I will not give up on their humanity and the possibility (at least in principle) of redemption and healing.

Empathic Presence

9. **Empathic Presence:** *Even when others are in pain, disconnected from themselves, expressing intensity, or in judgment, I want to maintain a relaxed presence with their experience. If I find myself attempting to fix, offering advice, doing mechanical empathy, or turning my attention elsewhere, I want to seek support to regain my faith in the transformative power and the gift of just being with another.*

Although most people I have encountered appreciate being heard, far fewer are able to provide this experience for another. Even though more and more research is coming out suggesting that we are hard-wired for empathic understanding (the latest I saw described seven-month-old babies showing clear signs of understanding others' experience!), more often than not we are habituated to *acting on* rather than *showing* our understanding. I was particularly struck with this distinction when I was in Japan, where attunement to others is perfected to a degree that left me in awe, and where action without words is far more prevalent than any verbal checking with another. I remember a moment in which I was able to see an opening of recognition when I asked people if it was ever challenging for them when others did things for them without checking if that was what they wanted. That step of verbal connection, that pause before action, appears to me to be key to increasing the gifts of empathic presence.

The challenge of presence tends to increase when we are with a person whose expression contains any form of intensity, such as distress or judgment. In addition to the lack of practice in verbalizing our empathic understanding even if we have it internally, we are less likely to focus our attention on empathic presence to begin with. What makes it harder to offer our gift of presence in those circumstances and what can we do about it?

In broad strokes, I see the effect of intensity operating in two basic directions. One is that our care for our fellow humans gets activated when we see someone clearly in distress or suffering. The other is that our care for ourselves comes into the picture in the form, for example, of wanting to make ourselves available only for that level of intensity that we trust our organism has the capacity to handle.

Usually our reactions to these two broad categories aren't very consciously chosen. Habitually, we have learned to show our care by solving the other person's problem, "making them feel better," as it's so often described. Even after years of training and practice, many people continue to err in this direction. My hunch is that, in addition to so much early training, the habit remains so strong, in part because we also have so much discomfort about display of emotions, about people being in pain, or about people expressing themselves in ways that are not aligned with our comfort or values. This kind of discomfort adds to the pressure to make a shift in the other person's experience and delays our integration of the magical power of pure empathic presence.

Another common human reaction to another's suffering is most dramatically illustrated by the book of Job. The Biblical narrator tells us that Job is an exemplary human being. All manner of calamities befall him. His friends, unable to bear witness to his agony, insist on convincing him that his suffering is caused by some unknown sin of his. In the end, Job is vindicated. There really was no reason. It just happened. Suffering does.

In Biblical times suffering was seen as God's response to sin. Today's versions call on bad choices, mental diagnoses, or negative thinking instead of a punitive God. Does explaining someone's suffering, finding some cause or reason, make it easier to bear? Does the distance provided by an explanation protect us from the pain of another's pain?

Overcoming these challenges takes practice on both levels. In terms of our care for others, we can remind ourselves in any way we know how to self-connect about what we all believe anyway: that pure presence in and of itself constitutes an extraordinarily powerful vehicle of support for anyone who is suffering. It provides relief from being alone, it provides clarity and self-connection, and it provides perspective and understanding, among other things. As Thich Nhat Hanh says, just listening already alleviates a lot of suffering.

Another reminder that can help relates more to our inner experience and focuses on what it actually means to have empathic presence. Oftentimes in the culture at large empathy is blurred with identification or sympathy, as can be seen by language about it that refers to feeling what the other feels. I believe this is part of what we are sometimes afraid of: that being with a depressed person will get us depressed, that if someone we're with is angry we will get agitated. If we can remember that empathic presence is about opening up a space of being with another rather than with our reactions to another, that can often lessen the tension and allows us to relax into the trust.

Both of these reminders can work to transform the habitual response. However, to find our way to easeful embodiment of empathic presence will also take doing some emotional work necessary to remain relaxed in the presence of intensity. This can take the form of practice and stretching of our comfort zone. We may also be called to heal whatever has happened to us to bring us to discomfort with intensity. In that way, cultivating empathic presence also becomes a vehicle for becoming more of ourselves, less fearful, and stronger.

If you want to understand more fully what I mean by "bearing witness," or simply to be inspired by what some human beings are able to do with just the gift of presence, read Greg Boyle's *Tattoos on the Heart*. Greg is unafraid to look suffering in the eye. He lets his heart be pierced, again and again and again and again, by the unimaginable hardship of life in the barrios of Los Angeles. He created an award-winning program that offers jobs and training to gang members and ex-cons. They work alongside rival gang members in the same location. I found his work inspiring beyond what I can even describe.

It's his love that got me. The unprotected presence, ready for all that's there, finding the beauty, the heart, in whoever is in front of him, the downtrodden, the rough. Even after burying many dozens of young ones. Present and loving without blinking away, without explaining, without separating. A blueprint for how we can recover hope, and faith, and a sense of community with our fellow humans. All of them. All of us.

Making Empathy Concrete

Although talk of empathy is increasing, the "how" of empathy is still missing. People are hungry for this knowledge, and yet it's so elusive. Empathy is core to what makes us human. When we bring together our mind, heart, body, and imagination, when we can focus all our attention and become a witness to another's humanity, we enter the empathic space, and in some small measure life changes. How can we cultivate this capacity?

If, like me, words and thoughts are your primary entryway into another person's experience, reach beyond intellectual understanding for the human warmth we all wish for when we want to be heard. Let yourself feel and experience and resonate with the other's experience, and allow that feeling inside you to affect your tone of voice, bring softness to your being, and convey your care and humanity to the person speaking.

If your primary access is a felt sense of resonance, an experience of being at one with another person, complement it with putting your heart and mind on the other person. Empathic presence is about being with the other person's experience, so that they can have the benefit of your presence instead of your emotional identification with their experience. While we are habituated, in times of distress or loss, to experience another person's identification with us as being empathic, often enough it's because we don't even know what it's like to have someone's fully relaxed presence, complete focus dedicated to being with us. If you want someone to have that magical experience, keep your attention on them, make room for them to be in their experience without bringing yours in and while keeping your heart wide open to them. Imagine what it's like for them. Put words to what you discover, and share with the other person. Without your words, how would they *know* you understood?

If you can imagine easily, maintain your focus by thinking about the other person and staying clearly with the essence instead of the details of the storyline. Follow the thread of meaning of the person speaking instead of your curiosity. Bring your mind to bear on this focus, listen carefully to the words. Which ones have the most emotional charge? Those usually hold clues to what's going on for the person speaking. Is the person expressing judgments, frustrations with what is not happening, fear of what might happen? Focus your mind and attention on what they want. What may be leading them to speak to you right now?

If you have strong feelings about what the person is saying, you may be tempted to try to fix the situation, or reassure the person. Instead, it takes focus and determination to remember that your presence is the biggest gift you can give another, regardless of what the issue at hand is.

When we master the art and craft of empathic presence, we become laser-like. We can hear precisely what is wanted in each moment; we find words that convey our understanding and care and can touch another's heart; and we remain relaxed in the face of strong emotions knowing we don't have to do anything about them. Then we can discover that empathic presence is also a gift to us: the gift of being nourished by the trust of another, by witnessing pure, distilled, raw humanity in its unmistakable beauty.

Generosity

10. **Generosity:** *Even when I am afraid or low-resourced, I want to keep reaching out to offer myself to others and respond to requests. If I find myself contracting in fear and unwilling to give, I want to seek support to release any thoughts of scarcity and embrace opportunities to give.*

If gratitude is the fuel of life, as Marshall Rosenberg has suggested and as my own ongoing practice of gratitude has demonstrated to me, then generosity is probably the fountain of life, the generative source of everything happening. Perhaps the fuel of gratitude provides the energy to generate more and more and to give it to ourselves and others. Generosity comes from the same root as genesis and generation. I have an image of us as creating something, giving birth to new possibilities, by practicing generosity.

I am also struck by how living generosity to the fullest can almost be the entire practice. Perhaps this is true of any of the commitments – that if we live them fully, they become the entire practice. Perhaps in order to reach fullness with any of the commitments we would be called upon to stretch along the lines of other commitments. For example, if we focused only on self-care, and did it with the full intention of our entire being, wouldn't we eventually find generosity becoming an act of self-care? Wouldn't we find an incredible desire to give as a way of nurturing that need in us? Conversely, if we focus on generosity, wouldn't that lead us to better self-care so that we can be nurtured sufficiently to have access to generosity?

I see the true essence of generosity as the experience of utter joy and delight that giving can offer. It's no accident that Marshall Rosenberg conjured up the image of a small child feeding a hungry duck as a symbol of free giving. I wish for everyone living to experience, at least once, the complete abandon into giving that a young child who has not been severely hurt lives in.

Obstacles to Generosity

What happens to make this completely jubilant and natural expression of our humanity disappear and be replaced by contraction and challenge when asked to give? If, as I believe is the case, we inherently enjoy contributing to others when we have connected with our own and others' needs and can experience our giving as coming from choice, why is it that so much of the time we are not drawn to giving?

I see four core messages and experiences that serve as major obstacles.

Scarcity: Need I say anything here? Clearly the assumption that there isn't going to be enough interferes with the flow of giving. The real question for me is at the level of practice. What can any of us do to increase the *experience* of sufficiency that would nurture more generosity? And, while anyone is still experiencing scarcity, what can contribute to a practice of generosity? If giving is done through gritted teeth it's unlikely to offer the delicious expansiveness of naturally flowing giving. How can that experience be found?

Separation: So many people experience themselves as separate from others that sometimes I find it a miracle than any of us give anything to anyone. Giving, free giving that is not about exchange of any kind, rests on relationship, on recognizing the receiver, seeing the commonality, the shared experience. Many people find it easier to love and give to animals than to other people. Why is it that we experience our fellow humans as something separate? How can we rebuild our sense of interdependence that used to be so primal for humans? Some of the difficulty rests in the intensity of commodification that's happened in the last hundred years. The paradox of these developments is that at one and the same time we have become more dependent on many other people and less able to see this dependence. Since most of us don't know how to grow food, make clothes, take care of our own health, and many other essential life skills, we are less able to attend to our needs without the support of others. At the same time, having everything appear as commodity or service for exchange results in the illusion of self-sufficiency which deepens our sense of separation. Perhaps a practice of reclaiming generosity requires us to cultivate awareness of and practices to sustain interdependence.

Insignificance: One of the most tragic outcomes of growing up the way we do is that we lose any sense that we matter. In this way the commitment to generosity is intertwined, to some degree, with the commitment to risk our significance. If we don't trust that we matter, that our needs and what we want have room in the world, it is that much harder to open our hearts to others' needs, the very condition of being moved to want to give.

Coercion: Many people, probably most, are raised with an ongoing stream of do's and don'ts. If we look again at the small child feeding a hungry duck, the flow of that generosity arises from within, spontaneously. It's a world of difference from "Say thank you" that most children hear repeatedly. Why would anyone feel *joy* about thanking another person if they are *required* to say it? It seems that freedom, the experience of having choice, is essential to the quality of joy in life. Heard enough times, shoulds get internalized and lead either to less-than-joyful giving or to rebellion and an unwillingness to give, or to both, sometimes in the very same act. Reclaiming our sense of choice is, for many of us, a lifelong and ongoing practice. Key to it is the willingness to not give unless we are really clear that we want to give, and doing it with tender self-acceptance. This can send a powerful message to our own inner self that generosity is not a requirement, that it's a choice, that "no" is truly an option that doesn't immediately mean we are less than. Within that context of growing choice we have more room to reclaim the spontaneous, exuberant, and expansive capacity to generate more and more resources by giving fully.

Saying "Yes" Authentically

No wonder, then, that so many of us, so often, experience an immediate "no" when being asked to do or give something. In my experience, that "no" is usually reactive and disconnected, not a genuine response that comes from connection and from holding all the needs in front of me.

Given the challenges we face, cultivating generosity becomes a deep spiritual practice that can free us up to have a more open approach to life instead of living in habitual contraction. As we grow in our capacity to recognize our freedom to say "no," we can more easily consider the possibility of saying "yes." As we shift our source of trusting that we matter from how others respond to us to an inner knowing, we can more easily be available to hear others' needs without collapsing inside. As we move more and more towards assuming that both parties' needs can be met, we can explore strategies beyond those that appear to meet only our own needs. We can then cultivate a practice of making ourselves available to have our feelings affected and needs transformed by engaging with others openly, even in times of conflict.

The question remains, though, how to do this without losing ourselves. As is often the case, what is most needed is sufficient connection, within us, with our needs as well as the needs of the other person. Along the way we learn two significant distinctions that can help us navigate apparent conflicts.

The first is the distinction between giving up and shifting. In particular, learning how to differentiate between the communion of being with others' needs and the choice about what we will do. As we allow our hearts to be softened by the experience of others' needs through recognizing our shared humanity, many of us find ourselves overwhelmed by others' needs to the point of losing track of our own. Being touched by another's needs does not necessarily mean saying "yes." The desire to contribute to others' well being by actually attending to their needs may be strong. It's still not the same as a genuine shift if we don't at the same time hold softly and attentively our own needs.

The second distinction is between self-care and attachment to our own strategies. Just as much as we want to ensure we don't over-stretch, we want to remain open to shifting our strategies even as we maintain self-care and attention to our needs. Attending to our needs, and separating them from our strategies, is essential if we are to find a genuine "yes."

And so, in order to find an authentic "yes" we need to overcome both our habits – that of habitual "no," and that of habitual "yes." A true "no" comes from connection, not contraction. In fact, both "yes" and "no" can be authentic expressions of caring for both parties' needs. A true "yes" expresses a genuine shift, and is different from fear or helplessness. An authentic "yes" comes from connecting with a wider range of our own needs and making a full choice to honor more of them.

The point of engaging with these questions is not so that we become a "better person" by saying "yes" more of the time. The point is, rather, to have more ease in reaching inner and outer connection, as well as having more internal freedom to make authentic, non-reactive choices.

Interacting with Others

A core test of our true commitment to nonviolence is the actual choices we make in how we interact with others. Nonviolence is not just internal, nor is it just about social activism and what kinds of actions we will or won't take. Nonviolence is just as much about how we treat the people around us – our family, friends, colleagues, and opponents. In this realm, we bring courage to match the level of openheartedness we cultivate so that we can overcome fear of consequences and show up with authenticity and full integrity. My experience has been that when I do that, I almost invariably learn and grow from what others say to me. Embracing dialogue as a way of life changes how we engage and how we address conflicts and differences. The result is often transformational for all involved.

Authenticity and Vulnerability

*11. **Authenticity and Vulnerability:** Even when I feel scared and unsure of myself, I want to share the truth that lives in me with others while maintaining care and compassion for others and for myself. If I find myself hiding or protecting, I want to seek support to embrace the opportunity to expand my sense of self and transcend shame.*

If "Loving no matter what" is for me the deepest and most succinct vision of nonviolence, "Authenticity and vulnerability" is the one closest to my heart because it defines my own personal core path, and is one way of expressing another indispensable aspect of nonviolence: courage.

When people refer to Nonviolent Communication (NVC) as compassionate communication I always have a sense of loss, because compassion does not capture for me in full the depth and complexity of nonviolence. We can have compassion without the radical ripping of the heart open and making ourselves available to endure whatever will come our way in order to live in full integrity with love and compassion. We can have compassion without the radical truth-telling that nonviolence rests on. It's not an accident to me that Gandhi called what he was doing "experiments in truth."

This commitment contains two aspects of stretching. One is for those who have been hiding the truth. The invitation is to come out and expose it, overcome the fear, overcome the shame, trust inner wisdom, accept self, and be bold.

The other is for those whose only way of sharing "truth" has been in the form of judgments and criticism without regard to how it will affect others. This invitation is to embrace care, to soften the truth without giving up on any bit of it, to hold the other while sharing the truth.

Both of these require letting go of protection. Because I have been in both places (although I have never been "nice," I was simply afraid to say certain things about myself), I have a viscerally clear sense of how criticism and judgment are a form of protection, a way of hiding, sometimes even from myself, the depth of pain, fear, helplessness, or despair that are at the core of the expression.

This speaks to me of the depth of the needs for belonging and acceptance, both in me and in others, and of the anguish in moments when they seem to be in conflict with authenticity. I know many people who choose to let go of authenticity in order to gain acceptance and belonging, and who nonetheless suffer because they ultimately don't trust the acceptance. For as long as acceptance depends on hiding the truth about who we are it remains suspect, temporary, elusive. What if people found out the hidden truth? I also know the experience of losing belonging and acceptance because of choosing to be authentic in ways that can be challenging for others. This is still work in progress to me. I have the contours of a path, without full clarity on where it leads. I know I want to grow in my flexibility about what feels authentic to me. I also, at the same time, want to grow in my willingness to risk losing everything for truth. I know how to grit my teeth and express truth anyway. What I want to learn more and more is how to remain relaxed and soft in my expression when I am stretching my limits.

The path of authenticity and vulnerability calls on us to trust two things at once: that every truth can be connected with deeply enough inside us that we can say it with care, and that whatever comes our way in response we can survive emotionally. We can use this faith to keep experimenting with speaking our truth, to keep undefending ourselves until there is nothing left but the soft, unprotected, and glorious heart that we each have.

Vulnerability as a Spiritual Path

The path of vulnerability includes: understanding what generates so much fear about stepping into more vulnerability in our lives; learning to sit with the discomfort to create more self-connection; finding ways of redefining vulnerability as strength; discovering an inner sense of safety; and securing support in inhabiting more authenticity. More than anything, though, the path of vulnerability is about choice: How can we muster inner strength to understand, face, and transform our fears so we can have the aliveness and authenticity that come from the willingness to share our truth?

Usually when we think of the meaning of the word "vulnerability" we think of it as an experience of being exposed in a way that could lead to hurt. When we talk about choosing vulnerability rather than having it simply happen, we are embarking on an extraordinary journey of changing our relationship with fear.

As Chogyam Trungpa says, "true fearlessness is not the reduction of fear, but going beyond fear."

What does choosing vulnerability look like? Here is a personal example. After a painful breakup with a partner many years ago, I took on the practice of examining myself closely for months to see the ways that I had contributed to the relationship not working. Every time I found something, I shared what I found with my former partner. I felt exceedingly vulnerable – as if I was providing my former partner with ammunition, a way to "prove" that it was my fault that the relationship ended. I also loved the practice. I was being true to myself instead of protecting myself. And after a few months it meant we could be friends again.

There is no final arriving, no end point to the path. In each moment the balance of our needs may shift. By inquiring into the lived truth of this moment we become present and step out of stories about what things mean. In each moment, we solve the emotional equation of that moment: With all of the needs that are on the table for this moment, what's the action to take in this moment? What needs rise in significance in this moment? Which needs are less important in this moment?

When we start working with vulnerability we discover what someone expressed in a workshop I led on the topic: "I don't think the fear will ever completely disappear, so I have to find a way of accepting the fear." The point of being on the path is to find the freedom, not necessarily to always have to be vulnerable, but to have the option to be vulnerable when we choose.

Living Undefendedly

My spellchecker doesn't recognize the word "undefendedly." My heart does. I feel the difference, immediately, between defending myself or not. One protects and closes, keeping me safe and apart, less available. The other allows my heart to be affected, without a shield, keeping me open, soft, and strong.

When I first started thinking about the choices Jesus made in his life and understood him to have decided to love no matter what, I also understood immediately the power of removing protection and embracing an uncompromising vulnerability. Jesus did not let fear of consequences stop him. He had no protection. What an awesome, fierce strength. Inspired by this vision I choose, as an ongoing practice, to remove protection, layer after layer, to make myself available to life, accessible.

I practiced Tai Chi for a few years. Towards the end of that period I started learning "push hands." I learned that yielding, which requires overcoming the impulse to stiffen up and defend, makes for more strength. When my body stiffens to protect, it's easier for the other person to push me, and I can lose balance. My stiff body gives the other person leverage for pushing. When I yield, on the other hand, the other person cannot push me. If I yield long enough, I even gain freedom of movement when the other person continues to follow me past their balance point.

If someone says something that's painful, I have a choice. I can defend, protect, wear a shield, and move away from the pain. This tends to surround me with tension, in my heart and in my body. I have less freedom in that way. I can also remain open, allow the pain, soften myself towards it, towards the person who said whatever it was. With that option I have more strength, less fear, more options for how to respond.

That softness, without protection, can also disarm others, reach their heart more easily. This particular kind of strength is one of the foundations of nonviolence, what gives it power. Undefending myself rests on tremendous faith in the fundamental humanity we all share. What captures this dazzling experience of humanity is the core needs common to all.

The practice of undefending, core to any serious engagement with nonviolence, rests on a deep trust that underneath whatever veneer and protection anyone else carries lives a human heart just like mine. Whatever others did, their hearts also long to be loved. They, too, feel vulnerable. In fact, as James Gilligan so lovingly reminds us in his book *Violence: Our Deadly Epidemic and Its Causes*, apparently an astonishing majority of incarcerated violent offenders are full of shame and untold rates of self-loathing. At the heart of their shame he uncovers precisely the longing to be loved, so deeply unfulfilled as to create shame for even having the desire. Their hearts, in other words, are just as vulnerable as mine and yours. They defend it to such a degree that the result is violence towards others.

If I can respond without tension to what comes towards me, if I can actively look for the tender heart behind any action or word, I convey a deep message. I thereby tell others that I don't have a reason to fear them. Once their humanity is mirrored back to them, they are more likely to respond in kind.

No wonder that nonviolence requires learning to undefend. The less I defend, the less likely I am to respond with violence. Undefending nourishes my capacity to choose. On the other end, the less I defend, the more capacity I have to disarm others' tension and protection. My heart, my soft and strong heart, de-escalates violence and conflict by being exposed in its vulnerability.

Courage in the Face of Fear

Just as one must learn the art of killing in the training for violence, so one must learn the art of dying in the training for non-violence. Violence does not mean emancipation from fear, but discovering the means of combating the cause of fear. Non-violence, on the other hand, has no cause for fear... He who has not overcome all fear cannot practice ahimsa. – Gandhi, *All Men Are Brothers*, 104

This quote has been haunting me ever since I first discovered it some years ago. I think about it several times a week. I find it so intense, so fascinating, and at one and the same time inspiring and discouraging. I know that the practice of nonviolence – whether in the social activism context, or in daily life – requires tremendous courage.[68] In moments of great challenge this statement sometimes helps me find the courage to face my fear and continue anyway. At other times, in moments of darkness, the continued existence of such basic fear in me becomes so disheartening. If, after all these years of rigorous training and practice, I am still so often paralyzed, what is the point of even trying to teach nonviolence?

If nonviolence – ahimsa – is about love, is moving forward through the fear enough? Is it possible to act on pure love when we are afraid? Are there different kinds of courage, one protected one not? What exactly are we choosing when we embrace nonviolence – either as a path, or in a particular moment?

Since 1996 my own path of nonviolence has been embracing vulnerability. I have been systematically undefending and

[68] Although for most people the consequences of vulnerability in daily living are not exposure to potential physical violence, the fear of judgment, ridicule, or social isolation are just as real *emotionally* as the possibility of literal death, perhaps because early in life social isolation can indeed threaten our very survival.

unprotecting myself. My sustenance and inspiration for this path come from experiences that are very remote from my own life. I choose to face the risks of social isolation, humiliation, and loss of respect when I break social taboos, sometimes, by saying things that most would not say. I do this more and more over time. I lean on Gandhi, Jesus, and Martin Luther King, Jr., images of love and courage, in the most literal way to help me walk through abysses that sometimes seem bigger than my individual capacity.

Not Knowing

I am not settled. I face my fear and walk on, risk the consequences, and learn to survive them. Does this mean I will be less afraid next time? Will the responses affect me less next time? If I am vulnerable – enough – will there eventually be fewer consequences, more openness to the vision I am bringing forth, to my own individual self, to my own human fallibility? If I survive enough times, will I find more ease in the midst of the fear to unprotect my heart? I mean, not just gather my strength and move forward, but most literally lay down the armor that surrounds my innermost part and walk forward, embracing life as it unfolds in that moment? What exactly am I hoping for? What exactly am I trying to teach?

More questions arise. What can I tell people about how to act when fear is all-consuming? What did the students in the Civil Rights Movement do? Did they *feel* fear when they were sitting at the lunch counters ridiculed and beaten up? Did they continue despite the fear, or was there some vision, conviction, love, unity, or anything else that transcended the fear completely for the moment? What made it possible for them to do what they did that is missing in our time?

The very act of writing this is part of my practice. I am writing about being unsettled, unsure, struggling with questions I don't know how to answer. This is not a clear, confident, upbeat, or optimistic message. So why share it? Because truth is what I am after, whatever its flavor. Because exposing my uncertainty may invite you, the reader, into self-acceptance, and the willingness to let down your guard. Because knowing you are not alone in your struggle may just be what you need to keep going on your path. Because breaking down the isolation we live in may well be vital for deepening our collective exploration of how to face the challenges of our time and survive as a species.

Availability for Feedback

12. ***Availability for Feedback:*** *Even when I want to be seen and accepted, I want to make myself available to receive feedback from others in order to learn and grow. If I find myself being defensive or slipping into self-judgments, I want to seek support to find the beauty and gift in what is being shared with me.*

Why is receiving feedback challenging? Whenever any one of us gives feedback that is tainted with criticism, judgment, or our personal upset, we create a situation that requires a lot more capacity and skill from the person who receives our feedback. In other words, a big part of why receiving feedback is so challenging is because so few people around us know how to give feedback. If we are committed to a life lived in full responsibility for ourselves, we won't wait. Waiting for others to offer us usable, digestible, manageable feedback will not likely provide sufficient feedback for our growth and learning.

The alternative is to stretch our inner muscles, seek feedback, and grow in our capacity to fish the pearl that's in what may otherwise be someone else wanting to be heard for how upset and angry they are with us. How do we do that, and how do we grow in our capacity to do that?

Overcoming Defensiveness

One of the first things we discover if we begin the journey of making ourselves available to feedback is that defensiveness usually arises from a deep desire to be seen and accepted. The primary antidote, then, is to grow in our own self-acceptance. Then we will find it easier to hear feedback, because we can relax into ourselves and receive it as *information* rather than confirmation that there is something wrong with us.

When I receive feedback, I watch for my reactions. As soon as I feel any kind of contraction, I take it as a sign that I am lacking sufficient inner resources in the moment to receive more feedback. That kind of contraction is the precursor to defensiveness. I can ask the other person to pause so I can be more present. I did this for years, and these days it's rare that I even feel the contraction. The primary tool I used to help me navigate those moments was a small reminder I would say to myself internally: "Even if this thing said about me just now is true, there is still nothing about me that's worse than anyone else that's ever lived." Over time, and with other practices I used to reach self-acceptance, I have come to a place of hardly any defensiveness left in me.

If you want to have a fast-track course of learning about feedback, you can enlist the people in your life in support of your learning. You can start with your closest people, the ones you would most trust love and care about you, who would be willing to do it in order to support you. Invite them to talk about things they may have been happy to let go of bringing up because of their love and trust. Let them know how much of a gift their honesty would be for you. In the process, you will discover how much more intimacy this added level of honesty can bring to your relationship, even if it's uncomfortable for both of you along the way.

Then branch out to people who are not so close to you, whose feedback you may not find so much ease in receiving. As you work on your defensiveness, feedback, even angry feedback, is not going to be as scary. Be clear inside yourself what is leading you to seek feedback from each person you approach, and communicate this clarity to them. And, in the end, remember to thank them, even if you are in pain.

Metabolizing Feedback

Sometimes we "buy" our availability for feedback at the cost of self-judgment. We may have enough self-acceptance to hear the feedback without reacting, and not enough to make use of it in a self-loving way. My experience leads me to conjecture that the more we step outside the societal comfort zone in which we live, the more feedback will come our way. My own experience has been of hearing more feedback than I can possibly integrate. In order to be able to discern with clarity what I want to do with the feedback, I find it essential to understand both what the feedback actually is, as well as relate it to my own personal goals for learning and growth. I don't know of a way of doing that with tenderness if I follow the route of self-judgment. I know this well, because I have so little self-judgment left that I feel the difference immediately when it comes up.

Once I am fully at peace, I want to give my full attention to understanding the feedback. This involves empathic listening. What is the essence of what the other person is saying? Without specifics, I have no capacity for learning, and so I want to make sure I have sufficient clarity about the actual details of what happened that this person is talking about. If I don't know, I ask. I also want to understand at the deepest level why this is important to the person giving feedback even if the words are focused entirely on me, even if the words are full of blame and criticism. Understanding what's important to the other person really helps me know whether or not I want to take on making changes, or work out something else with the person.

Once I have full understanding, I connect with my own interests and goals in terms of my growth. Is this feedback aligned with areas of focus for my growth? If not, I want to remember that I don't *have* to work on anything and everything that someone says is an issue for me. I am the one who sets the priorities around my growth. Connecting with the effect of my actions on others may shift my priorities, or it may not.

If I want to use the feedback to support my growth, I then focus on truly assessing my capacity to create change. I may choose to do a daily practice in this area, or I may choose to take incremental steps to implement the changes I want. On a number of occasions I even enlisted the support of the person who gave me the feedback in monitoring my own movement towards my goals. Change is extraordinarily vulnerable, because to whatever small degree it challenges our sense of self, of our mastery, and again and again our self-acceptance. I have seen myself and others slip into harshness and violence towards self in the commitment to change behaviors or choices. I want to maintain tenderness all the way through, whether I succeed or fail. Whatever I take on, I want to remain open to the way of life. We cycle and circle and loop and spiral, learning things again and again, falling and getting up, and eventually something gets fully integrated and becomes a seamless part of who we are.

The gift of feedback is about increased honesty, connection and even intimacy with the people who share it with me, and about increased opportunities for me to grow where I want. Keeping this clarity and avoiding the trap of taking blame or pushing back increases the chances that feedback serves its true function: a gift that one human being gives another freely for the benefit of both.

Openness to Dialogue

13. **Openness to Dialogue:** *Even when I am very attached to a particular outcome, I want to remain open to shifting through dialogue. If I find myself defending a position or arguing someone else out of their position I want to seek support to release the attachment, connect with my needs and the needs of others, and aim for mutually supportive strategies to emerge out of connection with needs.*

I have often reminded others (and myself in the process) that our commitment to nonviolence is only tested when people do things we don't like. How are we going to respond when we see an individual, a leader, a group, or even a nation, acting in ways that are not aligned with what we want to see happen in the world?

Nonviolence gets its power from love, from breaking down the barriers of separation and cultivating compassion for everyone, from the courage to face consequences to our actions, from the willingness to stand for truth, from the fierce commitment to overcome fear and act in integrity.

Responding nonviolently to what we don't like, then, invites us to find ways of bringing love, courage, and truth to the situation even while we are trying to transform it. What can our actions look like when we come from this perspective? We either engage in dialogue, when such is available, or we engage in nonviolent resistance.

Both aim to create an outcome that works for everyone through the recognition that only solutions that work for everyone are sustainable. Any solution that is forced on another person, group, or nation simply has too much potential to breed resentment, even hatred, and therefore to backfire at the soonest opportunity of the forced party to seize power again. Knowing this, the choice to engage in nonviolent resistance, which is, in effect, a form of force, walks a complex and fine line. Because this book/volume is primarily about individual choices in daily living, I leave the full discussion of this complexity, and especially how we can choose how much force to use and in what ways, to another context.

This deep commitment to an outcome that works for everyone is the connecting link between nonviolent resistance and dialogue. Dialogue, unlike nonviolent resistance, requires two (or more) people or groups that are willing to talk with each other. However, dialogue doesn't require both parties to agree to be in dialogue, only to agree to talk. The discipline of dialogue, at its heart, is a commitment to pursue the goal of an outcome that truly works for everyone even when others are only looking out for their own interest.

Dialogue and Conversation

Most conversations are simply monologues delivered in the presence of a witness.

— Margaret Millar

Dialogue is a conversation ... the outcome of which is unknown.
— Martin Buber

While every dialogue is a conversation, not every conversation is a dialogue. What are the features that distinguish dialogue from other forms of conversation? If we accept Buber's characterization of dialogue, what makes it possible for the outcome to be unknown?

Listening: I know I have embraced dialogue when I recognize in me a sense of openness to the other person's experience. Part of what makes so many conversations different from the true magic of dialogue is that so often we use the time during which others are speaking to think about the next thing we are going to say, without giving our ears and hearts to the person speaking. This is even more pronounced when whoever is speaking is someone whose actions, words, or opinions we are opposing. This, after all, is the context for this exploration: dialogue as a response to a situation we don't like.

Openness to change: An unknown outcome means that something along the way has changed from whatever it was that could have been predicted as an outcome. Especially if we are unhappy with how things are, this willingness takes active dedication and commitment. Without it, I don't trust my own integrity. If I am unwilling to change, to be affected by what I hear sufficiently to consider options that are new to me, on what grounds am I expecting the other person to change?

Holding everyone's needs: At bottom, embracing the spirit of dialogue is a commitment to caring for everyone who is part of the dialogue, even if they have taken actions that deeply concern me. I love what I see as the radical gift of this commitment. Without it I could so easily be tempted to impose solutions on a less-than-willing person just because I believe they address my own needs better. With this commitment in place I work for an inclusive solution even when the other person may still be advocating for their needs only. This, to me, is where the strength of the commitment to nonviolence gets tested: I want to be able to hold enough love and trust, both in myself and in the humanity of the other parties, that I will stay the course until we are connected, until we have some solution with which we can all live. I have seen it happen on a small scale, and I continue to have faith that such dialogue is possible at all levels.

Honoring Our Limits

The commitment to dialogue may appear to ask of us to have infinite capacity. Always be open to dialogue? With anyone? About anything? Any time they want it? Many people balk at this idea, both in the name of autonomy and in the name of conserving resources. When do we get to honor our limits?

A key to coming to peace with this commitment is the distinction between the *openness* to shifting through dialogue and the *act* of having an actual conversation with a particular person – inner and outer aspects.

I have found repeatedly that the experience of that openness in and of itself is transformative. I can tell the difference, sometimes in a very visceral way, when I am or am not open in that way. I know how attachment *feels* because I have had the experience so many times now of not having it, and the immense freedom that comes with that. It's not about not wanting, even wanting passionately; it's not about not having opinions, even strong ones; it's not about going along with anything or anyone. It's simply about the willingness to be affected by what I hear, or even by my own imagination about another's needs or perspective. It's about allowing connection with needs, my own and another's, to be the moving force of life, the source of creative strategies.

As to the act of being in conversation with another, that act happens on the material plane, and is therefore subject to finitude in a way that willingness is not. Willingness, like any inner state, has no limits. Our capacity to schedule, mobilize resources, and create the conditions for dialogue to occur, is humanly limited. I have often seen many of us get so confused by material limitations that we close ourselves down and disengage. Instead, even when I am not seeing a material way to engage in conversation with someone, I can still remain open to dialogue, and especially open to shifting through connection with needs.

If I am going to say "no" to participating in a dialogue, I want absolute honesty with myself that my choice is based on clear assessment of my resources rather than a subtle form of avoidance, closed-heartedness, or any other form of putting a barrier between me and another person.

And there are still decisions to make about the material plane. Here's what I aim for in making my decisions about when to engage in dialogue and when not.

Availability: Every day I choose, repeatedly, not to engage in dialogue with untold numbers of people in positions of power with whom I would love to be in dialogue. These are people whom I don't know personally and who I have no reason to believe would readily make themselves available to dialogue with me. I am quite confident that were I to succeed in being in dialogue, true dialogue, with any of these people, I would shift my beliefs, experience, feelings, or imagined strategies about any number of things. From time to time I have tried to create such dialogues, so far without success. Why do I call it my choice? Because I have a high degree of confidence that if I made it a point to engage in dialogue with a particular person, and put all my resources into reaching that person, I would eventually manage to do it. So far that has not appeared to me to be a fruitful use of my resources. That may change.

In a less dramatic way, I have also had the experience many times of reaching for dialogue with someone unsuccessfully. I even remember times of desperately wanting to find a way to reach a strategy that would include the other person's wishes and perspective, and feeling helpless to do so without dialogue. One such time I had the epiphany that led to the distinction I made earlier between openness to dialogue and the act of dialogue. I realized that even if I don't have access to the other person I can still choose to have an imaginary dialogue with that person inside of me and represent their needs to myself.

And so, in terms of making my decisions, when someone else is actively choosing not to be in dialogue, I rarely pursue strategies to attempt to reach an agreement to be in dialogue.

Skill level: In determining whether or not to attempt an actual conversation with someone, I check in carefully to see if I have the skill level necessary to achieve the connection. This doesn't happen very often for me, less and less so over the years, and still I want to name it, because it still happens. I know a particular limit I have, which has to do with looping around without reaching understanding. I don't know how to dig myself out of such a place with another person. I seem to not know how to continue to engage when I feel helpless to create a shared tracking of where we are in the dialogue. I imagine for each of us we know where we get lost. When I have had such experiences with someone repeatedly and haven't managed to create a different outcome, I don't prioritize being in dialogue, and I look for other strategies to allow that person's needs and experience to affect me.

I want to distinguish this from its close cousin of emotional trigger. I know triggers, I know them well, and I don't ever consider them grounds for not engaging in dialogue. This is precisely where I see this particular commitment as an important stretch. Choosing not to be in dialogue because we are triggered is the quintessential experience I want us to learn to transcend so that we can use those moments and relationships as opportunities to deepen our capacity to be present. I wouldn't begin to say that I always succeed. That's not the point for me; the point is to keep aiming for that presence. It's only when I trust my overall presence and only doubt my actual skill level that I am willing to choose not to be in dialogue.

Other priorities in my life: This is a tricky consideration to navigate with full self-honesty. On the one hand, I know I want to maximize the efficacy of my work in the world, for example, or my commitment to be available to my sister Inbal who is facing cancer, or my self-care, and balance those with being open to dialogue. Just because someone wants me to change my strategies or beliefs is not an automatic reason to shift my priorities. Again, material limitations exist.

On the other hand, I want to be vigilant with myself so I don't use this as an excuse to discount other people, to charge forth with something I want without consulting with others, to subtly slip into thinking I am more important than others, or to allow my triggers to trick me into thinking that there is good reason not to be in dialogue instead of being honest with myself to recognize I want to work on the triggers. The more visible I become in the world, the more vigilant I want to become about my own availability to dialogue. No easy solutions here; only consciousness.

Resolving Conflict

*14. **Resolving Conflicts:** Even when I have many obstacles to connecting with someone, I want to make myself available to work out issues between us with support from others. If I find myself giving up on someone, I want to seek support to remember the magic of dialogue and entrust myself to the process of healing and reconciliation to restore connection.*

When mutuality and connection are as fragile as they are in contemporary U.S. culture, and when the culture continually reinforces messages about scarcity, protection of our needs, and hostility towards others' needs, conflicts and breakdowns in mutuality arise with remarkable ease and frequency. Indeed, many of us experience a steady diet of conflicts in everyday life (e.g. disagreements with employees or supervisors, or struggles with spouses, children, and other family members) as well as ones that are foundational to the overall social structure (e.g. race relations and class antagonism).

Having little, if any, experience of restoring mutuality through empathy and dialogue, we tend to polarize and lose connection, either temporarily or permanently. We lose the ability to see the other as a full human being like us. Depending on the nature and outcome of the conflict, we can despise the other as "needy" and weak or too demanding, see the other as uncaring or brutal, or manipulative, or judge ourselves as wanting too much. In less personal contexts, we can see others as exploitative or destructive of human life, or uneducated and lazy. What we don't see under conditions of conflict is others' full humanity, their separate existence full of needs remarkably like our own. As Samuel and Pearl Oliner point out, mistrust leads to misinterpretation of the other. Misinterpretation, in turn, exacerbates the mistrust and tends to escalate conflicts.

As I was beginning to study Nonviolent Communication (NVC) and learn about conflict and dialogue, I encountered a sentence written by Thich Nhat Hanh as part of his version of the "Right Speech" precept: "I will do everything in my power to resolve every conflict, however small." Every time I think about this phrase, which is surprisingly often, I have a little shock at the power of the last two words. I think about the many relationships that turn into empty shells because people give up on connection one small conflict at a time. They choose not to work things out, believing they are letting go when in actual fact they erect invisible subtle barriers, small initially, that grow and grow into thick walls that make the memory of connection appear like a fantasy. Some conflicts appear "too small" for many of us to give energy to working them out.

On the other end of the spectrum are conflicts we don't resolve because they are "too big." We are afraid of being overwhelmed. We are afraid of hurting the other person by bringing up something difficult to work out. We are afraid of making things worse. We are so angry we don't even know how to talk to another person. Moving away and giving up seems easier.

Small or large, conflicts that are not worked out can diminish our humanity. Those that we move into and out the other end of successfully expand our hearts, deepen our connections, increase our knowledge of self and other. So why don't we?

Without the tools for resolving conflicts, the attempt to bring up a difficult situation often does "make things worse." We are all such sensitive, tender creatures with hearts that have so many longings that we carry. Our unskillfulness often does trigger pain in others, and if we don't know how to respond, and they don't either, the pain, the anger, the awkwardness, and the ensuing distance and resignation can, indeed, be devastating. We lack models of conflicts that get worked out. How many of us grew up frequently seeing people around us willing to engage in conflict? If our choice is between escalation and avoidance, I can easily see why avoidance would feel attractive.

As with "Openness to Dialogue," the problem of finitude arises here, too. How many conflicts can anyone participate in with full integrity and still have a life? I lack imagination about how to truly live up to this commitment in the literal sense of it. I do know the difference between choosing not to engage in conflict resolution because of a clear and open-hearted choice to attend to something else, and choosing not to engage out of fear, overwhelm, or giving up on the other person.

What matters to me – for me, for others who join me in living this commitment – is the *in principle* willingness, the state of open-heartedness towards the work of resolving the conflict, the clarity that not working out a conflict is a clear loss, the willingness to receive support from others (mediation, restorative circle, or some other support), and the curiosity about all the learning that can come from engaging in conflict.

Within a society like ours, engaging with conflict, establishing true dialogue with another, is enormously difficult. This is because trust in others' basic humanity, and hence in their independent desire to restore connection with us, is minimal and brittle. This is understandable, because so often that desire all but disappears in moments of challenge. Nonetheless, and despite the enormous difficulty in overcoming societal messages of separation and mistrust in order to learn empathy and cultivate mutuality, I have ample experience to know it is not impossible. The incredible paradox of empathy is that when it is successfully used to restore connection, the outcome of conflict more often than not actually meets both parties' needs. Empathy is a way of transforming, rather than simply resolving, conflict.

While I still often experience the habitual dread about taking on a conflict with a friend or colleague, over the years it has softened, the internal clench is shorter, and the choice to walk towards the conflict easier. I almost invariably feel enormous gratitude for what emerges. I know that no conflict is ever all about the other person or all about me. There is always something to learn – about me, about the other person, about the relationship, or about being human overall. Each time, something in me opens more and more. I so long for that openness, that radical simplicity of engagement, to become first nature for all of us.

Relating to Life

Rounding up the set are three commitments that speak to how we see ourselves in relation to life as a whole. Where we see our place in the web of life brings us to an awareness and conscious embracing of interdependence. Key to a nonviolent life is our capacity to accept life, which allows us to engage with life when we want to see change from a place of peace and clarity instead of fighting with life. Lastly, we can embrace life in celebration and nourish our capacity to engage in this way of living.

Interdependence

*15. **Interdependence:** Even when I experience separation or deep isolation, I want to open my heart to the fullness of the interconnectedness of all life and to cultivate awareness of the countless ways that our actions and experiences affect each other. If I find myself retreating into self-sufficiency, separation, or mistrust in my own gifts or those of others, I want to seek support to remember the beauty and relief of resting in interdependence, including the many ways each of our lives depends on the gifts, actions, and efforts of others.*

As I see it, interdependence is both a way of interpreting reality and a conscious choice about how to live within that reality. In that sense interdependence is similar to needs. Needs, too, are a way of making sense of reality, as well as a conscious practice. The analogy continues, for me, in one more way. In both cases, my understanding is that what we choose is not whether or not interdependence, or needs, exist or have an effect; what we choose is how we relate to them. And, in both cases, the more consciousness of interdependence, or needs, we bring to our choice, the more likely we are to be satisfied with the result.

So what does interdependence mean as a conscious practice? How has it become one of the commitments? The core of it for me has been continuing to increase my awareness of the multiple layers and forms of relationships and effects we have on each other and the environment within which we live.

Transcending Self-Sufficiency

Since independence is such a strong component of modern life, if we are to move closer to a conscious practice of interdependence, sooner or later we will be called upon to embrace our dependence on others. This may not be easy at first, since having our dependence masked in so many ways allows us to maintain an illusion of autonomy. The first step on this journey is often learning to transcend the injunction to be self-sufficient.

Transcending self-sufficiency means opening to the limitations of our *capacity* to attend to our needs without letting go of our *responsibility* to attend to our needs. How so? By asking for all we want. Aiming to ask for more and more leads us to confront fears and cultural imperatives. Asking provides opportunities for others to fulfill their need for contribution. Asking supports us in cultivating non-attachment as we practice making requests and letting go of outcome. Asking supports humility. Asking also supports power, and the possibility of having the life we want.

Transcending self-sufficiency in a cultural context, if we want to live as full, alive human beings embedded in a web of connections, also means offering our support to others even when they don't ask, even if almost invariably they say no to our offers. Everyone else has likely been socialized in the same manner, and is also unlikely to ask. Offering is then a form of modeling, alongside our own asking, that caring for others is what we value, that supporting each other is essential for living. Sometimes we walk a delicate line between acting on our care for others and supporting them as a substitute for their own self-responsibility. We are likely to make mistakes, because this is such uncharted territory. I would rather err on the side of offering too much support than too little, because I rarely trust people to have emerged from the conditioning sufficiently to ask for all they want. I know I have been at it for years, and I still don't ask for all of it.

Part of asking is about knowing that we matter, each and every one of us, which goes back to risking our significance yet again. It's about mattering to ourselves sufficiently to hold our needs with care and attend to meeting them, and to be open to receiving support and love to meet our needs. And it's about not letting shame interfere with love and presence when we begin to think that what we have to offer is not enough or not the right kind of support. It's about the freedom to show up with the fullness of our love, power, and longings.

Caring for Everyone

Interdependence is also about caring for others. Ultimately, my goal is to be able to hold everyone's needs with care. This *is*, after all, the world I am dedicating my life to creating: a world in which *everyone*'s needs matter. I am aiming to live, day in and day out, as if this world already exists. I am aiming to care for others' needs whether or not I trust that they care for mine. I am aiming to care for others' needs alongside caring for my own, not instead of.

Holding everyone's needs with care means learning to stay open even in conflict, even when feeling helpless, even when having no imagination about how we can meet our own needs unless we let go of caring for others. It means learning to keep holding the focus on everyone's needs, so we don't give up on ours, and don't give up on others'. Aiming for caring for everyone puts us face to face with the uncompromising truth that every choice we make has consequences, both for us and for the rest of life. Caring for everyone invites us to also care for ourselves more, so we don't fall into the dangerous trap of "altruism" or "selflessness." Caring for everyone invites us to be larger and larger agents of change in our life and beyond. This allows us to increase our sphere of influence and power, first within and ultimately around us, to match the level of care.

Nothing is Separate

Another aspect of cultivating interdependence and living in it is about developing more and more ways to remember and integrate non-separation. When I read Sharif Abdullah's *Creating a World that Works for All*, one of the ideas that really stood out to me was that when the Exxon Valdez crashed, it was delivering my oil to me. It wasn't someone else's oil. I was using it just like the vast, vast majority of people in this country. This was radical non-separation for me. It has stayed with me, and continues to inform my investigations about how to approach the current cluster of challenges we are facing in the world.

A very personal and radical form of this awareness came to me in the form of a poem by Chun Yu (chunyu.org), a fellow member in a writing group. Chun is a polymer scientist, environmentally concerned citizen, poet, and Buddhist practitioner. In her poem – *The Game of Bonding – the Story of Plastics*, from which I am quoting passages below, she practices non-separation in bringing together all parts of herself. She also invites the readers to practice non-separation. What would it be like to transcend the duality, to recognize continuity even with a substance that so many consider dangerous? Below are parts that stood out to me from this poem and my musings about them. I see Chun as thinking beyond our familiar categories, and I love the idea of more of us doing that in our daily living.

What are plastics
But the same materials made of
You and me?
Hydrogen, oxygen, carbon, nitrogen…
What are they, but like us

Right away my breath changes as I grasp the depth of unconscious separation I had created.

Nature/God made, or man made
Can both sustain or destroy lives.
But as for fundamental existence of matters
There is no increase, no decrease,
No creation, no elimination,
As the Heart Sutra says and
As the physical law understands.
Thus no liking, nor hating
Shall be applied
Towards the same matters made of us.

Buddhism and physics come together to remind me of my own practice of transcending right or wrong, preference for joy over pain. I open wider.

Now we have waves, waves that are man made,
of plastics, of covalently bonded forms

The anguish, my utter helplessness about creating any change rise to the surface. How could this have happened? What can we do about it? Miles and miles of plastic covering the ocean. Will we ever learn?

We're nature/god's
failed students
who are punished by our mistake of
not being able to learn the total truth, the way,
before trying our hands on alchemy

I am struck by the compassion I hear in this, the simplicity. We, and our actions, and all that has happened, including plastic, including our mistakes, are part of life, part of nature. How exacting to recognize that there is nowhere that is outside of life.

> What makes anything evil is
> our own inability to bear its consequences.
> Yet, in nature's time/god's eyes everything is degradable,
> including the consequence itself.

In moments I can open wide enough to trust this simple truth. It's only my scale, the small human scale, that zooms in on one particular aspect instead of a larger picture. I am grateful to Chun and to all the teachers who remind me of the larger scale.

Challenging Tradition

In May, 2000, I graduated from a Ph.D. program in Sociology at UC Berkeley. For the last four years of my studies I was part of a dissertation support group that consisted of four women from the department. We met every week for most of that time. Each week one of us had a turn, and could get whatever support we wanted. Sometimes it was having everyone else read a chapter and provide a critique. Sometimes it was making room for one of us to express and be heard about her challenges with her husband. Sometimes it was strategizing about how to proceed with our work given constraints and life challenges. Our interdependence was clear to all of us. To this day I am not certain that I would have managed to get to the finish line without this ongoing support.

So, when one of us was approached to do the graduation speech that year, we cooked up a secret plan of delivering a two-person speech without letting anyone know ahead of time. I was that second person. Kim DaCosta, the official speaker, invited me to join her on stage, and we delivered a speech together. I am including here the speech we delivered as a tribute to the possibilities of creative challenge and of exposing truth with love.

Department of Sociology Doctoral Student Address
Graduation, University of California, Berkeley
May 20, 2000
Kimberly DaCosta and Miki Kashtan

* KIM

When I was first approached to give this address, I could not say no fast enough. Preoccupied, as many of us are, with my work and family responsibilities, it was the last thing I wanted to add to an already hectic schedule.

But when those who were encouraging me to do this said I should because I'm an "inspiration" to other students, I realized I should take on this responsibility - not under any pretense that I can indeed inspire you, but to challenge that very idea. Rituals like graduation, with their individual speakers, and focus on individual achievement, emphasize uniqueness, exalt the individual, and portray us as "exceptions." In so doing they obscure the social conditions which make what appear to be individual achievements possible. In an effort to counter this individualist perception, Miki Kashtan (a fellow graduate student) and I decided to craft this address together, to make visible one of those forms of social support, namely our dissertation study group, that helped both of us achieve this goal.

But also to symbolize what sociology is particularly well-suited to do. Sociology provides the tools to uncover the social within the individual - the relations between people, institutions, history, and ideas that we embody.

* MIKI

Sociology can help us see what common sense often obscures. Common sense knowledge, for example, says that people are selfish by nature, and that they will always look out for themselves and do anything for material gain. Sociology teaches us that some societies are structured in ways that encourage more competition, while others foster more cooperation; sociology teaches us that it is society which pits our needs against each other and makes it so difficult for us to work together, while making it look like it's just the way people are; sociology teaches us that it is society which obscures the role of others in making our own very individual achievements possible.

* KIM

Each of us can no doubt point to a variety of institutions and people that have supported our educational achievements. Our professors, this university, and for many of us, foundations that provide us with scholarships. Yet these institutions and the people who inhabit them are already recognized and rewarded with social prestige for their work. What about the unseen sources of support that just as certainly make this day possible for us? As a mother of three, to use one small example, my education would not have been possible without access to quality, affordable childcare, which itself depends on the conscious commitment of institutions to make available such programs, and, of course, on people who are willing or compelled to do what is too often underpaid and undervalued work.

We are here, but there are others who could also be here, if we had a different set of priorities. For as the very institutions that support our educations decline, other oppressive ones have expanded. For example, while no new campus of the University of California has been built since the 1960s, some twenty prisons have been built since 1984. And while California spends roughly $6,000 a year per college student, it spends more than 5 times that amount per prison inmate. In other words, for each one of us invited into elite educational institutions, there are thousands locked out, and, for that matter, locked up.

* MIKI

Common sense tells us that people get locked up, are unemployed, or suffer economic hardship because they bring it on themselves, somehow, because of their individual weaknesses, or genetic predispositions, or because they don't work hard enough; sociology teaches us about the historical, social and systemic forces that create oppression and domination, and with them the conditions of people's suffering.

We, who are now graduating, know this. We, who spent several years learning sociology, have a responsibility to make this kind of knowledge available to those who have not studied it with us. We can counter complacency and insensitivity by educating those around us. We can contribute to people's hope by showing them that there is another way, that crime, despair, economic inequality, and environmental degradation are not natural disasters, but rather human made, and can be changed.

* KIM

Each of us will be looked upon at some point, whether we want to be or not, as inspiration by someone else. Many of our fellow PhDs will be teaching in universities and no doubt our degrees and awards will impress some of our students. But rather than emphasize our uniqueness, we can better serve our students if we expose the social "within" the individual so that they not only expand their understanding of what's possible for themselves, but for our society as well.

* MIKI

In every situation we can choose to go along with the flow, or challenge it. We can choose to cooperate when others compete; to be honest when others deceive; to show our feelings when others hide; to trust people when others are cynical. Challenging the flow is not easy or comfortable. But the reward is an enriched, joyous and courageous life, and the knowledge that we are contributing, however imperceptibly, to creating a world in which more people have more of their needs met more of the time.

I want to thank our families and our communities for helping us get to this moment, and congratulate all of us who are graduating today for the incredible effort and commitment we brought to this endeavor.

Accepting What Is

16. ***Accepting What Is:*** *Even when change happens (welcome or unwelcome, small or large), things fall apart, people don't come through, or calamities take place in the world, I want to remain open to life. If I find myself contracting away from life or drawn to ideas about what should happen, I want to seek support to find a sense of peace with unmet needs, and to choose responses and actions from clarity about how I want to interact with and respond to life.*

Many of the commitments have a flavor to me of being a possible bedrock, a place that we can land and through which we can look at everything. This is particularly true of this commitment. I know for myself that being able to land in this spot, especially in a moment when I am in the midst of an emotional storm or of intense agitation, is an exceptionally powerful avenue towards peace. Any time I am able to accept what is, my range of actions in the world expands, and the energy with which I take action is softer.

At the same time, I know very little about cultivating acceptance. I know for myself there are areas of life where I have extraordinary ease in having acceptance, and others that are uniquely challenging for me. Among the former are just about any natural disaster, illness, and death. The latter are made up entirely of matters of human choice. They may even be small in the large order of things, with consequences that have no long-term effect. I can even have compassion for the person making the choice, and still have tension inside me, a great distress, and difficulty in fully relaxing. It's not the intensity of the situation that determines my acceptance, nor how much my needs are met or not.

What exactly does it mean to accept what is? It certainly is not about *liking* it. I don't like it if there is an earthquake or if someone gets ill. And yet I am able to accept it. I see that it's something about recognizing that there is nothing I or someone else could do about it that allows me to accept. In the realm of human choice, however, it seems that despite my overall shift away from right/wrong thinking and the release of obvious and explicit ideas about what "should" happen, I continue to harbor semi-unconscious "should" ideas. If an unpleasant outcome seems to be preventable, then it's harder to accept. That means that I likely think that if something is preventable, then it *should* be prevented. This is not so in all areas, only in things that constitute care towards others.

Accepting what is means letting life be, whatever form it takes. In those times that I struggle to accept, I very clearly sense the energy in me of fighting reality, which is not the same as wanting reality to be different. I can want reality to be different. I can want a different outcome, or a different choice, or a different effect, and still be in acceptance. I know the difference.

When I am fighting reality, sometimes I am able to shift into acceptance, and many times I'm not. When I say that I don't know how to cultivate acceptance, what I am saying is that I don't have a clear sense of being able to *will* it, which I can do with many other commitments. Acceptance is a purely internal *attitude*, not an action. What's there to *do*?

If non-acceptance is about fighting reality, then, perhaps, cultivating acceptance is about softening that fight. Perhaps it is about grieving the huge gap between what I see as possible and what I see as our collective actions. Perhaps it's about continuing to engage with any area in which I find any shred of "should" thinking and connecting with the depth of longing, vision, and beauty that lead to the thinking. These are ongoing practices. In the moment, the only practice I have found so far is engaging with others, receiving support for my struggle, and opening up to life through that. Here's one example.

Uncertainty, Human Limitations, and Acceptance

I had a conference call scheduled with members of my community. There were technical difficulties. When the call materialized, ten minutes late, most people had given up, and only five participated. It soon became clear that the people who had promised they would fix the technology in advance had not done so.

The Habit

I am sure this kind of dilemma is familiar to many. We each have our own peculiar ways of responding in such moments. My own habitual response became clearer to me as I was working my way in real time through this issue on the call. Simply put, in the past I had been putting attention and energy, mind and heart, on understanding how the unwelcome result happened, and what can be learned to prevent it in the future. This kind of focus is one of the deepest sources of stress for me: always working on eliminating possibilities for error, forgetfulness, or inattention. It's as if I have been trying to make something go away that cannot: the irreducible uncertainty of life and human interaction. I don't think I am alone in this. In fact, I imagine we all have a collective illusion about our limitations. If only everyone paid attention fully, if only everyone took responsibility, if only … then there would be no unwelcome outcomes. From here it becomes so easy to blame – others or ourselves, as the case may be.

The Alternative

With the help of others on the call, I found an alternative to my habitual response. I saw that I could open up *for real*, not just in concept, to the irreducible uncertainty of life. There is never going to be anything definitive that I or anyone else can learn, integrate, or put in place that would take away this uncertainty. The very attempt to do so feeds my sense of helplessness and creates the stress. Even following the call, I am only beginning to imagine what life could be like. Instead of helplessness, I can see simply mourning what happened, being with the sadness of the results and their effect on me and others, especially, in this case, all the people who were looking forward to the call and couldn't get on it.

The difference between the two emotional states is immense. Helplessness is full of tension and contraction, and is about moving away from life and what is happening. There is no peace in it. Mourning, even when intensely painful, flows with life. My heart opens, and I know and accept the consequences. The shift from helplessness to mourning is not about having no pain; it's about how I relate to life. Am I opening to acceptance, or am I in some fundamental way fighting life? It was the empathic presence of others that allowed me to jump-start myself into acceptance, which then made everything easier.

Then, and only then, I could notice what *was* happening instead of being entirely with what *didn't* happen or what *should* happen or what I can do to make it *never* happen again. One of the people on the call brought to my attention that I said, several times, that the call wasn't happening, when, in fact, we were on the call, connecting, learning together, and even having fun and laughing.

I know I am done working my way through something when I get to a place of feeling grateful for it. That's when I know that I have assimilated the events, and am open to life again. Sometimes it takes years. Some things I may not finish while alive; I am quite sure of that. On that call, I found my way to gratitude within a few minutes. I could see that the depth of learning, in community, with support, that I was experiencing came about precisely because this mishap had happened and I was in acute helplessness at a time I could receive support. Whenever something doesn't happen, something else does. Life continues, and we have only so much say about what it will look like. I can fight life, or I can join the ride, with the mourning and the laughter, the pain and the joy.

Celebration of Life

17. ***Celebration of Life:*** *Even when I am faced with difficulties, personal, interpersonal, or global, I want to maintain an attitude of appreciation and gratitude for what life brings me. If I find myself becoming cynical or experiencing only pain and despair, I want to seek support to connect my heart with the beauty and wonder that exists in life even in the most dire circumstances.*

When I wrote the initial list of commitments, I started out thinking I was basically going to write about how I am living. Little did I know… Fairly quickly I shifted into some kind of almost altered consciousness, almost like channeling something that was bigger than me. Through this process something was mirrored back to me, my own limits became clearer, and I was humbled in a very satisfying way, most noticeably with this commitment. When I "discovered" this commitment, I knew this one was "for me." At the time I had not yet been through a year of gratitude practice, and so was far from any flow in this area. I knew I was invited, by something in me that pointed to something larger than me, to stretch to embrace life differently.

The year of daily gratitude practice that I then committed myself to was a resounding success. It was the longest practice I have undertaken, the only daily practice I have ever stayed with consistently, and an incredibly gratifying experience. In the course of that year I had a sense of having changed; I had become, in some ways, a different person. Of course, the experiment was not perfect. I can't say that this practice is the only thing I did that year, and therefore the "cause" of my inner transformation. I only know that this change happened during that year, and I have a strong suspicion that this change was real.

I am also not surprised, because I read research that after three months of weekly meetings in small groups, those who were sharing things they were grateful for were physically healthier than those who were sharing things they were annoyed about.

I stopped the practice because I felt done. I knew that it had been integrated, and was no longer necessary as a practice. I still often do my practice, though with a different purpose. On days when I feel depleted, lacking resources, or particularly stressed, I rely on gratitude to nourish me, give me some energy, release some of the stress. Or to soothe myself and come to peace when I am full of adrenaline from being engaged intensely just before going to bed. It's become a resource I can use to support my living.

I have heard Marshall Rosenberg say that gratitude is a kind of fuel, and I completely know what he means. Now that gratitude and celebration are so integrated into my way of responding to life, I notice more and more things to celebrate, and I am regularly moved to tears by what I notice.

From time to time I have been challenging myself to stretch even further. Instead of reviewing a whole day to find things to celebrate and enjoy, I look for what happened in the last minute that I could appreciate. I never get stuck any more, though I used to. And it never feels phony, which it sometimes used to. I feel free to explore and learn and enjoy in these ways.

As I focus on what I can celebrate and be grateful for, I become more attuned to noticing these aspects of life. This means, in a very real sense, that I then end up having more to celebrate, more to be grateful for. My life literally becomes better.

Section 2:

Practices

Acquired Spontaneity

There is no such thing as a difficult piece. A piece is either impossible or it is easy. The process whereby it migrates from one category to the other is known as practicing.

— Louis Kentner, *Piano*

Embracing and living a radical consciousness of nonviolence challenges most of how we have been trained to think, to feel, to speak, and to act. For most of us, when we discover this consciousness, when we awaken from the socializing to which we have been subjected, we realize that the old way is deeply ingrained in us. It's not a surprise to me that so many revolutionary movements have not succeeded in creating the change they envisioned. It takes practice to integrate a new way, no matter how much we love the new way, nor how much it may feel aligned with our deepest heart's desires. Even with the help of the commitments, integration remains elusive: they point the way, and they don't necessarily constitute specific practices.

Because I am so hungry for and committed to freeing up my consciousness from the deeply embedded structures of thought that I have inherited, I have been happily embracing one practice after another over the years, sometimes several in parallel (not recommended!). The effort has paid off in spades. I feel incredibly free from some pervasive social norms, almost entirely shameless, and have a sense of flow in my actions and speech much of the time.

I call this acquired spontaneity. It's no longer effortful for me to speak without judgments, for example, because I have created new pathways in my brain that are available to me by dint of having been used again and again and again.

I am offering some of the practices that have been most helpful to me so far. Some of them are not yet fully integrated. All of them have invigorated and excited me beyond words. I owe much of my freedom to this ongoing form of practice.

One key to this kind of practice is that I only do it when I notice forms of thought or speech that are not aligned with how I want to act. I am quite confident that at least early on I didn't really notice all the times that I engaged in the behaviors I was trying to change. Part of the practice is about increasing my own awareness over time by being gentle with myself when I notice, so that there won't be any internal fear of waking up to awareness.

Each of these practices is based on a similar principle: whenever I notice myself using a certain way of speaking, or behaving a certain way, I pause and revise myself on the spot. This takes some swift consciousness to do in the middle of a conversation. If I am not immediately able to do this seamlessly, I explain to the other person what I am doing, and ask them to wait until I figure out my preferred way of expressing myself. This happens a lot in the early days of any practice. I have noticed, however, that with each successive practice the integration happens faster.

I Don't Have to Do Anything

This was an early awakening in me, to realize and take to heart that I really and truly don't ever have to do anything; I only choose to do what I do based on ever growing awareness of what my needs are, and what my willingness to face consequences is. It's an ongoing balancing act at the heart of which there is always choice. Becoming aware of that choice is empowering. Forcing that awareness on anyone else is generally infuriating to them.

I want to illustrate this discovery with two stories, and then share the specific practice I have chosen.

The Story of Annalisa

I was once visiting a friend, and for a short period of time her granddaughter, then eight, was the only one at home. Let's call her Annalisa. We embarked on a delightful conversation, which she stopped at a certain point, saying: "I have to go clean my room." The following dialogue ensued:

> **Miki**: "No, you don't."
> **Annalisa**: "Yes, I do. My mother told me so."
> **M**: "You still don't."
> **M**: (*in response to silence, and a completely incredulous look on A's face*) "She may punish you if you don't clean up your room, and you still don't have to."

A: (*pausing to integrate, looking puzzled and then smiling with clarity*) "I see. I want to go clean up my room, because I don't want to be punished."

While some parents may find what I did with Annalisa horrifying, I believe I simply exposed the truth that was there already. Time and again I have told parents that they cannot make their children do anything, although they do have the power to create consequences that their children will dislike, and they can restrict their children's access to resources. No one can give someone else choice, nor can they take it away. The choice is there. It's only the options that are limited, not the choice.

Facing Disappointment

I was once at a reception honoring the director of a movie I loved and for which I helped create and promote study guides. Thinking that the reception was going to last 2-3 hours, two other friends and I had made dinner plans with a fourth friend who wasn't at the reception. We were all excited to participate in lively conversations and planning of our next steps, and deeply engaged. When we realized that the reception was continuing well into the evening and that going to our dinner engagement meant we would be missing the rest of the event, we went around the room saying our goodbyes to the people who were staying.

I noticed that my friends were saying to everyone something along these lines: "We really want to stay but we have to leave now, because we have dinner plans." I, already aware that we didn't really have to, was mesmerized by this statement. I then asked myself why I was choosing to go to dinner if I didn't have to. I realized quickly that as much as I hated missing the rest of the event, the thought of facing our dinner date's disappointment was overwhelming and significantly less welcome. I then was able to leave with complete acceptance of the truth, and without any resentment.

This happened in 1995, and my practice of NVC was almost brand new. If this were to happen today, I like to believe that I would call the friend, explain the situation to her, and attempt to reach a collaborative decision with her about whether or not to keep the dinner plan or reschedule. That *is* a possibility, and I have done it many times.

The Practice

The practice was born from the memory of this story. It's absolutely simple. Whenever I hear myself say that I "have to" do something, I stop myself, check inside, and express what I was saying without using those words by focusing on what it is that's leading me to make the choice I am making.

I am only satisfied when I am completely able to replace every "have to ..." with "I choose to because I want ...." I have never once not found the clarity. Over the years, the frequency of my using these words has diminished to essentially nothing.

Owning and Choosing My Values

I had known even before NVC that motivating myself or anyone else through "should" thinking was counter-productive. Now, having worked with so many people over the years, I am even more confident of the tragedy of this one word. As soon as I am told that I should do something, my joy in doing it leaks out of me faster than I can even notice. Our love of freedom is so deep, and this way of motivating ourselves challenges our sense of freedom in a very fundamental way. Of all the practices, this one has on occasion brought on active glee to me from the smell of reckless freedom.

The more I have reflected on this topic, the more confident I am that motivating people through "should" is an expression of lack of faith in our fundamental desire and openness to give and to serve. Of course this starts early in life. We have inherited a system of upbringing predicated on the idea that we need to be tamed, that left to our own devices we won't do anything useful. This is the legacy we need to overcome in order to access our own values, our own open-hearted generosity, and our choice about giving.

In addition, this practice can support us in strengthening the faith in ourselves and ultimately in human beings overall, that we will do things without coercion, without guilt, and without shame. Ultimately this is the core faith that makes my vision possible: that there would be enough goodwill and generosity to make everything happen that is needed by all of us; that we can treat ourselves and others with care; that we can all access responsibility and our deepest values softly if the space is given to us.

The Joy of Giving[69]

When Yannai, my sister Inbal's son, was three-and-a-half, his grandparents were visiting and were staying in the downstairs room. At about eight o'clock in the morning Yannai started banging a pole on the floor upstairs. There ensued the following dialogue:

> **Inbal:** "Seeing you banging on the floor, I am worried about our guests. I would like them to be able to rest as long as they want. Would you be willing to stop banging or to bang on the couch instead?"
>
> **Yannai:** "I don't want to, but I'm willing."
>
> **I:** "How come you don't want to?"
>
> **Y:** "Because it's not waking me up!"
>
> **I:** "So how come you're willing?"
>
> **Y:** "Because I want to consider you."

He then put down the pole, without any of the sense of resentment and anger that people often exude when they are doing something against their will. Inbal expressed her gratitude to her son for meeting her need for cooperation, and they moved on with their morning.

When Inbal shared this story with a group of people at one of her workshops, one man said: "But of course, your son was clear that if he didn't do what you asked you would take the pole away!" "No," she replied, "I would not have taken the pole away. In fact, I believe that because my son knew that I would not physically take the pole away from him, he was willing to put it down even though it was not what he wanted."

As I see it, the ongoing absence of coercion and "should" thinking was the context within which Yannai could find and cultivate his organic and genuine desire to care for the well-being of his mother.

The Practice

Whenever I notice myself using "should" thinking (and this hasn't happened now in many months, possibly years), I pause to translate. The practice here is a bit more elaborate, because of wanting to

---

[69] Adapted from an article written by Inbal Kashtan.

recover the fullness of my own values even when my inner access is
blocked. Even if my "should" thinking is about other people, I still
want to access *my* values and release the sense of expectation and
judgment that tends to hang on should thinking.

Instead of "I should …" I aim for "I want to … because I …."
The linguistic turn is simple. The internal shift is not. It's easy to say
"I want to eat fewer cookies because I want to care for my body"
instead of saying "I should eat fewer cookies." It's not so easy to
access our desire to care for our body sufficiently to make the
difference, to access the desire so deeply that it can serve as a loving
motivation to eat something else rather than a self-admonition.

Similarly, instead of "you (or someone else) should …" I aim for
"I would like you to … because I …." Again, even though the
behavior I want to encourage is in another person, the motivation is
still within me. That's completely revolutionary if we think about
interactions with children, for example. Imagine saying to a child, "I
would like you to go to bed now, because I care about your physical
health" or "because I want to have some rest and to focus on
something else now." That spells an entirely different relationship, to
me.

I come back, however, to this as an inner practice, even though I
may exercise it in interaction with others. It's a practice designed to
wake me up to what's truly important to me, and to let go of hiding
behind an impersonal authority that decides who should do what.
None of us know that.

Owning Choices with Care

I imagine each one of us, on any given day, wouldn't be able to count
the number of times we use phrases such as, "I gotta run," or, "I
couldn't get back to you earlier," or a host of other similar
expressions. They all serve the same basic function: they make it look
like our choices are beyond our control, defined by forces outside
ourselves.

When I became aware of the pervasiveness of this kind of
speech, I developed a strong wish to find a way to take full
ownership of my choices without losing the care that I believe is
served by the denial of choice. Clearly, we can't ever do everything.
We make choices and set priorities all the time. My belief, after some
years of the practice I am about to describe, is that it's entirely

possible to be truthful about our choices while at the same time affirming our care and connection with the person with whom we are speaking.

The Practice

The practice is simply telling the truth, the full truth, and nothing but the truth about the source of our choices. Instead of, "I'm sorry I couldn't get back to you sooner," I might say, "Between X and Y on my plate, I didn't find a way to make it a priority to get back to you sooner. I am sad about it, because this new project with you is important to me, and I plan to make it a higher priority as soon as X ends." I only want to say this if it's true. It may be that I didn't get back to the person because it's not a priority. Then I want to own that, too, with care: "I didn't get back to you sooner because I was reflecting on how to let you know that I am choosing not to engage with this new project while still supporting you and our connection." In a more personal context it may be: "I didn't get back to you sooner because I knew I had some challenging things to say to you about our friendship, and I wanted to be ready to do it with full love in my heart, which I am now happy to say I have."

I imagine some of you are reading this with some horror. You might be thinking, "Isn't this 'not nice'"? I know I am going a bit out on a limb here. I also know that the more I learn how to do this with soft and relaxed love in my heart, the more I get relief and appreciation from others. When we don't want to connect with others, they often sense it anyway, and the hurt is doubled by not having it acknowledged and the perennial enigma about why. We can create much more connection with others, even through discomfort, by sharing the gift of our true choices.

A word of caution

This is a fairly advanced practice that requires a lot of inner knowledge and capacity for creative framing. Initially, you may want to do it only internally while continuing to use the old phrases. If your choice is between the old phrases and "brutal" truth without cushioning it with love, I would still prefer that you use the old phrases. We are all so sensitive; we've had the experience so many times of being emotionally bruised, told we are not wanted, or ignored, dismissed, or ridiculed for being human, for wanting connection and respect. I want to keep that in mind when I speak, so that I minimize the risk of the person in front of me feeling significant pain.

Letting Go of Predicting the Future

On any given week I have dozens of experiences of people telling me that they were going to do something and then not doing it. Most of these are small things that don't amount to anything much, and some are significant. I am not outside this circle, either. How many times have I said, "I'll call you back as soon as I am done with this email," only to lift my head an hour later having totally forgotten about it?

I came to believe that I have no way of knowing what the future holds. This is not just a spiritual platitude. It's a basic and simple truth. Owning this truth supports me in being more honest. I created this practice for the purpose of cultivating humility and trust.

I now delight in finding ways of expressing a strong commitment and a sense of responsibility without saying that I will do something. I only the say the truth: "I plan on being there tomorrow at 2 pm" or, "I have it written in my calendar that you and I are getting together for a hike on Monday morning." I am liberated by this the same way I am liberated by any truth.

Sometimes I slip, still, and say that I will do something. I then wonder: Do I want to stop and correct and call attention to the shared myth that we know what's coming? Usually I don't. And some of the time life reminds me of the truth of uncertainty in those times when I slip and then indeed don't do what I said I would do. It's not that I am particularly "flakey." On the contrary, I actually have a reputation of being impeccable in tracking and performing things (and I am trying to lower people's expectations of me as a way to create more spaciousness in my life). It's just that I am more aware of life's happenings.

My biggest example is that I was scheduled to go teach in Japan on April 20th, 2011. In all my conversations about April I was consciously choosing to say "I am scheduled to go to Japan in April." I didn't say "I am going to Japan." I ended up not going, because I didn't want to expose my body to the risk of radiation given the strong history of cancer in my family and the work that I still want to do in the world. Life is just like that. We never know, for real.

Alternatives to Buts

Many people have become aware of the role that the word "but" plays in communication and seek to transform that dynamic. I sometimes stop people in the middle of a role-play after they say something like, "I totally get why you are upset about what happened," and everyone hears the "but" hovering over those words. In those cases, the person recognizes that what they were going to say next is, "but I want you to hear that ..." Essentially, what happens conversationally when a "but" shows up in someone's speech is that everything that preceded it gets erased from the other person's radar screen. I have often told people that they may as well throw out all the words that come before their "but" because in any event the other person won't hear them.

Some people strive to replace the word "but" with the word "and." I don't believe this does the trick. The problem is not simply with the word. The problem goes deeper and has to do with the energetic flow of meaning. Using a different word doesn't change the quality of thinking. What I focus on, instead, is on creating a different thought structure in what I convey. In speech, this takes the form of dividing the expression into two parts, and making contact with the other person separately about each piece.

In the above example, this would mean having the focus of attention be on the person who is upset rather than on the person who is speaking (the one whose actions resulted in the upset). Instead of "I totally get why you are upset about what happened," it might look like, "I want to see if I really get why you are upset about what happened. Is it because ...?" This expression ends with a question mark, invites further dialogue, and stays with the person who is upset. There is no tug back to the person speaking. Once this part of the interaction is complete, then the person speaking can bring attention to what they want to say, and without a but.

In writing, which is where I have discovered all my many buts, I rewrite the sentence so that it doesn't require the juxtaposition of two different pieces. I was astonished to discover how much of my thinking was built on contrast and comparison instead of looking at each thing in its own right. I am still in process on this one. I am already finding so much richness and benefit. Even now, I eliminated a but in the previous sentence, and I find the result more satisfying in terms of the ideas I am trying to convey.

No More War

I remember the day when I learned that the word "seminal" comes from the word "semen." I knew right then and there that I wasn't going to use that word again, not in a world in which male imagery is used for describing what is human. The experience was so powerful for me that this decision was integrated permanently, and I haven't once used this word to my memory.

A couple of years ago I had a similar shock experience when I realized in full how much our language is riddled with war metaphors, and violent metaphors more generally.

Since the fundamental intention of all my practices is to enhance my capacity to live nonviolently, I took on, with relish, the intention of eliminating from my language any words that I know are related to war or to violence. It's been incredibly educational. I now see and hear them everywhere, always eager to find alternatives. Not only is it liberating, I also love the challenge and the playfulness of looking for alternatives that will convey the fullness of whatever I want to say without invoking the field of violence into which all of us were born.

Any time we use words that imply violence in any form, we reinforce inside our brain the neural pathways that we have built around the legacy of our culture. Every time we find alternatives we strengthen the thin tendril of possibility within us that trusts that we can create a world where war is truly obsolete. I dedicate my many practices to the hope of making that dream a reality.

Anchoring Change in Practice

Whatever else may be true about "human nature," I know us to be very malleable. We become what we practice.

Time and again I ask people in workshops how many of them were asked, regularly, when they were growing up what they were feeling, or what they wanted. Usually no one raises their hands, and sometimes there are one or two people. Without the practice that we could have gotten in connecting to our hearts in this way, we are not likely to become adults who have this capacity.

Because we were formed through practice, I also believe that if we want to create change in who we are or how we act, practice will be an essential component. Practice complements the emotional journeys (see pages 135-9) we take to recover our full selves. In fact, an emotional journey *is* a form of practice – choosing to take steps that will bring us closer to our emotions. While such a practice provides the healing, we still have our habits to transform. This is where I have found a different kind of practice, the kind I described at the beginning of this section, to be extraordinarily valuable: small steps that model the way I want to be, and gradually over time result in new habits.

Both with myself and in my work with others I have relied on two forms of practice. One is a daily practice: something that I do every single day. While I provide several examples here, I myself have only used one consistently. A daily practice is akin to meditation, and in fact some of the examples I provide later are forms of meditation, whether they are used as a daily practice or not. It is a training of the mind and heart, and sometimes the body as well, that provides the scaffolding for change to take place in a gentle and self-loving way.

The other is the ongoing practice of becoming aware of specific behaviors or thought patterns I want to change, and then engaging in the new behavior right then and there. This can be more exacting, or demanding. In those circumstances where this kind of practice has been a fit, I have found it to be quite effective in creating rapid change.

Are you ready for practice? Only you would know. Perhaps you have never tried practice, or you tried and didn't like the results. Or you are using some practices in your life that satisfy you. My hope is that you will consider the practices in this section – those I have described before that I have myself done, and those that I describe below, or those that you will create for yourself based on my suggestion. Whichever form of practice you experiment with, you may want to remember that when we start a new practice we are usually not good at it, or else we wouldn't need to practice.

Deciding which Practice to Use

In writing about my practices here I noticed that my experience of one of them is different from the others. I simply don't remember to do it. When I remember, I do it. I just don't remember as often as with the others, and I have seen no shift in that phenomenon. I also haven't seen any integration in the underlying habit.

This led me to notice that this practice challenges a deep place in me that continues to hold a belief that is opposed to the practice. I began to wonder if that's what makes it hard to remember.

The practice, like most of my ongoing practices, is quite simple and straightforward: whenever I feel some distance from someone I am with, I look for and name to myself three ways in which this person and I are similar. I really don't believe it gets simpler than this. What makes this so difficult for me, as well as necessary?

My intuitive sense is that the obstacle is the belief in my difference, which is one of the deepest aspects of my sense of self. I am not used to seeing myself as belonging, or of there being room for me in the world (though in the last while this is in the process of shifting). I can see that I look for differences, and assert them to myself internally. I have had this habit for decades, as far back as conscious memory goes. Learning empathy, and especially participating in role-plays in which I took on roles of people radically different from me, have transformed my heart's ability to find commonality. While I am teaching or writing I have no difficulty feeling the continuity with other people. However, when I am in the daily course of life, I still engage in the old habit of latching on to differences, and creating some internal distance and aloneness in response.

Given how this has unfolded, I am now thinking that I want to consider taking this one on as a daily practice instead of an ongoing one that I use when I remember (since I simply don't). I want my ongoing practices to be easy to remember, without strife, just the practice itself. If I make it my daily practice, then I can review my day and notice all the people I separated inside from, and apply the simple practice to them. I don't have to remember in the moments I feel distance from people; I can just do it once a day.

If my theory is correct, then you can apply it as you think about creating a practice for yourself. If you find a practice that you want to take on and that challenges deep-seated ideas that you have about you or the world, it may make more sense to have it be a daily practice, done at a particular and regular time every day, without having to remember or re-decide.

Tips for Creating a Useful Practice

For me and others I have accompanied over the years, I find that the single most important quality in a practice is that it be concrete and specific. Practice goes beyond setting an intention. It starts with connecting the intention to specific actions that can move us in the direction we want. I may have an intention to become more loving in my life. An action can be reviewing the people in my life and coming up with specific steps I can take with them that would align with my vision of what it means to be loving.

Practice also needs to be doable, so we don't get discouraged. Going beyond our limits will result in a practice that's not sustainable and will thus be more likely to be dropped. If I struggle with generosity and I take on the practice of giving away 10% of my income to charity every month, I am not likely to follow through for a long time. If, however, I take on the practice of giving away all the change I collect in the course of the week once a month, it's more likely to be manageable for me. I want it to be enough of a stretch to be a practice, to take me outside my comfort zone, and not so much that I go into my alarm zone.

It helps if the practice is rewarding in and of itself, either because I can see results and experience satisfaction from having them, or because the very act of doing the practice contributes to my well-being. If I want to increase my sense of power in the world, and my practice is to examine all the ways I gave my power away, I am less likely to enjoy it than if I choose a subtly and profoundly different practice of reviewing situations in which I gave my power away, and writing down what I might have done that would have preserved my inner sense of power. Doing the latter can nourish my sense of hope that I *can* become more powerful over time.

Finally, whatever else you do, build in something that will allow you to be kind to yourself about the practice. If this is a challenge for you, you may want to begin your practice journey specifically with a self-acceptance practice. It makes all the difference in the world, because no matter what, you will have days and times when you don't follow your practice, and will need love to keep you going. Self-judgment is not conducive to learning.

Creating a Daily Practice

Here are some examples of practices I have either engaged in or proposed to others who engaged in them. Either way, these are practices that have brought benefit to some people. If you want to build your own practices, you can read these for inspiration and guidance. For your own sense of balance and ease in life, it probably makes sense to do only one practice at a time until you fully integrate it and can pick another.

Shifting to Needs Consciousness: Meditating on Needs

If you have ever participated in meditation of any kind, you probably know that most forms of meditation involve returning attention to an object of focus whenever attention wanders. Some meditation practices focus on the breath (many forms of Buddhist and Yogic meditation), some on certain bodily sensations (some forms of Vipassana meditation, for example), some on specific words (mantras in transcendental meditation), and some on specific sequences of ideas and images (some forms of Jewish meditation).

In an entirely similar manner, you can develop a meditation practice that focuses on connecting with needs. The object of focus is the line "I have a need for _____." Just as with any other form of meditation, your mind will likely wander. You will likely hear internal responses, such as: "But this need cannot be met; why bother?" or, "Yeah, but this person is not going to change," or, "I should just grow up and get over this petty wish of mine," or, "This is not just about some personal need of mine. This is about everyone's right to dignity." The aim of the practice is to bring your attention back to the need you are meditating on, without harshness. Rather than punishing yourself for wandering, just gently bring your attention back.

Encountering and connecting with needs is different from naming them as checklist items. Whenever we do this practice, we can take a moment to breathe, to really experience the flavor of that need being inside of us – exactly what it feels like, what the sensations of having this need are, and what this need means to us.

Self-Acceptance: Mourning and Learning Daily Practice

1. What's something you did today about which you have some regret or mourning ?

2. What needs of yours were not met by what you did? What feelings arise when you notice these unmet needs?

3. Take some time to connect with each need. Shift your focus from how this need was not met, to the need itself (consulting the Human Needs list at Appendix A may be helpful). You can use the phrase: "I have a need for...." Notice what feelings arise now.

4. Shift your focus now to understanding yourself at the time you acted. How were you feeling when you did this? What needs were you trying to meet by doing it?

5. Again take time to connect with each need. Shift your focus from trying to meet the need, to the need itself. You can use, again, the phrase: "I have a need for...," which allows you to touch the need itself rather than the experience of whether or not it was met. Notice what feelings arise now.

6. Spend a moment reflecting on both your unmet needs and on the needs you were trying to meet. What feelings arise in this moment?

7. What would have been another option for you to try in that moment that may have met your needs more fully? (If this question triggers any self-judgments, take time for self-empathy.)

8. Do you have any requests of yourself or others around you in relation to this situation?

Gratitude

I described my own practice of gratitude earlier ("Gratitude in the Midst of Difficulty," page 173). My primary focus for my practice was on the people who contributed to my life on any given day. For others it may be grace, or nature, or systems and structures. The point is the experience of being grateful, and I find the content less important. It's more about the effect of opening our hearts in this particular way.

Another gratitude practice can be more of a meditation on gratitude, which would consist of bringing attention again and again to everything I could possibly connect with about which I am grateful. Then, when the attention wanders, to bring it back to the focus on gratitude again.

Power

So many of us have, at best, an ambivalent relationship with power, that the direct practice of power may be challenging to choose.[70] Nonetheless I recommend it as a strong move towards taking full responsibility for our lives, and as a way to increase in our capacity to take leadership and support the whole.

I have found this practice to be most useful in the morning. I review my day, what I know of what's coming, not counting the unannounced, unplanned forceful flow of life. For each piece of my coming day that I remember, I ask: What can I do to be more powerful in that situation? What would bring more leadership? How can I be more intentional about attending in the moment to everyone's benefit?

Blocked access to power looks different for different people. My particular version looks like collapsing in the face of obstacles; paralysis and helplessness; giving up and resigning; or becoming abrupt, intense, or unpleasant as a way to scramble out of helplessness. Sometimes powerlessness shows up as waiting, just waiting – for the right person, the right circumstances, the right opportunity, the right project – so life could start, finally.

You can also answer the following questions in addition to the broad reflection I suggested earlier. In order to make use of these questions, it's important that you know yourself clearly and gently enough to recognize your own habitual responses when your access to power is blocked.

---

[70] This ambivalent relationship stems from confusing *power*, which is the capacity to mobilize resources to attend to needs, with *power-over*, which is a choice we make about how we use power.

1. Think of an upcoming situation during the day in which you anticipate being challenged in terms of maintaining your sense of power.

2. Imagine yourself in the situation. Imagine the other players. Imagine the actions others might take that would be particularly challenging for you.

3. How might you wish to respond in the moment you imagine? What would be the inner obstacle? What are the messages that you tell yourself that create the obstacle (e.g. "There is nothing I can do;" "I am not adequate for this challenge;" or, "I will be kicked out of this meeting if I speak up")?

4. Once you've identified the message, look inside for what you most want in that moment (e.g. a vision of what to do, sufficient skill to pull it off, or courage to meet the consequences).

5. What do you want to remember to tell yourself in the moment that might help you overcome the inner obstacle and act powerfully?

Power and Gratitude

You may want to engage in a double practice of starting your day with a power practice and ending it with a gratitude practice. This creates an arc to the day. In the morning, the power practice is about thrusting ourselves into the world, preparing to meet life. We gather our strength, our inner resources, all we have, to create, to bring our gifts and longings to fruition. By night, the gratitude practice is about surrender. We can let go of any illusion that we can do anything on our own. For me, it's about entrusting myself to life. We can focus on receptivity, on the gifts that life brings to us.

Gratitude, nourishment, relaxation, inspiration, and beauty serve as fuel for life. Challenges, when we can meet them with inner resources, serve as the fire that strengthens us. We become bigger, stronger, more able to face life, to prevail, to imagine new strategies to address obstacles, and new capacities to accept life. Without fuel, without grace, the challenges become overwhelming. Without the stretching, we run the risk of losing vitality, clarity of path, or our compass. I know I want both, in ample measure, for me and everyone.

Choice

1. Review the day, and identify moments in which you are satisfied with the degree of choice you experienced (regardless of your satisfaction with the actual choice you made in the moment). You can focus on one particular area, or on your overall capacity to exercise choice.

2. What contributed to your ability to make a conscious choice?

3. Pick a moment in which you didn't bring as much consciousness to your choice as you would like. What kept you from making a fully conscious choice?

4. What would you have wanted to do in the situation you picked? What might have contributed to your ability to bring more consciousness to the moment? What needs might have been attended to by making a different choice?

Responsibility

Morning

Review the day ahead of you, and identify moments or situations you imagine might be challenging for you in terms of your sense of power. Imagine yourself in your full power. What can bring you to full responsibility (as discussed above in "Responsibility," page 277) in the moments of the upcoming day? What support do you need to embrace that full power? How will you secure the necessary support?

Evening

1. Review your day and identify moments in which you are satisfied with the degree to which you took responsibility for your experience, your choices, and your needs. You can focus on one particular area, or on your overall capacity to maintain self-responsibility.

2. What contributed to your ability to maintain self-responsibility?

3. Pick a moment in which you didn't maintain self-responsibility to the degree you would wish. What led you to relinquish your responsibility for your needs and for creating an outcome that works for you and others? Use the self-acceptance practice if you slip into self-judgment, so you can deepen your compassion for yourself in these challenging moments.

4. What would you have done if you had maintained your self-responsibility? What might have contributed to your ability to do so?

Emotional Openness

1. Review your day and notice which emotions were alive in you in the course of the day. Does any one of them stand out to you? Note the emotions, so you can develop some awareness over time.

2. Can you connect with needs that were alive in that moment, especially the needs that gave rise to the emotion?

3. If your heart was open and gentle towards the emotion, what made that possible?

4. If you were contracted in response to this emotion, what led to the contraction? What could you have done, or what can you do in the future in response to this emotion that would allow you to open your heart more to yourself?

5. What emotions are alive in you right now in response to this reflection? What needs are related to these emotions?

Authenticity and Vulnerability

1. Review your day and notice times when you have withheld aspects of your inner truth. What was the message that you didn't share?

2. Can you connect with the deepest truth underlying this message?

3. Is there any way that you could find to frame this truth in a way that holds with care your dignity, your safety, the other person's needs, the other person's humanity, and the overall nature of the relationship?

4. Imagine sharing this truth with whoever you were not comfortable sharing it with before. How can you support yourself internally to grow in your capacity to share such truths?

Holding Everyone's Needs with Care

Review your day and notice any times when you have either given up on your own needs or on someone else's. In each instance take a few moments to hold compassion for your choices, and imagine how you might have responded to the situation if you were to hold everyone's needs with care.

Then pick either of the two practices that follow – Empathy or Opening Our Hearts to Others – to explore the situation more fully. These practices can also be used independently of this one.

Empathy

Review the day, and identify moments in which you had an opportunity to respond empathically to a situation, regardless of whether or not you actually did. For each of those moments that you want to explore, consider the following questions:

1. If you are satisfied with how you showed up in that situation, connect with what made it possible, and how the choices you made about how you responded contributed to you and others. Take some time to celebrate your choices and the results.

2. If you are not satisfied, take some time to connect with the needs that led you to choose what you chose, and focus primarily on responding empathically *now*. This means running the scenario in your imagination or in writing and imagining how you might have responded if you remembered, chose empathic presence, focused your attention on the essential human meaning of the other person's experience, and picked the choice of response that fit the circumstances. This activity tends to strengthen the

recognition in your system of empathy as an option to go to, as well as integrating the skills you are using.

Opening Our Hearts to Others

1. Review your day and notice times when you kept your heart closed.

    a.   What was the situation?

    b.   What led you to close your heart?

    c.   What needs were met and unmet through this choice?

    d.   How would you like to have responded in the moment?

    e.   What needs might have been met and unmet with this other choice?

2. Notice times in which you succeeded in opening your heart in response to a challenging situation.

    a.   What was the situation?

    b.   What made it possible to open your heart?

    c.   What needs were met and unmet?

3. Write down any insights you have from this review, and any requests you may have of yourself.

Asking without Attachment to Outcome

1. Review your day and notice times when you have made demands instead of requests.

    a. What was the situation?

    b. What was the thinking that led you to make a demand?

    c. What can you now identify as the needs underneath this thinking?

    d. Can you imagine ways of attending to those needs without making a demand?

e. If not, make full contact with those needs and mourn the moment.

f. If yes, what request would you have made?

g. Now imagine a "no" to your request as a way of exploring how fully you let go of your initial demand.

h. Keep working with self-acceptance, mourning, and stretching until you have reached a satisfying level of self-connection.

2. Now notice times when you remembered to make requests

a. What made it possible for you to be open to "no"?

b. What made it possible for you to risk making the request? Since making any request involves the risk of receiving a "no," which we may interpret as meaning we don't matter sufficiently to the other person, how did you handle inside your need to matter?

c. Were you happy with the results of making the request you made at the time?

d. If not, is there some other request you would have preferred to make?

Connecting across Differences

This practice is designed to support the possibility of bridging across uncomfortable differences related to membership in different groups in society – political, racial, physical ability, etc. If you do not experience such challenges in your life, then this practice would not be relevant for you.

1. Review your day and notice times when you have successfully navigated an uncomfortable difference between you and someone else.

a. What was the situation?

b. What supported you in connecting across the difference?

c. What have you learned about yourself and others through this experience?

2. Now notice times when you didn't manage to create the connection you would want with a person different from you.

    a.   What was the situation?

    b.   What was the obstacle to connecting across the difference?

    c.   What needs does this obstacle point to?

    d.   How might you have attended to this need and moved towards more connection at the same time?

    e.   What skills or practices might you want to develop to allow for more success at connecting across differences in the future?

Nonviolent Communication as Practice

Discovering Nonviolent Communication (NVC) was one of the singular moments in my life, a concrete and tangible practice and a way of understanding myself, human life, and the world at large that provided relief, energy, healing, theoretical clarity, and a sense of movement and possibility. It was a big "Wow!"

Earlier in this section I wrote about how NVC is an everyday application of Gandhian principles. The entire set of commitments describes and invites us into the deeper consciousness that is my own understanding of what nonviolence means. I haven't yet talked about NVC as a practice. This is ironic, because a huge part of my gratitude to Marshall Rosenberg for inventing this process is precisely linked to its *practical* nature, both in terms of how easy I find it to apply in a wide variety of situations, as well as it being a form of practice in and of itself. In fact, I often tell people that NVC is my spiritual practice.

The consciousness that underlies this practice is not new. Gandhi, too, knew that he didn't "invent" much. As he said, "truth is as old as the hills." All the world religions have, at their core, the same set of principles, regardless of what their organizational or institutional practices have been. Love, non-separation, trust in life, and the empowerment to live fully are all there. Nonetheless, as a species we have set up social structures and forms of interaction that are not aligned with this deep consciousness.

What this means to me is that understanding this consciousness, even embracing it, choosing it, loving it, believing in it wholeheartedly, are not sufficient, because the old ways are so embedded in us, and we in them. Enter NVC, with a set of concrete practices to anchor our commitment to the consciousness.

Focusing Our Attention

The first level of the practice is learning to focus our attention in a particular way through four key distinctions. I have found that each of the following supports specific aspects of the consciousness, although not everyone will experience them in the same way.

Observing instead of Evaluating: This simple tool has the power to wake us up to the fact that we continually engage in internal storytelling. Then we can open up to the possibility that despite the conviction we have in our interpretation of reality, that interpretation is not necessarily so. We can observe someone taking an action. We cannot observe their intentions, the meaning that the action has for them, or anything else that so often goes into our descriptions of events. This is a practice of openness and clarity.

Example: "He was being mean to me" is not an observation. "He told others a secret that I asked him to keep in confidence" *is*. It doesn't contain an evaluation of his acts, nor an attribution of motives; it only describes what happened the way a video camera could have taped it.

Noticing Our Emotions as Distinct from Our Thoughts: This practice supports us in distinguishing between what's going on outside of us, and what's inside of us. I have already written about the commitment to taking responsibility for our lives, including our emotions. This practice supports us in doing so by focusing inward, and thereby removing any shred of making the other person responsible for our feelings. This is a practice of freedom.

Example: The word "attacked" doesn't qualify as pure emotion in this practice, because the word implies that someone is attacking me. The words "fearful" or "helpless" describe only my internal state.

Separating between Needs and Strategies: This practice for me is the absolute core element of NVC. Because needs are the primary force of life, the source of energy that motivates us to do anything we do, truly understanding what they are provides peace and inner openness like nothing else. As we get more and more capable in this particular practice (more so, in my experience, than any of the others that NVC provides), we become more and more able to choose our responses. In addition to being the motivation for action, needs are also the source of our emotions, and thus connecting with needs allows us the understanding of ourselves and the relief that comes with that. In addition, this practice also allows us the opportunity to understand others and cultivate empathy. This is a practice of connection with self and others as well as of choice.

Example: "I need you to come home in time" is not actually a need. Rather, it's a strong expression of my attachment to a strategy that, probably unconsciously, I believe would meet my needs. Which needs? It could be order, it could be respect, or peace of mind, or trust, or a host of other needs. Needs are universal and timeless. Any mention of person, location, action, time, or object is a clue that we are expressing, or thinking, a strategy and not a need. The acronym Plato (**P**erson, **l**ocation, **a**ction, **t**ime, **o**bject), courtesy of a student of mine, can help you remember this set.

Making Requests and Not Demands: This practice supports us in two moves at once, and I often think of it as the most difficult aspect of the NVC practice. On the one hand, this practice supports us in asking for what we want, which I already alluded to being essential for creating a life that works for us. At the same time, this practice supports us in being able to meet a "no" with openness to dialogue. The true "test" of a request is precisely when we hear a "no" – do we give up on ourselves? Do we judge the other person and give up on them? Do we penalize them, directly or subtly? If we recognize that "no" is simply a piece of information that tells us the other person has needs that wouldn't be met by our proposed strategy, then "no" is an invitation for us to remember interdependence, and specifically the focus on holding everyone's needs with care. This is a practice of power and of non-attachment.

Example: Part of what makes this practice so difficult is that words by themselves don't really give us enough clarity to know if we are open or not to shifting our strategy of choice. We can say words that sound like a request, and then discover that it was actually a demand when someone says no and we get angry. That said, some words lend themselves more easily to being understood as requests, and thereby reducing the chances that they will be heard as demands by others when we don't mean them to be. For example, "Would it work for you to do the dishes today?" is more likely to work than, "Can you do the dishes?" or even, "Please do the dishes." Similarly, "Are you open to having a conversation now?" is less charged than, "Let's talk about this." Ultimately, it's only in actual practice that you will discover the words that work for you.

Grounding Our Practice

Focusing our attention is something that is always available to us internally, regardless of what words we use in our speech. At the same time, many of us have found it tremendously useful over the years to have a formal practice to support our focus. This is in complete analogy to having loving kindness as a focus of attention, and certain forms of meditation as a formal practice that supports that awareness.

The practice of NVC, being language-based, contains a formal form that hundreds of thousands of people all over the world have been using for about forty years (though the form has evolved and is different from the original practice that Marshall Rosenberg created in the '60s).

I find it critical to distinguish between a practice context and life. Just as much as I am not likely to meditate in the middle of interacting with someone unless we both agree to do this together, I want to make sure that I use the formal NVC practice only in contexts where an implicit or explicit agreement exists between me and others. At all other times I encourage people to speak in whatever way works most authentically for them in the moment. I trust that any of us that commit to the practice and show up to do it regularly will, over time, find different ways of expressing ourselves that sound natural to us.

Accordingly, I want to emphasize strongly that I am offering the formal practice template only for purposes of supporting people to engage in it with others' agreement, ideally in a group that gets together for this purpose, rather than practicing, so to speak, "on" others without their knowledge or consent. The reason is that early on in our practice, or whenever we are emotionally triggered (which puts us back into an earlier phase of our practice anyway), we are likely to sound stilted, and our tension about the situation will merge with our tension about the practice to make us sound cold and stiff, distant, manipulative, condescending, or outright hostile.

In addition, if we use these words when the consciousness is not integrated, we will not feel authentic. I remember once when a fellow NVC practitioner sent me an email where she was conveying a difficult message to someone. She wanted my feedback before sending it. I told her that in a number of places I saw her express herself with judgment and blame despite her efforts. She said that was true, and that the reason was that the "translation" didn't sound authentic. When we reach full integration, expressing ourselves in reference to our needs rather than to the wrongness of the other person no longer feels inauthentic. This practice may support us in getting there. I ask again: please use it only internally or with others who agree to it.

A Practice Template

The table below provides a very condensed and brief summary of the elements of the formal practice of NVC. The main fork in the road is the choice between expression and empathy, within each of which we have four components to our words which reflect the distinctions I named earlier in this piece. If you are interested in learning more about the actual practice of NVC, please consult the resources below rather than attempting to use this table on your own. I am offering it here for reference and illustration rather than as a path to learning and practice.

Expression	Empathy
Observation	[Observation]
When I see/hear . . .	*[When you see/hear . . .]*
Feeling	**Feeling**
I feel . . .	*Are you feeling . . .*
Need	**Need**
Because I need . . .	*Because you need . . .*
Request	[Request]
Would you be willing...?	*[Would you like...?]*

In addition to pointing our attention directly to the distinctions I presented earlier, I find this template to be powerful in a few other ways:

Taking Responsibility: Notice that the first three lines of the expression are focused on "I," which subliminally encourages me to be responsible for my own experience. It is only when I ask for what I want that I turn to the other person.

Presence: Notice that when I am focusing on empathy, the general preference for not including observation and request invites me to stay focused on the other person in this very moment, without trying to "solve" any problem. In addition, since the template of empathy focuses on the other person's experience without including me in any way, I am relieved of making myself responsible for the other person's feelings.

Dialogue: Both the expression and the empathy forms end with a question mark, formally inviting the other person's experience and response, thereby keeping us in permanent dialogue until we have reached satisfactory connection and resolution.

Integration and Authenticity

One of the reasons that this practice is so challenging is that many people long for the inner transformation that NVC signifies and yet are still tethered to their own past experiences and to social norms that are designed, often, to maintain surface harmony and manageability at the cost of aliveness, authenticity, and empathy.

At the same time, people who are looking to NVC to help them become more alive and spontaneous may at first fear that adopting NVC practices will have the opposite effect. They want to have ease and flow, to speak in ways that feel natural to them. Or they say that NVC is just too hard, or impossible for them.

The role that practice plays is in reducing the gap between what we long for and what we can embody. This gap can otherwise lead us to oscillate between unconscious behavior that's steeped in separation, scarcity, powerlessness, and right/wrong thinking, and a conscious choice to apply the forms of NVC as "correct form," without being in true connection with the new consciousness of interdependence, sufficiency, and choice. As we practice, our internal landscape changes, and our awareness is awakened. Eventually we integrate the results of the practice into our automatic speech, and thus are able to transcend the stiltedness so often associated with early learning of NVC and be our authentic selves more and more of the time.[71]

Resources

In writing this book it wasn't my intention to write a book about NVC practice. I am so thrilled that a number of books already exist that serve that purpose in a way I wholeheartedly support. If you are

---

[71] For a longer discussion about the potential challenges associated with this form, you can read my blog piece on the topic: baynvc.blogspot.com/2012/06/basic-pitfalls-of-using-nvc.html

inspired to find such books, based on what you read here, you can find plenty of titles through Puddle Dancer Press, the NVC publisher, at nonviolentcommunication.com.

If you want to learn more about NVC in person, you can look for the possibility of trainers or other NVC enthusiasts near you by going to the website of the global organization that was created by Marshall Rosenberg – the Center for Nonviolent Communication – at cnvc.org, and looking for resources there. There are also many other forms of support you can find on that site, including email listserves that connect people across the globe.

If there isn't anything available near you in person, and if you want to explore further resources, you may want to explore the NVC Academy, at nvctraining.com, which provides both online and telephone-based instruction in NVC done by various trainers from different places in the world. I myself regularly offer classes through the NVC Academy. The advantage is that you can do this from the comfort of your own home, provided you have a computer and internet access. I also offer teleseminars through BayNVC, which can be found on the calendar at baynvc.org/calendar.

Learning NVC is a journey that takes a lifetime, as any of us who have been on it for some time know deeply. I see it as offering the potential of relatively quick and profound transformation along the lines I have outlined in this section.

I know I am longing for companionship in living this consciousness, and for the faith that enough of us will do this to turn the tide in the world.

Section 3:

Final Reflections

Current Notes about My Personal Journey

Imagine what it's like to have at one and the same time a sense of porous sensitivity to all I see in the world juxtaposed with having such a clear vision as I portrayed here, and having it be completely palpable and "real" rather than appearing to be utopian. I oscillate between an immense expansiveness of possibility and ongoing pain about where things are and the level of suffering I see and know of. I am permanently at odds with the world as it is.

Yes, I have found vision. Yes, I have found courage. Yes, I have found more wholeness than I believed possible. Yes, I have found integration. Yes, I have almost reached my goal of being 100% shameless. No, I am not pain free. No, I have not yet come to see myself as fully part of life. No, the daily challenges of being a woman have not ceased.

I am not a Contradiction

I walk toward conflict with love. I tell the truth. I ask for what I want. I offer what I have. I listen to another. I am nourished by intimacy, laughter, depth. I do not distract myself. I don't need a break from being conscious, and mindless activities don't tend to satisfy me.

I love heart engagement with ideas and intellectual play with care and commitment. Practical exploration of theory and political understanding of the ordinary. Personalizing the structural and finding social context for the individual. Authentic contact with the other and deep sinking into kinship with the similar. Allowing emotion in the formal and bringing order to the inner chaos. Connecting while working and efficiency without control. Wanting fully without attachment. Deep bonding with full autonomy.

I practice a secular spirituality. I thrive on vision and attend to detail. I open to despair and delight in little pleasures. I have major goals and projects and throw myself into the flow of the moment. I am comfortable with the technical and scientific and adept at attending to the human psyche.

I am a woman and my role models are men. Jesus. Gandhi. King. Fierce, uncompromising, world-embracing, visionary love. I embrace the path of vulnerability without protection, secrets, or anything to hide, and I am afraid of people being upset.

I love a lot and am willing to disappoint people. I have endless care and remarkable obliviousness. I live a dedicated life, committed to transforming the legacy of oppression and separation into a future of collaboration and care. I have faith without personal trust, clarity about possibilities without patience to attend to seeds.

I experiment with leadership without coercion. Power without domination. Inviting without demanding. Teaching others and learning from and with them. Knowing what I want and letting things happen.

I burn with passion for change and aim for acceptance of what is. I cultivate humility and confidence. I flow with intensity and access tenderness. I am rarely angry and often helpless.

I am porously sensitive to touch, smell, taste, sound and sight, and I can withstand and endure much. I get hurt easily and stay present with strong feelings. I know and see so much pain and suffering and I tune out news and the media. I am a social critic and I have compassion for all. I know of interdependence and I hold it all alone.

I live in loneliness.
I risk my significance.
I am not a contradiction.

A Female Visionary
in a Man's World

I don't think I can truly imagine what it would be like to live in a society in which, as a woman, I have restricted legal rights, or am socially isolated, or am required to hide my body and face, or am barred by norms from entering certain occupations. I regularly have bouts of despair and deep anguish knowing just how many women have exactly those kinds of experiences.

I have immense gratitude to the women whose vision, effort, and dedication have made it possible for me and many other women to live in societies where none of the above are true. I am also grateful to the men who supported them in those struggles.

I am also under no illusion that I live in anything other than a man's world. Despite the rhetoric of gender equality, more often than not we have tacitly been expected to become like men in order to "earn" equality. There has been, for example, a much larger entry of women into men's occupations than the other way around. Even societies that experimented with conscious goals of equality (such as the Kibbutz movement in Israel) have not challenged that tacit agreement. The result, indeed, has been a sad absence of any radical re-alignment of society, and the values and norms continue to reflect the experiences of men, whether it is women or men who abide by them.

Especially as a visionary, especially because I have consciously chosen to unprotect and un-numb myself, I experience an ongoing butting up against reality that wears me out. On a daily basis I live in a world that isn't mine. I live in a world in which I experience obstacles to my visibility and my leadership. People are less likely to take me seriously because I am a woman. My heart breaks when I acknowledge without holding back that women, too, participate in this way of responding to another woman.

On a daily basis I encounter the persistence of different interpretations being assigned to the exact same behavior in a woman and in a man. The woman would be called domineering when a man would be seen as taking leadership. She would be seen as being less serious about her work if she gets married or has children; he would be seen as getting grounded and solid. The examples abound to such a degree that I feel hopeless about enumerating them – those who know already know, and those who don't I don't know how to reach.

I don't know how to keep myself from losing energy and hope when I encounter these mines on my path. I want to know how to keep going undeterred.

Imagine that you tuned into a radio station and listened to a group play music. Let's say it's a men's only group. When the piece is over, the announcer comes on air, and says that these men are not only talented, but also attractive, and adds that in case you don't believe it, you could look at the record cover and you would agree with him about their attractiveness.

Doesn't that story sound entirely implausible? Wouldn't you find it absolutely odd if a radio announcer did this? Why is it that it doesn't seem odd when a radio announcer speaks like this about women? This story is true. The announcer, on a "respectable" European classical music station, said exactly those words about a women's ensemble, and I heard them.

I am tired.

On Whose Shoulders Do I Stand?

From the time I was about nine and for a good number of years thereafter, I had a role model. I knew I wanted to be a scientist; I read about Marie Curie, and I wanted to be like her. She remained my role model for quite a number of years, until I no longer wanted to be a scientist. I am so glad that I had at least some years of internalizing a female figure I could look up to, be inspired by, and see as a possibility for myself.

Since I started walking the path of nonviolence, I haven't yet found such a woman. Not that they haven't existed. I have some embarrassment and lots of grief that I haven't found my way to mobilize myself to pursue research in this area, to find the women, whether known or not, who have embodied this particular combination of human qualities I admire so much in Gandhi and in Martin Luther King, Jr.: the ability to love everyone, including those whose actions are harming us, the courage to do what it takes to confront the situation and transform it without losing the love, the fierce truth telling, and the creative commitment to transcend the conditions that create the violence and conflict in the first place.

I have been told by many of my students that often enough they find themselves in a challenging moment and derive inspiration by asking themselves, "What would Miki do in this moment?" Sometimes they even find the courage to do something different from their habitual behavior. When I find myself in difficult situations or challenging moments, I often ask myself, "What would Gandhi do in this moment?" I find that invoking him supports me, serves to remind me of my own commitment to uncompromising nonviolence, and increases the chances that I will respond to the situation in manner I won't later regret.

I am grieving the absence of a woman about whom I can ask myself the same question, not only because I have such a longing for a sense of belonging, continuity, and hope about what I can do. I also wish to have a woman because in two important ways I am not satisfied with the models I inherited from these men.

One is the model of top-down leadership. Given the different roles into which women and men have traditionally been placed, I find it substantially more likely that a woman would have come up with a non-authoritarian and effective leadership model than that a man would do it. There is still no alternative I am aware of that operates with significant leadership and coordination without authoritarian rule. The only alternative that's been created, to my knowledge, is an absence of leadership, based on long-standing models such as the Twelve Step movement (initially started by a man, Bill Wilson) and the Catholic Worker (initially started by a woman, Dorothy Day). I am still left with questions, because for certain effects a large-scale and coordinated movement appears to me to be necessary, and dispersed small localized groups appear to me less effective. Is there a way to scale up without losing the distributed sense of power? More often than not I feel quite alone in trying to figure it out.

This difficulty is intertwined with my other concern about the model that Gandhi and MLK left behind. In 1990 I saw the movie *Dry White Season*. This movie tells the story of a white South African schoolteacher who discovers the horrors of apartheid through a series of experiences. As he is confronted with this reality, he loses connection with his family, who continues to hold on to their sense of innocence and their privilege. He then loses his job, joins the underground opposition movement, and is assassinated within weeks.

I returned home from that movie distressed to my core. It didn't seem to me that his death contributed in any measure to the cause for which he fought. It seemed utterly futile and meaningless. The whole project of nonviolence, at that time still new and foreign to me, was in question. If we are committed to no act of violence, I thought, then why would we make ourselves potential targets for violence? I couldn't settle for a long time. What finally brought peace to me was the realization that top-down charismatic leadership makes both the leader and the movement as a whole more vulnerable. If the charismatic leader gets eliminated, the entire movement falls apart. Instead, I have since come to believe that the more leaders can make themselves dispensable, the more robust the movement they create can be.[72] Although I think of myself as a having a fairly small sphere of influence, I still strive to make myself as dispensable as possible, so that whatever I have to contribute is more likely to be robust and sustainable. I keep wondering if my upbringing as a woman makes me more likely to experience dispensability as relief and inspiration rather than constraining.

I am, indeed, tired.

And I won't stop.

[72] This is one of the reasons I held such a sense of hope and curiosity about the Occupy Movement in its early days. Although there clearly were leaders to this ostensible "leaderless" movement, they remained invisible and in some significant way not so important. Most of the leadership took place spontaneously and was distributed in a way that made repression or personal reprisal by the government more difficult, even if it was ultimately successful in terms of dismantling the encampments. Although under the radar, the Occupy Movement has continued to operate in some creative ways. As of the writing of this comment, in 2013, I remain curious and intrigued about projects like the Rolling Jubilee or Occupy Sandy.

Making Room for Being Different

I can't remember a time when I didn't feel different, even when I was very young. Being different is as familiar to me as breathing and eating. I have had a storyline for most of my conscious life that says there is no room for me in the world.

What I came to see in the last year, an insight I am discovering again and again and then forgetting, is that I can be different and there can still be room for me. I also had a shocking realization that the idea that there is no room for me leads to feeling separate, and has been hampering my effectiveness in the world.

Being different is not something I can or want to change. My responses to many things are different; what I like and dislike tends to be different; I often want different things from what others around me want; my sensitivities are generally far more pronounced than those of people around me; I see things others don't see (and don't notice things that others do); I articulate things differently from how others do. I have complete acceptance of all of that in me, almost all the time. It took years of work to get to where I like who I am and feel at peace with myself about where I am.

The difficulty has always been what to do with my difference. In my habitual way of being, whenever I have had a response that's different from another person's, I could only see two options. One was to hide my response, suppress my difference, not ask for what I want, and endure the pain of inauthenticity, which is for me pretty excruciating and vivid. The other was to express my response, share my difference, or ask for what I want, and risk (and often experience) the pain of disconnection or conflict.

More and more I am beginning to find a way of being fully authentic that creates   more connection instead of less. Sometimes I can see the possibility that there can be room for me to express my responses, what I want, what I like, what I feel sensitive about alongside the other people with their responses, likes and dislikes, and what they want, however different the two are. Neither of them negates the other. There need not be separation between us just because we are different.

I want to continue to grow in this area, because I am aware of how much this belief limits my effectiveness. Because I have lived in an either/or consciousness about being different, and specifically assuming that my responses would not be welcome, I have been holding a layer of protection around myself that was invisible to me. When I have chosen to hide, I would become stiff and less flowing. It's easy to see why that would result in less receptivity to me. Even when I have chosen to express myself, and despite all the years of working on vulnerability, I have often done it with edges because of the protection. The result is that often people experienced themselves being judged by me, whether or not that was true. It's my separation, my protection, that came across as judgment. Once again, the result would be less receptivity to me. In both cases my lack of trust acted as a self-fulfilling prophecy.

I have the contours of a path, without full clarity on where it leads. I know I want to grow in my flexibility about what feels authentic to me. I also, at the same time, want to grow in my willingness to risk losing everything for truth. I know how to grit my teeth and express truth anyway. What I want to learn more and more is how to remain relaxed and soft in my expression when I am stretching my limits.

If I can learn and master the possibility I now see for bringing myself forward with much more openness and humility, making room for myself and thereby allowing room for others, I imagine something fundamental can shift in my experience of being alive. I can, perhaps, finally come to a place of true belonging, and thereby reach and connect with more people without separation between or within.

I anticipate that in a manner similar to how I have worked with other core issues in the past, I will likely cycle and circle and loop and spiral, learning things again and again, falling and getting up, and eventually something will get fully integrated and become a seamless part of who I am.

I'd like to believe that in addition to my own strengthening, writing about this aspect of my challenge and trying to make sense of it may support others in gaining more courage to move closer to the edges of their confidence, so that more and more of us choose to bring forth our gifts and vulnerabilities. I have no doubt they are all needed for the immense task of making the world work for all of us.

Getting from Here to There - Taking on the World

Although Gandhi is primarily remembered as a nonviolent, even spiritual, strategist and political fighter, it is not usually well understood how far everything he did was founded on his deeply exacting spiritual practice. He referred to his work as "experiments in truth" and even said that he chose to be a political leader as an extension of his spiritual practice, not because he was specifically drawn to politics. He felt compelled to do it as part of his search for truth. I'd like to believe, though I am not as certain of this as I would like, that any one of us would reach a similar inner compulsion at some point along the journey. This is not such a simple hope, though. As Michael Nagler, preeminent Gandhi scholar, said, "Of all the truly great masters in Indian and for that matter much of humanity's spiritual traditions, he was the most pronounced in taking his awareness/compassion 'out' to the social/political world."[73] Not everyone makes the step from personal liberation to social commitment

How far can a human heart open before the suffering of others propels us to take some action to create change in the world beyond our own living? How much freedom can we experience before we want to share it with the entire world? How much generosity can we cultivate before we recognize that our own resources, alone, can only go so far, and begin to dream of a worldwide flow of giving and receiving? How long can we live, individually, based on a consciousness of needs before we will begin to envision entire systems based on putting human needs at the center?

There is no doubt that our very presence in the world becomes an inspiration when we can reach a stage on our path, a level of inner freedom and acceptance that allows us to live, more and more of the time, the radical principles of nonviolence. When we demonstrate and come back again and again to empathic presence regardless of circumstances, people around us will notice. When we speak truth even when the consequences frighten us, and especially in the face of power differences, we encourage others to be less afraid. When we

---

[73] Personal communication, 2013.

aim to care for everyone's needs, not only our own, and without ever giving up on ours, we model a possibility and implicitly invite others to join us.

Still, if we want *everyone*'s needs to matter in the world, I trust we will eventually conclude, as I did, that something more than being a one-person endeavor to mend the tears in the human fabric will be necessary.

We would not be the first if we walk that path. The struggle for a better world has been with us for a long time. In the last century alone there have been more than 300 movements in the world that were designed to change an oppressive regime, free a nation from an occupier, or break away from a larger entity. While many have succeeded (and many more of the nonviolent ones succeed than the violent ones, as documented by Erica Chenoweth and Maria Stephan[74]), we have yet to create a world that truly works for all, or a society that is fundamentally based on honoring human needs.

Indeed, Michael Nagler also suggested that this combination of the spiritual and the political may well be a twentieth century phenomenon. If so, what could be the reasons for that confluence? Gandhi is not unique in this way. If we look at other major spiritual traditions we see a lot more Catholics, for example, doing the same thing than in previous centuries.

Although speculative, perhaps this could be because of the appearance of more hope than previous eras had that the political may be amenable to moral/spiritual influence. This has much to do with the history of Western politics, which had reached quite a pitch of moral fervor in campaigns like slavery abolition, franchise extension, factory acts and idealistic revolutions, trade unions and socialism. All of these were equally a response to the new capitalist era, when history moved faster, long-established freedoms were taken away, and people were thrown together in factories and cities where they could reach critical mass in organizing together.

So some gifted spiritual people, who in earlier eras might have found little hope in the political arena, now began to see more possibilities. Perhaps in our times, as a result of the gap between a strong discourse of equality and democracy on the one hand and continued political and social oppression on the other, insults of

---

[74] See Erica Chenoweth and Maria Stephan, *Why Civil Resistance Works*, for more details.

political repression now feel more deeply damaging to the soul, , than they previously did?

In this context, the chronology of Gandhi's life may be significant. Gandhi – a man of his times in the sense of the above – was deeply hurt by the early insults he suffered at the hands of the British, and his soul had burned *before* he began the spiritual quest for truth that healed him of those hurts. His journey then flowered in a way that enabled him and others to do something practical about the pain "out" in the world and not only inside the individual.

It may well be that spiritually-questing people who, unlike Gandhi and King and Aung San Suu Kyi and others, have not been deeply, personally hurt and insulted by social/political harms in a conscious way are often hard to enlist in actual campaigns to do something practical about the hurts suffered by others: they tend to be more in love with the spiritual solution than with actually applying it to particular cases. They may never really exert themselves as heroically as the cases might require.

If you yourself are drawn to this possibility of combining a spiritual quest with practical action in the arena of social transformation, I invite you to read *Reweaving Our Human Fabric*, where I offer ideas and much practical guidance about what groups of people working together to create change can do to minimize the risk of passing on the legacy of separation. If the task of living a full, human, nonviolent life as an individual in a world of separation, scarcity, and powerlessness is challenging, you can only imagine what it would take to overcome that legacy sufficiently to maintain the commitment to nonviolence on the deepest level while attempting to transform institutions and establish new ones. I hope that some of the principles and practices I offer in that volume will make that task a little easier for those who undertake it.

An Eighteenth Commitment

For those of you reading this book who are already working for social transformation, or are seriously considering it, I offer an eighteenth commitment to be added to the core ones I presented earlier.

Nonviolent Struggle: Even when afraid of consequences, I want to be ready to struggle with others in support of transforming social structures using nonviolent means to create a world that embraces everyone's needs. If I find myself retreating into the comfort of my life or developing anger or hatred towards those whose actions I want to transform, I want to seek support to bring my intention back to maintaining love and care for the humanity and dignity of everyone and using the least amount of force necessary to support an ultimate solution that works for all.

Appendix A - Human Needs

(without reference to specific people, location, actions, time, or objects)

This list is, by necessity, incomplete. It is offered as a reflection tool rather than an exhaustive and prescriptive list. The list builds on Marshall Rosenberg's original needs list with categories adapted from Manfred Max-Neef. Neither exhaustive nor definitive, it can be used for study and for discovery about each person's authentic experience.

Subsistence and Security
Physical Sustenance
Air
Food
Health
Movement
Physical Safety
Rest / sleep
Shelter
Touch
Water

Security
Consistency
Order/Structure
Peace (external)
Peace of mind
Protection
Safety (emotional)
Stability
Trusting

Freedom
Autonomy
Choice
Ease
Independence
Power
Self-responsibility
Space
Spontaneity

Leisure/Relaxation
Humor
Joy
Play
Pleasure
Rejuvenation

Connection
Affection
Appreciation
Attention
Closeness
Companionship
Harmony
Intimacy
Love
Nurturing
Sexual Expression
Support
Tenderness
Warmth

To Matter

Acceptance
Care
Compassion
Consideration
Empathy
Kindness
Mutual Recognition
Respect
To be heard, seen
To be known, understood
To be trusted
Understanding others

Community

Belonging
Communication
Cooperation
Equality
Inclusion
Mutuality
Participation
Partnership
Self-expression
Sharing

Meaning
Sense of Self

Authenticity
Competence
Creativity
Dignity
Growth
Healing
Honesty
Integrity

Self-acceptance
Self-care
Self-connection
Self-knowledge
Self-realization
Mattering to myself

Understanding

Awareness
Clarity
Discovery
Learning
Making sense of life
Stimulation

Meaning

Aliveness
Challenge
Consciousness
Contribution
Creativity
Effectiveness
Exploration
Integration
Purpose

Transcendence

Beauty
Celebration of life
Communion
Faith
Flow
Hope
Inspiration
Mourning
Peace (internal)Presence

© 2009 Inbal, Miki and Arnina Kashtan

Appendix B:

Key Assumptions and Intentions of Nonviolent Communication (NVC)

Assumptions Underlying the Practice of NVC

Our ideas about individual and collective human nature have evolved and will continue to evolve. These ideas shape our expectations of what's possible, the social structures we create, and how we interact with ourselves and other people. Therefore the assumptions we make can have a profound effect on the life we live and the world we collectively create.

Following are key assumptions that NVC practice is based on. Many traditions share these assumptions; NVC gives us concrete, powerful tools for putting them into practice. When we live based on these assumptions, self-connection and connection with others become increasingly possible and easy.

1. **All human beings share the same needs:** We all have the same needs, although the strategies we use to meet these needs may differ. Conflict occurs at the level of strategies, not at the level of needs.
2. **All actions are attempts to meet needs:** Our desire to meet needs, whether conscious or unconscious, underlies every action we take. We only resort to violence or other actions that do not meet our own or others' needs when we do not recognize more effective strategies for meeting needs.
3. **Feelings point to needs being met or unmet:** Feelings may be triggered but not caused by others. Our feelings arise directly out of our experience of whether our needs seem to us met or unmet in a given circumstance. Our assessment of whether or not our needs are met almost invariably involves an interpretation or belief. When our needs are met, we may feel happy, satisfied,

peaceful, etc. When our needs are not met, we may feel sad, scared, frustrated, etc.

4. **The most direct path to peace is through self-connection:** Our capacity for peace is not dependent on having our needs met. Even when many needs are unmet, meeting our need for self-connection can be sufficient for inner peace.

5. **Choice is internal:** Regardless of the circumstances, we can meet our need for autonomy by making conscious choices based on awareness of needs.

6. **All human beings have the capacity for compassion:** We have an innate capacity for compassion, though not always the knowledge of how to access it. When we are met with compassion and respect for our autonomy, we tend to have more access to our own compassion for ourselves and for others. Growing compassion contributes directly to our capacity to meet needs peacefully.

7. **Human beings enjoy giving:** We inherently enjoy contributing to others when we have connected with our own and others' needs and can experience our giving as coming from choice.

8. **Human beings meet needs through interdependent relationships:** We meet many of our needs through our relationships with other people and with nature, though some needs are met principally through the quality of our relationship with ourselves and for some, with a spiritual dimension to life. When others' needs are not met, some needs of our own also remain unmet.

9. **Our world offers abundant resources for meeting needs:** When human beings are committed to valuing everyone's needs and have regained their skills for fostering connection and their creativity about sharing resources, we can overcome our current crisis of imagination and find ways to attend to everyone's basic needs.

10. **Human beings change:** Both our needs and the strategies we have to meet them change over time. Wherever we find ourselves and each other in the present, individually and collectively, all human beings have the capacity to grow and change.

Key Intentions when Using NVC

Having clarity about our intentions can help us live and act in line with our values. We hold the following intentions when using NVC because we believe that they enrich our lives and contribute to a world where everyone's needs are attended to peacefully.

Open-Hearted Living

1. **Self-compassion:** We aim to release all self-blame, self-judgments, and self-demands, and meet ourselves with compassion and understanding for the needs we try to meet through all our actions.
2. **Expressing from the heart**: When expressing ourselves, we aim to speak from the heart, expressing our feelings and needs, and making specific, do-able requests.
3. **Receiving with compassion**: When we hear others, we aim to hear the feelings and needs behind their expressions and actions, regardless of how they express themselves, even if their expression or actions do not meet our needs (e.g. judgments, demands, physical violence).
4. **Prioritizing connection**: We aim to focus on connecting openheartedly with everyone's needs instead of seeking immediate and potentially compromised solutions, especially in challenging situations.
5. **Beyond "right" and "wrong"**: We aim to transform our habit of making "right" and "wrong" assessments (moralistic judgments), and to focus instead on whether or not human needs appear met (need-based assessments).

Choice, Responsibility, Peace

1. **Taking responsibility for our feelings**: We aim to connect our feelings to our own needs, recognizing that others do not have the power to make us feel anything. This recognition empowers us to take action to meet our needs instead of waiting for others to change.
2. **Taking responsibility for our actions**: We aim to recognize our choice in each moment, and take actions that we believe will most likely meet our needs. We aim to avoid taking actions

motivated by fear, guilt, shame, desire for reward, or ideas of duty or obligation.

3. **Living in peace with unmet needs**: We aim to work with our feelings when we experience our needs as unmet, connecting with the needs rather than insisting on meeting them.

4. **Increasing capacity for meeting needs:** We aim to develop our internal resources, particularly our NVC skills, so we can contribute to more connection and greater diversity of strategies for meeting needs.

5. **Increasing capacity for meeting the present moment:** We aim to develop our capacity to connect in each moment with our own and others' needs, and to respond to present stimuli in the moment instead of through static stories about who we and others are.

Sharing Power (Partnership)

1. **Caring equally for everyone's needs:** We aim to make requests and not demands, thus staying open to the other's strategies to meet their needs. When hearing a "No" to our request, or when saying "No" to another's request, we aim to work towards solutions that meet everyone's needs, not just our own, and not just the other person's.

2. **Increasing capacity for needs-based sharing of resources:** We aim to develop and practice needs-based strategies for sharing our world's resources with the goal of meeting the most needs for the most number of people and for the natural environment.

3. **Protective use of force:** We aim to use the minimum force necessary in order to protect, not to educate, punish, or get what we want without the other's agreement, and only in situations where we find that dialogue fails to meet an immediate need for physical safety. We aim to return to dialogue as soon as we have re-established a sense of physical safety.

© 2012 Inbal Kashtan and Miki Kashtan

References

Aristotle, *Politics*, Cambridge; New York: Cambridge University Press, 1988.

Zygmunt Bauman, *Modernity and the Holocaust*, Ithaca, NY: Cornell University Press, 1989.

Ann Berlak, "Teaching for Outrage and Empathy in the Liberal Arts", *Educational Foundations*, 3(2): 69-93, Summer 1989.

Gregory Boyle, *Tattoos on the Heart*, NY: Simon and Schuster, 2010.

Erica Chenoweth and Maria J. Stephan, *Why Civil Resistance Works: The Strategic Logic of Nonviolent Conflict*, NY: Columbia University Press, 2011.

Lewis Coser, "Georg Simmel's Neglected Contributions to the Sociology of Women", *Signs*, 2(4), 1977, 869-876.

Rick Fantasia, *Cultures of Solidarity: Consciousness, Action, and Contemporary American Workers*, Berkeley: UC Press, 1988.

Sigmund Freud, *The Problem of Anxiety*, NY: The Psychoanalytic Quarterly Press and W.W. Norton & Co., Inc., 1949 [1925].

Peter Gabel, "A Spiritual Way of Seeing", *Tikkun*, 2013, 28(2): 17-22.

Ernest Gellner, *Reason and Culture: The Historic Role of Rationality and Rationalism*, Oxford and Cambridge: Blackwell, 1992.

James Gilligan, *Violence: Our Deadly Epidemic and Its Causes*, NY: G. P. Putnam's Sons, 1992.

David Grossman, *On Killing: The Psychological Cost of Learning to Kill in War and Society*, Boston: Little, Brown, and Company, 1995.

Agnes Heller, *On Instincts*, Assen, The Netherlands: Van Gorcum, 1979.

Arlie Hochschild with Anne Machung, *The Second Shift*, NY: Avon Books, 1989.

Kenneth Isaacs, *Uses of Emotion: Nature's Vital Gift*, Westport, CT: Praeger, 1998.

Emmanuel Kant, *Anthropology from a Pragmatic Point of View*, Carbondale, IL: Southern Illinois University Press, 1978 [1798].

Louis Kentner, *Piano*, NY: Schirmer, 1976.

Maxine Hong Kingston, *Veterans of War, Veterans of Peace*, Kihei, HI: Koa Books, 2006.

Alfie Kohn, *No Contest: The Case Against Competition*, Boston: Houghton Mifflin, 1992.

Alan Lew, *This Is Real and You Are Completely Unprepared: The Days of Awe as a Journey of Transformation*, Boston, MA: Little, Brown, and Company, 2003.

Jean Liedloff, *The Continuum Concept*, London: Duckworth, 1975.

Alisdair MacIntyre, "Epistemological Crises, Dramatic Narrative and the Philosophy of Science", *Monist*, 60(4): 453-472, October 1977.

Manfred A. Max-Neef, *Human Scale Development: Conception, Application and Further Reflections*, NY, NY: The Apex Press, 1991.

Alice Miller, *For Your Own Good: Hidden Cruelty in Child-Rearing and the Roots of Violence*, NY: Farrar, Straus, Giroux, 1983.

--------, *Breaking Down the Wall of Silence: The Liberating Experience of Facing Painful Truth*, NY: Dutton, 1991.

Stephen Nathanson, *The Ideal of Rationality*, Atlantic Highlands, NJ: Humanities Press, 1985.

Karl Popper, *The Open Society and Its Enemies*, Princeton, NL: Princeton University Press, 2013 [1945].

Sulamith Heins Potter, "The Cultural Construction of Emotion in Rural Chinese Social Life", *Ethos*, 16(2): 181-208, June 1988.

Minnie Bruce Pratt. "Identity: Skin, Blood, Heart", in Elly Bulkin, Minnie Bruce Pratt, Barbara Smith, *Yours in Struggle: Three Feminist Perspectives on Anti-Semitism and Racism*, Ithaca, NY: Firebrand Books, 1984.

James W. Prescott, "The Origins of Human Love and Violence", *Pre- and Perinatal Psychology Journal*, 10(3): 143-188, Spring 1996. (available online at violence.de/prescott/pppj/article.html.)

Howard B. Radest, *Humanism with a Human Face: Humanism and the Enlightenment*, Westport, CT: Praeger, 1996.

Nicholas Rescher, *Rationality: A Philosophical Inquiry into the Nature and Rationale of Reason*, Oxford: Clarendon Press, 1988.

Marshall B. Rosenberg, *Nonviolent Communication: A Language of Compassion*, Del Mar, CA: Puddle Dancer Press, 1999.

--------, *We Can Work It Out*, Del Mar, CA: Puddledancer Press, 2004.

John Ralston Saul, *Voltaire's Bastards: The Dictatorship of Reason in the West*, NY: The Free Press, 1992.

Andrew Bard Schmookler, *The Parable of the Tribes: The Problem of Power in Social Evolution*, Berkeley: UC Press, 1984.

Adam Smith, *The Wealth of Nations*, NY: Knopf, 1991 [1776].

James William Stockinger, *Locke and Rousseau: Human Nature, Human Citizenship and Human Work*, unpublished dissertation, University of California, Berkeley, 1990.

Iris Young, "Breasted Experience" in *Throwing Like a Girl and Other Essays in Feminist Philosophy and Social Theory*, Bloomington, Indiana: Indiana University Press, 1990.

Acknowledgments

Just about every time I read acknowledgments to any book, the author makes it clear that the book couldn't have happened without the support of others. This is obviously true of this book, too. Because of what it is about, I want to acknowledge more than the formal aspect of that, to uncover and expose the process, thereby making it more human and accessible, in honor of all of our journeys of liberation.

I will start with Marilyn French and Riane Eisler, whose books had the most singular effect on my worldview. *Beyond Power*, French's magnum opus that is not very widely known, was my first exposure to the possibility that life could have unfolded differently, and therefore still might. *The Chalice and the Blade* made it ever more concrete and gave it shape and clarity. I never looked back. It would have been entirely impossible to write this book without the 180 degree shift from cynicism to faith in human nature that they instilled in me.

My father, despite the immense difficulties and traumas I have endured at his hands and words, is also the source of much that I recognize as me. The endless conversations about things that matter, a daily occurrence in our family, and, especially, the unwavering respect for his daughters, despite being disappointed about not having a son, allowed all of us to grow up to be engaged, active human beings. My love of all things intellectual comes from this legacy, which he and my mother both nurtured in us. My mother, in addition, knew from the start that I couldn't be made to fit the existing structures of life, and did her best to mitigate the harshness of his attempts to assault my soul. As much as I still have challenges in my relationship with her, she nourished in me a particular strength related to withstanding the encounter with a world often hostile to me. I doubt I would have reached the stage of being able to write without her.

My two sisters are the most reliable source of support in my life, and a constant reminder of what human relations can be. They keep me sane when the world closes in on me, they celebrate my successes and help me survive the dips. Seeing what we can do with each other inspires me to imagine what can be possible all around. They are always in the back of my mind and heart when I dream about a different way of living. Beyond our extraordinary personal and familial connection, they are also my closest colleagues and collaborators over many years. The experience of teaching together, developing materials together, wrestling with spiritual, intellectual, and moral questions together, and writing together are woven through this book.

Marshall Rosenberg provided me with a coherent framework for being able to make sense of human beings and human life. Everything that I've done in the last 17 years is directly influenced by him.

Neil Smelser, my dissertation advisor, helped bring the quality of my writing to a new level with his tireless commentary on my dissertation. Although he wasn't involved in the writing of this book, a lot of the content and framing came directly from my dissertation research, and thus his hand is in it. His biggest contribution to me is the possibility of receiving a critique without crumbling.

I want to thank my colleagues, the large network of certified trainers in Nonviolent Communication, for the many substantive conversations, some in person and most on our email listserve, that have helped refine my thinking and practice. There is an element of co-creation here that is irreducible. We are all students of Marshall Rosenberg, and we continue to learn with and from each other.

This book was born in the most unexpected way. In the fall of 2010 I was given an astonishing assignment by Andrew Harvey, the well-known mystic, spiritual teacher, and author, whose insight and advice I value highly. He started by recommending to me that I use writing as my daily practice instead of meditation or anything else. That sounded nice, though I didn't fully take in until months later that "daily" means every day, nor could I yet imagine what committing to writing would do to support me in all areas of life.

Then came the more shocking part of the assignment. Andrew told me to write a book, whereupon I announced to him that I was already doing that. He didn't go for it. He told me what book he wanted me to write. I don't remember the exact words, and still the message rings clear as day even now. He wanted me to write a book in which I would put out the entirety of my message to the world, without trimming, editing, or holding back. He named, specifically, what he called "the prophetic vision", words which were very challenging to take in, along with the practical applications, the personal struggles that made me who I am, and everything I know that can be useful to others. I immediately recognized the depth of liberation and courage he was calling me to, as well as a discipline that would serve me.

Knowing myself to be prone to self-doubt, I asked my colleague and friend Lynda Smith to read the first draft of everything that I wrote for this book. A former editor of the *San Francisco Chronicle*, Lynda nonetheless knew exactly how to focus on the necessary task and ignore the less important one. She resisted any pull to offer line edits, and instead only provided encouragement and general structural ideas. I needed all of that encouragement to get to the finish line of the very large manuscript that emerged. Nine months later I completed the task. The significance of that number did not escape me. I had more than 500 pages of single-spaced text.

Janet Thomas, my first formal editor, engaged with me for a few months that were quite challenging. She wanted me to write a different book from the one I wrote, and we found ourselves struggling, ultimately deciding we were not a fit to work together. I still remain eternally grateful to her for "forcing" me, with support from Lynda, to get clearer and clearer on the focus and order of the work.

Dave Belden then stepped in and hasn't yet left his post as my editor, project manager, and supporter in so many ways I could not even name them. Dave was formerly the editor of *Tikkun* magazine, and brings to the task his extraordinary experiences and understanding of the dynamics of social and personal change. This book is significantly stronger because he challenged me on various ideas. He also supported me in saying what I wanted to say and in choosing to publish the book ourselves, rather than going with more commercial advice to reduce it in various ways, which he might have advised for someone else. He is also the person who brought it to print and I am deeply impressed with his esthetic sensibilities along with his perseverance and intellectual rigor.

All in all, it took me two years and three editors after the initial draft was completed to do the extraordinary task of figuring out how to organize the material and what I wanted to do with it all. Doug Reil of North Atlantic Press declined to publish this book through a process that ended up, like my earlier encounter with Janet Thomas, strengthening and clarifying the content. At some point, in part through the engagement with him, it became absolutely clear that the only way to manage the sheer size of this project was to divide it into two books in some fashion that held the integrity of the vision and would still allow people to engage with each of these books independently rather than as two volumes of one book. I don't know how Dave, Lynda, and I would have managed to find a way to divide that unruly manuscript into two coherent books without Doug's push.

This task is now complete. This book you are holding in your hands now stands alone, not as a prelude to the other one.

Two people volunteered their time and expertise to take on vital tasks. Ali Miller (in Berkeley) pored over the text and proofread the entire book with loving attention to detail and immense respect for my intentions. Mili Raj (in New Delhi) worked with us to create the cover design, bringing her extraordinary artistic sensibilities and willingness to revise designs forever and again, purely out of her faith in what I do and her desire to support this work in being published.

My final gratitude goes to the many hundreds of people in five continents who have shared pieces of their lives and journeys with me in workshops, private sessions, and when I've worked within organizations. Their trust and wisdom are woven through this book even though I haven't referenced most of these encounters in the text. In moments of great despair, seeing the palpable difference that supporting the journey of liberation provides has given me strength to continue.

Full Table of Contents

Index

P

parenting   39, 45, 49-50, 53-4, 56, 58, 73-4, 76-8, 80-2, 96-7, 119-20, 151-2, 179, 182, 347

peace   18, 163, 168, 221, 223-4, 226, 317, 321, 337, 339, 342, 370-1, 385-6, 393-4, 396-8

personal change, healing 36, 51, 183, 214-17, 405

Popper, Karl 88-9

power   160-1, 178-9, 199, 202, 218-20, 225-6, 249-50, 277-81, 311-12, 319, 325, 330-1, 357, 361-3, 370-1

practice   4, 56, 124, 194-5, 234, 261, 269, 304, 329, 341, 350-1, 356, 362, 369, 372-3

   ongoing   272, 293, 304, 306, 338, 355-6

   simple 204-6, 257, 357

Pratt, Minnie Bruce 204-6

Prescott, James 112, 148

presence   65, 106, 108, 144, 149, 162-3, 218-19, 234, 239, 241-3, 264-5, 288, 290-1, 299-303, 323

privilege   104-5, 155, 175, 193, 196-200, 202-4, 250, 384

R

racism 136, 203-4, 209

radical consciousness   4, 20, 52, 56, 124, 130, 138-9, 179, 183-4, 186-7, 192, 196, 200-1, 206-10, 345

rationality 19, 26-34, 38-9, 49, 83, 87, 115-16, 132, 238

reason 13, 15, 26-7, 29-31, 33, 83-4, 87-9, 91, 93, 144, 160, 223-4, 285, 300, 372

rebellion 33, 178-9, 306

relationships   3, 5-6, 25-7, 92-3, 95-6, 134-5, 161, 206-7, 214,

218-19, 235-6, 249-50, 288, 310-11, 396

resentment   133, 161, 281, 347, 349

responsibility   127-8, 214, 264, 267, 277-81, 283, 290, 329, 334-5, 339, 352, 363-4, 370, 373, 397

Riane Eisler 403

Rosenberg, Marshall   13-15, 23, 91-3, 157, 174, 178, 190, 225-7, 242, 261, 304, 369, 372, 375, 404

S

scarcity   2, 12, 18, 39, 90-1, 98, 123, 128, 239, 265, 267, 287, 289, 295, 304-5

science 29, 34, 68, 117, 200, 214

self-acceptance 17, 166, 175, 228, 267-71, 314-17, 367

self-care   264, 284-8, 304, 307, 323

self-connection   168, 170, 191, 300, 310, 367, 395-6

self-judgments 17, 169, 228, 264-5, 268, 315-16, 358, 360, 364, 397

separation 2, 4, 16, 18-19, 39, 41, 90-1, 179, 182, 266-7, 305, 327, 329, 386-7, 390

shame   7, 110, 132-3, 140-2, 147-50, 159-60, 166, 168, 204-5, 262, 268, 270, 297, 309, 312

sharing resources 102, 105, 396

Smith, Adam 28

social context   44-9, 51-2, 56-8, 61-3, 65, 109-10, 139, 380

social order 3, 11-13, 19, 36, 38-9, 43, 52, 77, 79, 108, 110-11, 138, 183, 186, 191

social structures 4, 6, 12, 36, 51, 123, 194, 250, 261, 325, 369, 390, 395

About the Author

For over twenty years, Miki Kashtan has been pursuing a passionate vision of a world that works for all, learning, developing, and teaching principles and practices that make such a vision a true possibility. A co-founder of Bay Area Nonviolent Communication (BayNVC.org) and certified trainer with the international Center for Nonviolent Communication, she has inspired and taught people on five continents through mediation, meeting facilitation, consulting, retreats, and training for organizations and committed individuals. Miki blogs at *The Fearless Heart* and her articles have appeared in *Tikkun* magazine, *Waging Nonviolence, Shareable,* and elsewhere. An Israeli native and New York transplant, she has lived in Berkeley and Oakland, California, since 1989. She holds a Ph.D. in Sociology from UC Berkeley. This is her first book.

If you would like to contribute to Miki's work, or to pay for copies of this book for her to give to others who cannot purchase it, please donate at baynvc.org and indicate in the memo line what your gift is for.

17679287R00228

Printed in Great Britain
by Amazon